TOTAL QUALITY MANAGEMENT

A Survey of Its Important Aspects

C. Carl Pegels
School of Management
STATE UNIVERSITY OF NEW YORK AT BUFFALO
BUFFALO, NY 14260-4000

boyd & fraser publishing company
I(T)P™ **An International Thomson Publishing Company**

Danvers • Albany • Bonn • Boston • Cincinnati • Detroit • London • Madrid • Melbourne
Mexico City • New York • Paris • San Francisco • Singapore • Tokyo • Toronto • Washington

Acquisitions Editor: DeVilla Williams
Production Editor: Jackie Bedoya
Production Services: Publication Services, Inc.
Composition: Publication Services, Inc.
Interior Design: Rebecca Lloyd Lemna
Cover Design: Rebecca Lloyd Lemna
Manufacturing Coordinator: Gordon Woodside
Marketing Manager: Karen Grantham

© 1995 by boyd & fraser publishing company
A division of International Thomson Publishing Inc.

The ITP trademark is a trademark under license.

Printed in the United States of America

For more information, contact boyd & fraser publishing company:

boyd & fraser publishing company
One Corporate Place • Ferncroft Village
Danvers, Massachusetts 01923, USA

International Thomson Publishing Europe
Berkshire House 168-173
High Holborn
London, WC1V 7AA, England

Thomas Nelson Australia
102 Dodds Street
South Melbourne 3205
Victoria, Australia

Nelson Canada
1120 Birchmont Road
Scarborough, Ontario
Canada M1K 5G4

International Thomson Editores
Campose Eliseos 385, Piso 7
Col. Polanco
11560 Mexico D.F. Mexico

International Thomson Publishing GmbH
Königswinterer Strasse 418
53227 Bonn, Germany

International Thomson Publishing Asia
221 Henderson Road
#05-10 Henderson Building
Singapore 0315

International Thomson Publishing Japan
Hirakawacho Kyowa Building, 3F
2-2-1 Hirakawacho
Chiyoda-ku, Tokyo 102, Japan

All rights reserved. No part of this book may be reproduced or used in any form or by any means—graphic, electronic, or mechanical, including photocopying, recording, taping, or information storage and retrieval systems—without written permission from the publisher.

Names of all products mentioned herein are used for identification purposes only and may be trademarks and/or registered trademarks of their respective owners. boyd & fraser publishing company disclaims any affiliation, association, or connection with, or sponsorship or endorsement by such owners.

2 3 4 5 6 7 8 9 10 BN 8 7 6 5

Library of Congress Cataloging-in-Publication Data

Pegels, C. Carl.
    Total quality management : a survey of its important aspects / C. Carl Pegels.
      p.   cm.
    Includes bibliographical references.
    ISBN 0-87709-274-5
    1. Total quality management.   I. Title.
HD62.15.P44   1994
658.5'62—dc20

94-30860
CIP

Contents

I. INTRODUCTION TO TOTAL QUALITY MANAGEMENT   1

1. **Management Approaches to Improve Productivity and Quality**   3
   Introduction   3
   What Is Total Quality Management?   4
   Other Definitions of Total Quality Management   5
   One Executive's View of How to Achieve Success   6
   Ten Years of the Toyota Production System in the United States   10
   Managers as Sponsors, Facilitators, Leaders, and Coaches   11
   Industrial Evolution at an Automotive Supplier   12
   Conclusions   13

2. **Total Quality Management Defined in Terms of Reported Practice**   15
   Introduction   15
   Origins of the Total Quality Management Movement   16
   Where Does Total Quality Management Fit In?   17
   Primary Improvement Strategies Employed by Organizations   18
   Secondary Improvement Strategies Employed by Organizations   20
   Quantified Improvements Achieved   26
   Conclusions   26

3. **Customer Focus and Customer Satisfaction**   29
   Introduction   29
   Customer Focus in Japan   31
   Customer Focus in the Travel Services Industry   32
   Customer Focus in Health Care   33
   Customer Focus in the Package Delivery and Financial Services Industry   34
   Customer Focus at the Leading Retailers   35
   Customer Focus through Value Pricing   36
   Conclusions   37

II. PRODUCTIVITY AND QUALITY IMPROVEMENT TEAMS THROUGH TEAMWORK AND TRAINING 39

4. **Human Resource Management and Employee Training** 41
   Introduction 41
   Requirements for a More Educated and
   Better Trained Workforce 42
   The Training Experts: Selected Corporations 43
   Motorola's Foundation Is Training 44
   The German Model for Apprenticeship Training 45
   Conclusions 46

5. **Human Resources Enhancement through Team Utilization** 49
   Introduction 49
   Japan's Participative Management Style 50
   The European Nissan Plant 51
   The Western View of Workers 52
   Japanese and American Management Views 52
   Effective Employee Development 53
   The Japanese Management Style 54
   Labor versus Capital 55
   Conclusions 55

6. **Group Dynamics and Team Development** 57
   Introduction 57
   Historical Background of Group Dynamics 58
   Span of Control of Small Work Groups 60
   Size of Small Work Groups 61
   Leadership Style of Small Work Groups 61
   Group Structure 62
   Pitfalls of Team Utilization 63
   Three Types of Teams 64
   Conclusions 64

7. **The Productivity and Quality Improvement Team** 67
   Introduction 67
   Objectives of Productivity Improvement Teams 68
   Training of Team Members and Facilitators 68
   Establishment of Productivity Improvement Teams 69
   Implementation of Productivity Improvement Teams 69
   Success Factors 71
   Cross-Functional Teams 72
   Conclusions 72

8. **Team Process Leadership Roles and Functions** 75
   Introduction 75
   Leadership Roles 76
   Stages of Team Development 77
   The Polite Stage of Team Development 77
   The Why-Are-We-Here Stage of Team Development 77

        The Struggle-for-Power Stage of Team Development   *77*
        The Productive Stage of Team Development   *78*
    The Team Spirit   *78*
    Conclusions   *79*

III. QUALITY AND PRODUCTIVITY IMPROVEMENT AND CONTROL TECHNIQUES   81

9. Brainstorming, Data Analysis, and Charting   *83*
    Introduction   *83*
    Brainstorming   *84*
    Use of Affinity Charts as an Alternative
    to Brainstorming   *85*
    Data Gathering, Tabulation, and Bar Diagrams   *87*
        Histograms   *87*
        Presentation Techniques   *87*
    Flow-Process Charting   *89*
        Recording Entries   *91*
        Application of the Flow-Process Analysis Chart   *92*
        A Proposed-Method Flow-Process Analysis Chart   *92*
    Conclusions   *95*

10. Cause and Effect Diagrams and Pareto Analysis   *97*
    Introduction   *97*
    Examples of Cause and Effect Diagrams   *97*
        Expanded Cause and Effect Diagram   *98*
        Staged Cause and Effect Diagram   *100*
    Pareto Analysis: A Problem Analysis Technique   *100*
    Principles and Applications of Pareto Analysis   *101*
    Conclusions   *105*

11. Statistical Control Charting   *107*
    Introduction   *107*
    Control Charting   *108*
    Averages Control Chart   *108*
    Other Types of Control Charts   *111*
        Proportion Control Charts   *112*
        Error Control Charts   *114*
    What Is a Process Variation?   *117*
    Decision Rules for Process Variation Control   *118*
    Motorola's Six Sigma Challenge   *123*
    Conclusions   *125*

12. Quality Function Deployment   *127*
    Introduction   *127*
    Description of Quality Function Deployment   *128*
    Illustration of Quality Function Deployment   *128*
    Application of Quality Function Deployment   *133*
    The Taguchi Method and Quality Function Deployment   *134*
    Conclusions   *135*

13. **Process Quality and ISO 9000 Standards** *137*
    Introduction *137*
    Components of the ISO 9000 Quality Systems Standards *138*
    ISO 9000 and Global Sourcing *140*
    ISO 9000—A New Approach to Productivity *141*
    Conclusions *142*

IV. IMPROVEMENT STRATEGIES *145*

14. **Productivity and Its Measurement** *147*
    Introduction *147*
    What Is Productivity? *148*
    The Productivity Level of the American Economy *149*
    Productivity Improvement through Empowerment and Control *150*
    Productivity Improvement through Engineering and Design Changes *151*
    Productivity Improvement through Incremental Managerial Changes *152*
    Conclusions *153*

15. **Benchmarking** *155*
    Introduction *155*
    Achievements of Benchmarking *157*
    Benchmarking the Product *157*
    The Process of Benchmarking *158*
    Benchmarking the Process *158*
    Benchmarking in the Administrative Sector *159*
    A Benchmarking Pitfall *159*
    Benchmarking Networks *160*
    Conclusions *160*

16. **Cycle Time Reduction, Time-Based Competition, and Managerial Use of Time** *163*
    Introduction *163*
    Cycle-Time-Based Competition in Day-to-Day Operations *164*
    Cycle-Time-Based Competition in New Product Designs *165*
    Cycle-Time-Based Competition and the U.S. Armed Forces *166*
    Managing Time for the Manager/Leader *167*
    Conclusions *168*

17. **Just-in-Time Operations** *171*
    Introduction *171*
    Just-in-Time Philosophy *171*
    Just-in-Time Purchasing *173*
    Just-in-Time at a Corning Plant *174*
    Just-in-Time in the Retail Chain Store *175*
    Conclusions *176*

18. **Flexibility and Adaptability of the Firm** *179*
    Introduction *179*
    Operations Flexibility in Japan *180*
    General Motors: Flexibility through Increased Plant Utilization *181*
    Flexibility in Managing the Computer Hardware Industry *182*

CONTENTS vii

        Flexibility through Product Modularization *183*
        Agile Manufacturing and Operations Systems *184*
        Adaptability in Strategic Alliances *185*
        The Adaptive and Flexible Corporation *186*
        Conclusions *188*

19. **Reengineering Systems** *191*
    Introduction *191*
    Pitfalls of Reengineering *192*
    Reengineering Management Information Systems *192*
    Reengineering in the Packaged Goods Transportation Industry *193*
    Reengineering at Ford Motor Company *194*
    Reengineering at IBM Credit Corporation *195*
    Reengineering at Boeing *196*
    Conclusions *198*

20. **Concurrent Engineering and Integration of Functional Areas** *201*
    Introduction *201*
    Alternative Means of Achieving Integration *203*
    The Traditional versus the Integrated Approach *204*
    Proposed Product Development Routing Integrated Approach *206*
    Proposed Frameworks for Integrating Functional Areas *206*
        The Three-Managerial-Level Approach to Functional Area Integration *208*
        Technical Aids—Flowchart and Cost Graph *209*
    Comparison of Organizational Alternatives and Alternative Tools and Processes *212*
    Implementation *212*
    Conclusions *213*

21. **Activity-Based Costing** *217*
    Introduction *217*
    Activity-Based Costing *218*
    Activity-Based Costing in Different Industries *221*
    Allocating Costs in Flexible Manufacturing Systems *223*
    Conclusions *223*

V. NEW TRENDS AND DEVELOPMENTS IN TOTAL QUALITY MANAGEMENT 225

22. **Innovation in Product Design and Development** *227*
    Introduction *227*
    What Does Creativity Contribute to Innovation? *228*
    Innovation in Basic Products *229*
    Innovation—New Products *230*
    Innovation in Health Care Information Technology *230*
    Innovation in Biotechnology *231*
    Innovation in Digital Technology *232*
    Innovation in Computer Hardware and Software *233*
    Conclusions *234*

23. External Sourcing and Global Movements in Manufacturing 237
Introduction 237
The Pros and Cons of Outsourcing 238
Local Sourcing by Japanese Transplants in the United States 239
Reducing the Number of Supplier Firms 239
High Cost of German Production 240
High Quality Level in Mexican Automobile Plants 241
Conclusions 242

24. Future of Total Quality Management 245
Introduction 245
Quality as a Focus for Management Improvement 246
Mentofacturing—Mento-Manufacturing—Mento-Operations 247
How Did Wal-Mart Do It? 248
Virtual Reality—What Is It? 250
The Workplace in the Twenty-First Century 250
Quality Experts, Consultants, and Associations 251
Conclusions 253

VI. APPENDICES 255

A. Evaluation of Functioning Productivity Improvement Teams 257
Introduction 257
Status of Implementation 258
Level of Activity 259
Effects of Staffing 260
Operational Impact 262
Changes in Employee Attitudes 263
Conclusions 263

B. Using Activity-Based Costing to Achieve Manufacturing Excellence 265
Introduction 266
Traditional Systems 266
Activity-Based Costing 266
What Is Manufacturing Excellence? 266
Objectives of Continuous Improvement 267
What Do Managers Need? 267
Product Costs 267
Conventional Product Costing Systems 268
   Overhead Activities Unrelated to Volume 268
   Overhead Rates Based on Direct Labor 268
Activity-Based Costing Systems 269
The Search for More Accurate Product Costs 269
   Eliminating Cross-Subsidies 271
   The Location and Consumption of Activities 271
   Using Activity-Based Costing to Focus Manufacturing Strategy 271
   The Impact of Sourcing Decisions 273
   Impact of New Process Technologies 273

Using Activity-Based Costing for Product Design   273
Using Activity-Based Costing for Continuous Improvement   274
Performance Measurement   274
Using Activity-Based Costing for Behavioral Change   274
Reducing Lead Times   276
Is Activity-Based Costing Consistent with Manufacturing Excellence?   276
Conclusions   277

Preface

The total quality management (TQM) approach is increasingly used by organizations to improve their operations, but specifically the processes used in all functional areas of their organizations. TQM has become popular because it promises to improve product or service quality, productivity, and firm competitiveness by improving communications within organizations and with customers and suppliers.

Total quality management is a comprehensive approach requiring lengthy and extensive education and training programs within organizations. This book takes an in-depth approach in order to teach students about critical areas of TQM, such as quality, productivity, flexibility, just-in-time, cycle-time reduction, teamwork, TQM techniques, benchmarking, activity-based costing, customer focus, reengineering, concurrent engineering, innovation, global sourcing, virtual reality, and competitiveness. The objectives of the book can be stated as follows:

1. Develop a set of teachable materials to instruct and familiarize students with the accepted TQM concepts, techniques, and approaches.
2. Develop a set of teachable materials that will train students in using TQM tools and techniques.
3. Develop a set of teachable materials that will enable students to evaluate the numerous concepts, techniques, and approaches covered in the book.

This book can be used to teach operations and production management students and operations planning and control students the four-umbrella total quality management concepts of quality, productivity, flexibility, and timeliness.

The text defines the concepts and examines the relationships of the concepts to each other; importance of the concepts to firm competitiveness and survivability; real world applications of the concepts; measures of how applications of the concepts have enabled firms to improve their operations; metrics that can be used to measure and evaluate the concepts; tools and techniques that can be used to train employees to implement and use the concepts; and use of the tools and techniques.

Many of the TQM concepts in this book aren't found in other current operations and production management books. This book is intended to fill this void. It can also be used successfully in managerial accounting, strategic management, manufacturing management, and other functional management courses.

Below we present a brief definition of the four-umbrella TQM concepts: quality, productivity, flexibility, and timeliness.

- *Quality* is an important ingredient of total quality management, but so is management. TQM therefore is a companywide approach to enhance the quality of the products or services delivered by the firm. These products or services are to be of the highest quality, and delivered in as timely a manner as possible at the best competitive price. TQM also involves the customer in the design of the product or the service delivery process.

    Total quality management is an umbrella term. Most firms use their own in-house TQM term. For instance, Motorola calls the TQM approach "six sigma" or "cycle-time reduction," Xerox calls it "leadership through quality," Intel calls it "PDQ" (for "product design quality"), and Hewlett-Packard calls it "total quality control." In all cases, the stress is more on the process than on the product or service.
- *Productivity* is the ratio of the output to a measure of all the resources used to achieve that output. Productivity is broader than just achieving the greatest output per employee. It means balancing all factors of productivity so that the greatest output is achieved for a given total input of resources.
- *Flexibility* is closely related to timeliness. It comes from contracting all lead times—factory throughput times, vendor lead times, new product development cycles, order entry and production planning cycles, engineering change order lead times, and other variable lead times. Flexibility enables firms to rapidly change over production lines from one product to another in order to minimize finished or work-in-process inventories. The concept is also used to measure a firm's ability to design and develop new products quickly to respond to market or competitive demands.
- *Timeliness,* or cycle-time reduction, is an expansion of the just-in-time concept. Just-in-time was largely focused on minimizing the presence of in-process inventories and on delivery of products and services in a timely manner. Cycle-time reduction focuses on all processes in the organization in order to reduce the cycle time to perform each process. The quicker a process can be completed, the quicker will be the turnaround time. Cycle-time reduction is especially important in reducing the time between receipt and delivery of an order.

The text is organized in five parts. Part One covers the approaches management can use to improve productivity and quality. Total quality management is defined in terms of the reported practices of well-known and respected firms. Customer focus and customer satisfaction are examined.

Part Two covers productivity and quality improvement through teamwork and training. Teamwork is increasingly viewed as important at all levels of the organization. At the lower organizational levels, it utilizes the creativity of employees and taps their knowledge of the jobs they are engaged in on a daily basis. At the upper level, it ensures that management makes decisions that have been thought through and evaluated thoroughly.

Part Three covers problem solving and control techniques such as cause and effect diagrams, Pareto analysis, statistical control charting, brainstorming, data analysis, flow process charting, quality function deployment, and requirements for ISO 9000 standards certification.

Part Four covers general TQM improvement strategies. These strategies are described, and cases of well-known firms using them are detailed. Strategies covered include benchmarking, cycle-time reduction, time-based competition, just-in-time operations, flexibility in process as well as design, adaptability of the firm, activity-based costing for proper pricing and cost control, reengineering, concurrent engineering, integration of functional areas, and productivity measurement.

Part Five covers new trends and developments in TQM. Topics covered include new product development, product innovation, supplier relations, external sourcing, global manufacturing, and future trends in total quality management.

The jury is still out on whether total quality management is a good identifier for all the topics covered in this book. The term TQM may disappear, but the approaches, techniques, and concepts described in this book will prevail. Firms that fail to use them will do so at their peril. The global competitive market demands that firms function at the cutting edge. They must remain competitive, and operational improvements must continue at an unabated pace.

I would like to thank the editorial, production, and design departments at boyd & fraser publishing for insisting on such a high-quality text, and for encouraging first-rate design and graphics. I would also like to thank the reviewers who helped shape the content and style of this book. I am especially grateful for the comments and insights provided by the following reviewers: William Cosgrove, California State Polytechnic Universiy-Pomona; Ellen Dumon, California State University-Fullerton; James Gilbert, University of Georgia; Janelle Heineke; Boston University; Terry Nels Lee, Brigham Young University; Glenn Milligan, The Ohio State University.

I also want to express my thanks to Valerie Limpert for an outstanding job of typing and proofreading several versions of the manuscript, and to my wife, Patricia, for providing moral support during the preparation of this book.

Dr. C. Carl Pegels
September 1994

Part one

Introduction to Total Quality Management

Management Approaches to Improve Productivity and Quality	1
Total Quality Management Defined in Terms of Reported Practice	2
Customer Focus and Customer Satisfaction	3

Introduction

The three chapters in this area will introduce what approaches management commonly uses to improve both quality and productivity.

Total quality management means different things to different people. We will attempt to define total quality management in terms of reported practice by numerous firms. You will find that quality is no longer the sole focus of total quality management. Most firms now consider productivity and the means of how to improve productivity to be as important as, if not more important than, quality.

Quality, for many progressive firms, is a given; that is, it is a necessity to be in business. However, productivity improvements never cease. Changes in technology, management, and processes provide opportunities for productivity improvement all the time. Hence, the term "continuous improvement" applies as much to productivity as to quality.

The beneficiary of all the total quality management activities, be they quality or productivity oriented, is of course the customer. As a result, customer focus and ensuring customer satisfaction are critical goals for the firm. Customers not only benefit from improved quality but also from improved productivity through lower prices.

Chapter one

Management Approaches to Improve Productivity and Quality

Outline

Introduction
What Is Total Quality Management?
Other Definitions of Total Quality Management
One Executive's View of How to Achieve Success
Ten Years of the Toyota Production System in the United States
Managers as Sponsors, Facilitators, Leaders, and Coaches
Industrial Evolution at an Automotive Supplier
Conclusions

Introduction

Improvement of productivity and quality requires a variety of approaches, tools, techniques, concepts, and ideas. Competitive indicators for a firm, such as productivity, quality, timeliness, flexibility, and ability to satisfy the needs and wants of the customer, form the topics discussed in this book.

We will begin with a discussion of total quality management (TQM). Total quality management started out as an approach to improve quality of products and services. It has, over the years, been expanded to fit a much broader definition. Now TQM covers such other performance factors and improvement activities as productivity, flexibility, just-in-time operations, benchmarking, timeliness, reengineering, concurrent engineering, customer satisfaction, keeping up employee morale, and improving communications (internally, among employees, and externally, with suppliers and customers). Also considered important are employee training and education, retraining on a regular basis, improving supplier relations, working with suppliers to improve their quality and productivity, and other issues. Hence, concern with quality has mushroomed into what can now be considered as the need for an organizational shake-up. The shake-up is so extensive that we can call it a major restructuring of the organization. Specifically, problem-solving teams, work teams, and other employee empowerment techniques flatten the organization because they remove most of the first-line supervisor and manager cadres.

The next topic in this chapter covers one executive's view of how to achieve success for a major multinational corporation. Do criteria that apply to General Electric apply to smaller firms? Possibly not all of them, but fundamental management processes do not differ all that much between large and small firms. Even the large multinational firms are subdivided into corporations, and the corporations are subdivided into business units or subsidiaries. The success of Jack Welch, General Electric's chief executive officer, is unquestioned. It therefore behooves management or the student of management to listen to what he has to say.

The most convincing proof of management restructuring is the case of the Japanese Toyota system installed at New United Motor Manufacturing, Inc. (NUMMI) in Fremont, California. NUMMI is a joint venture between Toyota and General Motors to build a car (the Toyota Corolla) and sell it under the Toyota and Chevrolet brand names. The venture was successful in terms of quality and productivity achieved in comparison with Toyota's Japanese operations and especially in comparison with General Motors' American assembly plants.

In this age of restructuring operations, flattening organizations, and experimenting with the numerous TQM approaches, we may want to ask the question, How do the upper middle managers manage their operations? To find out, we will take a look at five types of typical managers.

To conclude the chapter, we will take a look at what an American firm—an automotive supplier facing extinction because of inefficiencies and low quality—did to improve its operations in cooperation with its unionized workers. ■

WHAT IS TOTAL QUALITY MANAGEMENT?

Total quality management can be defined in a variety of ways. The shortest definition is probably *meeting and striving to exceed the requirements of the customer*. On the same theme, a more extensive definition is *providing the customer with quality products at the right time and at the right place*.

Both of these definitions are essentially qualitative outcome measures. TQM, on the other hand, is oriented around the process of achieving the outcomes stated above. Because the process must be managed, one could argue that TQM is essentially the effective management of a process that produces high-quality products or services according to exact customer specifications and expectations at the right time and at the right place. However, this definition does not say anything about the process or what is meant by quality. We could call the process a quality process that is intended to produce a quality product or service. The next questions then are, What is a quality process? What is a quality product or service?

A brief definition of a quality product or service is a product or service that has features, characteristics, and attributes that ensure that the product or service has the ability to satisfy a given need. A more extensive definition of a quality product or service is a product or service that satisfies the above definition but also has such other features or dimensions as performance, durability, reliability, maintainability, aesthetics, and perceptions of high quality (reputation). Ultimately, of course, it is the customer who determines the levels of all quality features and dimensions, and a successful supplier must try to satisfy the customer's expectations.

To produce a quality product or service requires a quality process. A quality process can be defined as product manufacturing or service delivery operations that utilize such accepted TQM processes as employee empowerment, employee education and training, solicitation of employee suggestions for improvement, utilization of teams for problem solving and for getting work done, utilization of the latest information and communication technology, utilization of concurrent engineering where appropriate, development of focused units, focus on cycle-time minimization, constant search for productivity improvements, and other aspects of TQM. However, it is important to keep in mind that TQM is more than a concentrated focus on quality process and quality product. One firm found that concentrating on quality alone can lead to problems in maintaining operations: it went bankrupt [4].

Other Definitions of Total Quality Management

A noted authority on management processes and practices, Richard Schonberger, identifies the basic pursuits of TQM, as reflected by practices and policies of enlightened companies and managers. They are:

1. Ever better, more appealing, less variable quality of the product or service.
2. Ever quicker, less variable response—from design and development through supplier and sales channels, offices, and plants all the way to the final user.
3. Ever greater flexibility in adjusting to customers' shifting volume and "mix" requirements.
4. Ever lower cost through quality improvement, rework reduction, and non-value-adding waste elimination [7].

The four objectives of continuous improvement are general categories. To be implemented, they must be translated and supported by specific operational tactics, strategies, and activities.

Figure 1–1 provides a framework for implementing Schonberger's basic pursuits. Note that the center block identifies five basic objectives, similar to Schonberger's four basic pursuits. The five objectives can also be viewed as performance indicators. Each objective must show continuous improvement if a firm wants to remain competitive.

The 24 tactics, strategies, and activities are shown to the right and left of the center block in the exhibit. Although we cannot describe each one in detail in this chapter, each tactic, strategy, and activity will be described, discussed, and explored in subsequent chapters.

In this introductory chapter to total quality management, it behooves us to list the guidelines of W. Edwards Deming, the generally acknowledged

Figure 1-1
TQM Objectives and Focus Areas

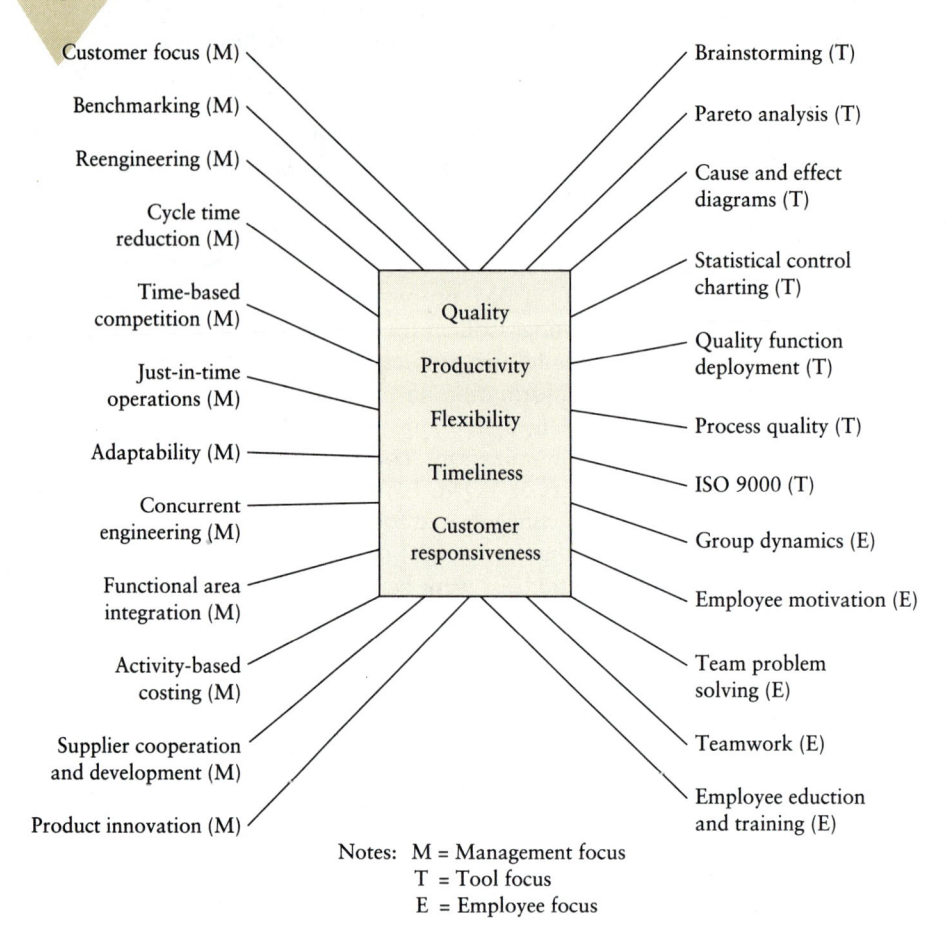

Central focus areas:
- Quality
- Productivity
- Flexibility
- Timeliness
- Customer responsiveness

Management focus (M):
- Customer focus (M)
- Benchmarking (M)
- Reengineering (M)
- Cycle time reduction (M)
- Time-based competition (M)
- Just-in-time operations (M)
- Adaptability (M)
- Concurrent engineering (M)
- Functional area integration (M)
- Activity-based costing (M)
- Supplier cooperation and development (M)
- Product innovation (M)

Tool focus (T) and Employee focus (E):
- Brainstorming (T)
- Pareto analysis (T)
- Cause and effect diagrams (T)
- Statistical control charting (T)
- Quality function deployment (T)
- Process quality (T)
- ISO 9000 (T)
- Group dynamics (E)
- Employee motivation (E)
- Team problem solving (E)
- Teamwork (E)
- Employee education and training (E)

Notes: M = Management focus
T = Tool focus
E = Employee focus

architect of quality assurance, quality management, quality control, or whatever name we want to give to his contributions. A listing of Deming's 14 points that management must follow toward a quality goal are listed in Exhibit 1–1 [2]. Note that Deming's 14 points are not just quality oriented. Deming's notion or definition of total quality management is much more comprehensive.

Schonberger's 19 principles of total quality management are listed in Exhibit 1–2. Note that Schonberger lists the 19 principles under eight categories: general, design and organization, operations, human resource development, quality and process improvement, accounting and control, capacity, and marketing and sales [7].

ONE EXECUTIVE'S VIEW OF HOW TO ACHIEVE SUCCESS

According to Jack Welch, chief executive officer of General Electric since 1981, only those companies that are the most productive and that deliver a top-quality product will survive and thrive in the world's global markets during the next decade. He calls the next decade the *value decade* and feels it will be based

> **Exhibit 1-1**
> *Deming's 14 Points toward a Quality Goal*
>
> 1. *Create and publish to all employees a statement of the aims and purposes of the company or other organization.* The management must demonstrate constantly their commitment to this statement.
> 2. *Learn the new philosophy, top management and everybody.*
> 3. *Understand the purpose of inspection, for improvement of processes and reduction of costs.*
> 4. *End the practice of awarding business on the basis of price tag alone.*
> 5. *Improve constantly and forever the system of production and service.*
> 6. *Institute training.*
> 7. *Teach and institute leadership.*
> 8. *Drive out fear.* Create trust. Create a climate for innovation.
> 9. *Optimize toward the aims and purposes of the company the efforts of teams, groups, staff areas.*
> 10. *Eliminate exhortations for the workforce.*
> 11a. *Eliminate numerical quotas for production.* Instead, learn and institute methods for improvement.
> 11b. *Eliminate Management by Objective.* Instead, learn and institute methods for improvement.
> 12. *Remove barriers that rob people of pride of workmanship.*
> 13. *Encourage education and self-improvement for everyone.*
> 14. *Take action to accomplish the transformation.*
>
> *Source:* Deming, W. E. *Out of the Crisis.* MIT Center for Advanced Engineering Study, Cambridge, MA, 1986. Deming revised his 14 points in 1990. Reprinted with permission.

on global price competition because delivery of top-quality products has become an accepted norm for survival [8].

Technology will be critical to remain a leader in industry, but in the process and operations area, that is largely a minimal requirement to be in business. In the product area, technology leadership will provide considerable advantages.

The value decade means that in all industries, especially those that are global or migrate easily across borders, value of the product in terms of lifetime costs will determine how successful you are going to be.

Welch sees better employee relations in the future. He feels that enlightened union leaders realize that job security comes from worker productivity, and many union leaders are strong supporters of improving productivity.

Employee development and upgrading of skills must be done through intensive and continuous training. Investment in people is a must for firms that want to be successful in the future.

Welch makes an interesting observation regarding incremental change. He feels that unless you institute major changes in an organizational unit, the bureaucracy in the unit will thwart your efforts to change and improve operations. In other words, if change is required, do it dramatically and in a revolutionary way.

Exhibit 1–2
Schonberger's 19 Principles of TQM

General

1. Get to know the next and final customer.
2. Get to know the direct competition, and the world-class leaders (whether competitors or not).
3. Dedicate to continual, rapid improvement in quality, response time, flexibility, and cost.
4. Achieve unified purpose via extensive sharing of information and involvement in planning and implementation of change.

Design and Organization

5. Cut the number of components or operations and number of suppliers to a few good ones.
6. Organize resources into chains of customers, each chain mostly self-contained and focused on a product or customer "family."

Operations

7. Cut flow time, distance, inventory, and space along the chain of customers.
8. Cut setup, changeover, get-ready, and start-up time.
9. Operate at the customer's rate of use (or a smoothed representation of it).

Human Resource Development

10. Continually invest in human resources through cross-training (for mastery), education, job switching, and multiyear cross-career reassignments; and improved health, safety, and security.
11. Develop operator-owners of products, processes, and outcomes via broadened ownerlike reward and recognition.

Quality and Process Improvement

12. Make it easier to produce or provide the product without mishap or process variation.
13. Record and own quality, process, and mishap data at the workplace.
14. Ensure that front-line associates get first chance at process improvement—before staff experts.

Accounting and Control

15. Cut transactions and reporting; control causes and measure performance at the source, not via periodic cost reports.

Capacity

16. Maintain/improve present resources and human work before thinking about new equipment and automation.
17. Automate incrementally when process variability cannot otherwise be reduced.
18. Seek to have multiple workstations, machines, flow lines, and cells for each product or customer family.

> **Exhibit 1–2**
> *Schonberger's 19 Principles of TQM (continued)*
>
> *Marketing and Sales*
> 19. Market and sell your firm's increasing customer-oriented capabilities and competencies.
>
> *Source:* Schonberger, Richard J. "Is Strategy Strategic? Impact of Total Quality Management on Strategy." Academy of Management Executive, 6(3), August 1992, 80–87. Used with permission.

This approach goes against the recommendations of proponents of incremental change or continuous improvement. Does Welch perhaps mean that if the entrenched leadership is unable to implement the process of continuous improvement, the organization should be changed in a dramatic and revolutionary way?

Welch believes in simplicity. According to him, the three most important measurements in a firm are customer satisfaction, employee satisfaction, and cash flow. He states that if customer satisfaction is improving, your global market share will grow concomitantly. Employee satisfaction generates productivity, quality, pride, and creativity. And cash flow, not profits, is the key measure of success.

One concept Welch feels strongly about is *boundarylessness,* a mouthful, to be sure, but very critical to General Electric. Boundarylessness means that an organization should use less segmentation, thus allowing unimpeded flow of information between the various units in the organization. Boundarylessness implies that employees at all levels of the organization should think in terms of the welfare of the total organization and not just of their respective organizational units. Boundarylessness breaks down barriers that divide employees, such as organizational hierarchy, job function, and geography, and any barriers between the company and its suppliers and customers. Achieving a continuous flow of information and ideas between and within business units provides considerable advantages.

Finally, Welch believes in raising as much intellectual and creative capital from General Electric's workforce as possible. He believes that trust is critical to achieve it. Trust makes people perform at maximum ability because they know they will be treated fairly and will be rewarded for it [4].

The ideas presented by Welch will reappear in various forms as we cover many of his ideas in detail.

TEN YEARS OF THE TOYOTA PRODUCTION SYSTEM IN THE UNITED STATES

One important area that this section will address is the work performed by work teams. Work teams will be extensively discussed in subsequent chapters.

The explosion of the use of work teams is part of the empowerment process, a process that lets groups of workers decide how to organize their work, find ways to improve productivity and quality, schedule their work (including overtime, if necessary), and, in some cases, even come up with work output standards.

In addition to empowerment, work teams have one important cost benefit. They essentially are self-supervising, thus eliminating the need for a first-line supervisor.

Because of the above structure, work contents, responsibility, and authority-inherent work teams, the impression is left that work teams are not highly disciplined and do not standardize their work. This is simply not true. Standardization of work and a highly organized structure of work is the norm in work teams and not the exception. This is not surprising. Most people prefer structure and standardization in their work. There may be exceptions, but someone who is a team worker and performs routine or repetitive tasks prefers and even thrives on structure.

A study of New United Motor Manufacturing, Inc. (NUMMI) found that the way work is structured and performed at NUMMI is exactly as described above. The author of the study even refers to NUMMI's work, as performed by work teams, as intensely Taylorist, after Frederick Taylor, the organizer of scientific management at the turn of the twentieth century [1]. The NUMMI study uses the following reasoning to explain the highly standardized work.

1. Routine and repetitive tasks require standardized work procedures in order to attain efficiency and quality, but if the work is organized by the workers in work teams, the work need not be dehumanizing or boring.
2. Hierarchy and standardization need not be coercive, because they can be based on the logic of learning that motivates workers and utilizes their potential contributions to job improvement.

NUMMI's utilization of work teams achieves three objectives. First, it improves overall productivity and quality. Second, it serves workers by providing them with increased motivation and job satisfaction, and by involving them in the design and control of their own work and thus altering the balance of power between labor and management. Third, it serves both management and labor by creating a formal system to encourage learning, institutionalize continuous improvement, and capture and communicate innovation.

NUMMI's production system has produced, since its inception in 1984, an efficiency level nearly as high as Toyota's Japanese plants. Its productivity in 1986 was higher than in any other GM facility. Quality of NUMMI, based on internal and external surveys, was much higher than at other GM plants and almost as high as at Toyota's Japanese plants.

The NUMMI production system is enormously effective because of its ability to make production problems immediately visible and to mobilize the power of teamwork. Teamwork implemented with trust and respect and with the above features creates real empowerment. The NUMMI system provides an enormously important benchmark for many organizations not now utilizing teams or not utilizing them effectively.

MANAGERS AS SPONSORS, FACILITATORS, LEADERS, AND COACHES

Who are the new managers of the newly restructured operations in the last decade of the twentieth century? How do they manage, what makes them tick, and how do they motivate and reward the people, and teams of people, working for them?

MANAGEMENT APPROACHES TO IMPROVE PRODUCTIVITY AND QUALITY

Many of the first-line managers are being squeezed out of the new, flattened organization structures, but that, of course, does not mean that all of middle management is eliminated. We will look at a few of the upper middle managers who are finding increasing opportunities to innovate, not always out of choice, but frequently out of necessity.

The motivation to be innovative for the upper middle manager is substantial. Managers who do well at work team building and encouraging and providing structures for entrepreneurship, and who along the way require extensive functional area experience, will be best positioned for promotion and potentially for the top job in the organization.

A *Fortune* article identified several styles of managers. We will take a brief look at each. The first is the Socratic manager. The Socratic manager's role is to teach, train, cajole, and comfort the people who work for him or her until they feel confident to do their routine jobs and to also, individually or in teams, hire new people and schedule vacations, production, maintenance, supplies, and other activities [3].

The Open manager believes that there should be no confidential internal information. Every employee should be fully aware of what the company's profits, costs, revenues,. and so on are. There should also be openness about compensation packages, including salary levels of all employees. Although this does not imply that everyone's salary is posted on the bulletin board, it does mean that if employees want to know what other employees earn, that should not be a secret. If an employee's salary is below the salary of a fellow worker, that employee is entitled to know why. The Open manager even uses that information to explain weaknesses to an employee and to show how he or she can improve.

The Renaissance manager is the one to manage concurrent engineering projects. Concurrent engineering combines employees from different functional areas to design, develop, and implement a designated project. The difficulty that the project manager has is the fact that all of his or her team members already have their own bosses in their respective functional areas. Therefore, the Renaissance manager must be able to win the respect of the people who work for or with him or her on a project. He or she typically does this by showing the employees a thorough understanding of their jobs, skills, and needs.

The Humane manager stays in close contact with the people who work for him or her. He or she realizes that people, especially those with families, are under a lot of stress, and that part of a manager's job is to see how stress can be reduced. In cases of children's illnesses or other problems, the Humane manager will suggest or provide flexibility in work schedules and make other efforts to reduce hardships on his or her employees. By showing that someone cares, the Humane manager provides a strong motivating force to employees, reduces stress, and generates a strong sense of loyalty not only to the Humane manager but also to the organization.

A fifth type of manager was proposed by Nohria and Berkley [9]. They identified the Take-Charge manager as a manager who has pragmatic judgment. He or she must carefully pick and choose the managerial ideas that promise to be useful and then adapt those ideas rigorously to the firm's needs. The process of picking and choosing the appropriate ideas uses pragmatic judgment.

The authors feel that the enormous flood of new ideas, tools, techniques, pursuits, and processes to improve performance has overwhelmed the typical manager. As a result, he or she has abdicated the responsibility of identifying and choosing what is appropriate and what will work in his or her particular environment. In other words, the manager must take charge of the situation.

As the authors point out, the job of the manager is to get results, not just blindly apply any new novelty or gimmick that is proposed by the latest management guru. Effective managers tinker with systems, evaluate alternatives, and use resources at their disposal to find effective and workable solutions. The challenge to the effective manager is thus to take charge and use pragmatic judgment in selecting new ideas or proposed solutions [6].

Industrial Evolution at an Automotive Supplier

Restructure and reorganize work and operations or go out of business is the choice many firms face. A.O. Smith, an automotive supplier to Ford, General Motors, and Chrysler, faced that choice in 1989.

Smith's operations were traditionally organized, with first- and second-line supervisors directing the workers. Wages were based on hourly wages plus supplementary payments for piecework. The performance indicators stressed output, not quality. As a result, in some cases as much as 20% of the production output of automobile frames had to be reworked or repaired before they could be shipped to Smith's customers.

Management realized that changes had to take place, especially when its customers demanded across-the-board price cuts. Working with its union representatives, Smith first tried quality circles, but union opposition turned that experiment into a failure.

As conditions worsened, the union leaders became supportive of, and provided leadership for, workplace changes. So management decided on a major restructuring change. The change consisted of the organization of work teams and the elimination of most first-line supervisors. Whereas the supervisor to employee ratio had been 1 supervisor per 10 employees, the restructured ratio reduced first-line supervision to 1 supervisor per 34 employees.

The newly organized work teams consisted of 5 to 7 workers per team. The team members were collectively responsible for their work output as well as for a variety of management tasks previously handled by supervisors. The management activities for the teams consisted of scheduling their own work (including overtime, if required), ordering maintenance work, and stopping production if too many defects were being produced. Although the added duties increased work for the work teams and their members, it also empowered them; they gained control over their workplace, which proved to be a strong motivator [5].

The above example provides an illustration of how work will be organized in the factory of the future. The idea of the worker as a robot who is directed by a supervisor is a phenomenon of the past. Employees are too valuable and too costly to be used as robots. Their initiatives and their knowledge of the job will increasingly be utilized to increase productivity and to improve quality.

The work team concept is also an important contributor to the effectiveness and efficiency of the worker. Work teams provide synergy but also serve as a strong control mechanism to supervise the slow or poor-quality producer. In most situations, work teams are sufficiently empowered to remove laggards, nonproductive workers, and non–team players from their teams. In unionized shops, workers removed from their teams are not necessarily laid off, but the threat of being removed from a team and being relegated to a lesser job is by itself a powerful motivator to produce and be a team player.

To what extent the work team concept can be extended to other than manufacturing types of operations will surely be explored in the future. The utilization of work teams in nearly all types of work situations holds great promise.

Conclusions

This chapter serves as the introduction to the general area of total quality management. Total quality management covers a much broader area than just quality of products and services.

Because of the increasing competitiveness in global and national markets, a firm's ability to produce high-quality levels of products and services is now assumed. Without high-quality, durable products, a firm is unable to survive for long. Therefore, the focus for most firms has switched from quality to productivity. This does not necessarily imply that quality is no longer important. What it does mean is that in the quality area, the focus has shifted to the process of manufacturing the products or delivering the services.

When one catalogs all the activities, techniques, tools, and processes that are now covered by TQM, we can only conclude that TQM in its entirety is really an approach to restructure the firm. The restructuring flattens the organizational chart of the firm, but it also addresses the other requirements of TQM.

The analysis of what TQM does and what it is able to achieve has been well cataloged. Firms who want to benefit from TQM have to think in terms of implementation of TQM, the most difficult part. But not implementing TQM will be very costly.

Discussion Questions

1. Define total quality management in your own words.
2. Describe the process aspects of TQM.
3. Describe the product aspects of TQM.
4. Describe the "value decade" as defined by Welch.
5. According to Welch, why is major restructuring preferred over incremental change?
6. Describe why structure of work is so important in work teams.
7. Describe a Socratic manager.
8. Describe an Open manager.
9. Describe a Renaissance manager.
10. Describe a Take-Charge manager.
11. Describe some of the benefits of work teams.
12. Relate the TQM objectives and focus areas in Figure 1–1 to Deming's 14 steps toward a quality goal.

References

1. Adler, Paul S. "Time-and-Motion Regained." *Harvard Business Review*, January-February 1993, 97–108.
2. Deming, W. E. *Out of the Crisis*. MIT Center for Advanced Engineering Study, Cambridge, MA, 1986.
3. Dumaine, Brian. "The New Non-Manager Managers." *Fortune*, February 22, 1993, 80–84.
4. Hill, R. C. "When the Going Gets Rough: A Baldrige Award Winner on the Line." *Academy of Management Executive*, 7(3), August 1993, 75–79.
5. Hoerr, John. "The Cultural Revolution at A.O. Smith." *Business Week*, May 29, 1989, 66–68.
6. Nohria, M., and J. D. Berkley. "Whatever Happened to the Take-Charge Manager?" *Harvard Business Review*, January-February 1994, 128–137.
7. Schonberger, Richard J. "Is Strategy Strategic? Impact of Total Quality Management on Strategy." *Academy of Management Executive*, 6(3), August 1992, 80–87.
8. Ticky, Noel M., and Stratford Sherman. "Jack Welch's Lessons for Success." *Fortune,* January 25, 1993, 86–93. (Excerpt from the authors' book *Control Your Destiny or Someone Else Will,* Doubleday, 1993.)

Chapter two

Total Quality Management Defined in Terms of Reported Practice

Outline

Introduction
Origins of the Total Quality Management Movement
Where Does Total Quality Management Fit In?
Primary Improvement Strategies Employed by Organizations
Secondary Improvement Strategies Employed by Organizations
Quantified Improvements Achieved
Conclusions

Introduction

Total quality management is a pervasive activity in many organizations. Organizations that have not yet adopted it feel impelled to jump on the bandwagon so as not to be left behind. What is this frantic activity all about? In this chapter, we describe what more than two dozen organizations are doing in the TQM field and thus give some structure to this area.

We were able to define 7 primary and 10 secondary improvement strategies in which at least one firm is engaged. Primary improvement strategies can be implemented quickly. Secondary improvement strategies require more advance planning and may be longer term.

Before we discuss both levels of strategies, it is useful to summarize some of the more important features of TQM. First, TQM stresses the importance of knowing who your customer is and what his or her expectations are, and then pulling out all the stops to ensure that your customer's expectations are fulfilled or exceeded. Second, empowerment of the employee and of groups of employees (teams) for the purpose of problem solving or just getting the work out is a critical component of TQM. The third

TQM focus is on designing and developing the product or service so it can be manufactured or provided in the most efficient and effective way. These are just three of the more important aspects of TQM; there are numerous others [12].

Total quality management is not just concerned with quality. Productivity, timeliness, flexibility, and profitability are also important performance measures in a TQM program. We will describe all features of TQM practice as reported by more than two dozen organizations.

Because of the overview nature of this chapter, none of the strategies, techniques, and activities are described in detail. However, nearly all of them will be examined further in later chapters.

Origins of the Total Quality Management Movement

To understand what TQM is all about and what it is intended to achieve, it is important to be familiar with its origins, which can probably best be found in the emergence of Japan as a global competitor in manufactured product markets. Before the second world war, Japan had a reputation for poor-quality products. It had to overcome this reputation to win back markets it had lost as a result of the war. Japan's emergence as a large exporting nation was preceded by overproduction of manufactured products in its own internal markets, which created intense internal competition. The search for markets for this excess supply resulted in Japan's growth as an exporting nation. Internal competition forced Japanese industry to focus on high quality at reasonable cost. History shows that Japanese industry was eminently successful at achieving its goal of high-quality products and large exports of its manufactured products. With that success, Japanese industry attracted the attention of the Western world; Western industry wanted to find out how Japan had passed it in terms of both quality and productivity.

Before we give too much credit to Japan's contributions to the TQM movement, it is important to note that nearly all of Japan's quality improvement activities followed extensive lecturing by W. Edwards Deming and Joseph M. Juran in Japan during the 1950s, and Feigenbaum's book, *Total Quality Control*, was first published in 1951 (before the lectures by Deming and Juran).

These three pioneers of the TQM movement have continued to contribute to the proliferation of TQM. Deming laid out his philosophies about quality in his 1986 book *Out of the Crisis* [3]. Juran, although not as well known as Deming, has been more prolific. His latest book is *Juran on Quality by Design* [8]. Feigenbaum's *Total Quality Control* has been revised several times [4].

One of the first Japanese industry practices to draw the world's attention was the quality circle movement, a worker team approach to solve both product and production process problems. The term "quality circle" was already outdated when it was first imported to the West because the problems Japanese quality circles worked on were more likely to be productivity than quality problems. Japan had already made considerable headway in solving its quality problems. However, the productivity problem is never solved; there is always a better way.

The next productivity improvement, also an import from Japan, to take hold in the West was the just-in-time movement. Its origin lay largely in the fact that the Japanese, in the early 1980s, had a $1500 per vehicle cost advantage over the Western automobile producers, and this cost advantage was attributed to the much lower work-in-process inventory and the much lower waste generated in Japanese auto plants. Just-in-time thus began as an inventory management/manufacturing management problem, but in subsequent years has been more broadly defined to include any management problem where timeliness of doing any activity or process is a critical component in productivity. The just-in-time movement is still very active and has contributed to substantial productivity improvements by reducing raw material and work-in-process inventories, reducing waste to a minimum, and producing overall improvement in manufacturing operations.

The operations flexibility movement, again a Japanese import, became the next area of productivity concern. Flexibility refers not only to flexibility in manufacturing operations but also to flexibility in designing and developing new products quickly. Although flexibility is getting little attention from the Western business press, it is still a critical component in a firm's ability to remain competitive. Whereas many Western firms are still attempting to become more flexible in current manufacturing operations, the Japanese focus on flexibility relates largely to flexibility in the design and development of new products.

Just-in-time and flexibility are, of course, related; a high degree of flexibility enables a firm to be more just-in-time oriented. Neither are easy to achieve in the short run. They both require extensive restructuring of manufacturing operations.

WHERE DOES TOTAL QUALITY MANAGEMENT FIT IN?

Total quality management can be viewed as an outgrowth of the origins of TQM. However, one can also argue that it is more than that. But how is it more? One can argue that TQM is more because its main driver is concern with the customer. What are the customer's needs? What are his or her expectations? What can we do to meet or exceed these expectations?

Another way to look at total quality management is to analyze the three words, especially the last two. The first word, "total," means that it is all encompassing. It also means that everyone in the organization must play a role in order for TQM to be successful. But the words "quality management" are loaded with potential meaning. Should the stress be on quality or on management? Does quality management mean good management or does it mean the management of quality?

In practice, TQM is what you make it do for you. It has generated a strong focus on customer satisfaction and close customer contact and coordination. But because many managers believe that the key word in TQM is "quality," the utilizers of TQM have a tendency to be heavily quality oriented. Quality is certainly a prerequisite of good management, but by no means is it the only measure. Ignoring productivity is done at one's peril. Although it has been argued that productivity follows quality, this is not always the case. Take, for instance, the case of the Saturn Corporation, G.M.'s subsidiary. Saturn appears to have been successful at producing an attractive, quality automobile, but so far it has been unable to do so at a satisfactory productivity level. Hence, managers who put too much stress on quality may want to put more stress on management.

In reality, the concept of TQM can be defined only on the basis of what it is to those who actively apply it in their operations. What managers in industry are doing in relation to TQM is, of course, not homogeneous. A variety of approaches and practices are utilized depending on the views of individual managers and on the perceived needs of their companies.

To determine what TQM is on the basis of recent American industry practice, we have analyzed what approximately two dozen firms in American industry are doing in TQM as reported by them in a variety of interviews and reported in detail by a number of business publications. Because the reports show only highlights of what each firm is doing, the picture presented for each firm is not necessarily complete. However, the information provided to the business publications must be important to the firms. Aggregating and evaluating all of the individual reports provides a good overview of TQM practices in American industry.

Based on the aggregate picture, we have developed a set of primary improvement strategies and a set of secondary improvement strategies. Strategies are long-term approaches that the firm plans to follow in order to achieve its long-term objectives. We will present our findings first for the primary strategies and then for the secondary strategies.

Primary improvement strategies employed by organizations

A primary strategy is usually viewed as a strategy that can be employed with minimal preparation and that can also be summarily suspended. However, to obtain maximum benefit it must remain in place over the long term. The primary strategies that firms have employed include the following:

1. Solicit ideas for improvement from employees.
2. Encourage and develop teams to identify and solve problems.
3. Encourage team development for performing operations and service activities resulting in participative leadership.
4. Benchmark every major activity in the organization to ensure that it is done in the most efficient and effective way.
5. Utilize process management techniques to improve customer service and reduce cycle time.
6. Develop and train customer staff to be entrepreneurial and innovative in order to find ways to improve customer service.
7. Implement improvements so that the organization can qualify as an ISO 9000 supplier.

This list of primary strategies includes most of the successful strategies employed by organizations in their quest to remain or become more competitive in their respective industries.

The first primary strategy, solicit ideas for improvement from employees, is being practiced by Eaton Corporation and Ford Motor Company. Eaton Corporation, a manufacturer of components and parts for the automotive and related industries, found that the best way to control costs is to get employees to understand how cost savings and improved productivity can benefit them. One press operator discovered that preheating dies before using them extends the die life considerably, thus generating considerable savings to the corporation. Awards for successful suggestions by employees are made in the form of prizes, gifts, and recognition [10]. Ford Motor Company utilizes a variety of tactics to improve performance, including employee suggestions. Over the last 10 years, Ford has made improvements that have given it a $795 per vehicle cost advantage over General Motors. Since 1980, Ford has reduced man-hours per vehicle produced from 15 to 7.25 [13].

The second primary strategy, encouraging and developing teams to identify and solve problems, is being practiced by Asia, Brown, Boveri, Inc.; New York Life Insurance; Goodyear Tire and Rubber; Eastman Kodak; and Eaton Corporation. At Asia, Brown, Boveri, structured teams are used to attack internal problems. At New York Life Insurance, team efforts are used extensively to correct operational problems. It was found that highly empowered teams are the best vehicle for problem resolution. At Goodyear Tire and Rubber, more than 2000 empowered teams are used to improve quality, generate cost-saving ideas, and find ways to improve customer service [1]. At Eastman Chemical Company, 150 improvement teams were formed to tackle problem projects [1]. At Eaton Corporation, worker-led teams tackle problems in order to find ways to improve quality and reduce costs [10].

The third primary strategy, encouraging team development for performing operations and service activities that result in participative leadership, is being practiced by British Telecom; New York Life Insurance; Goodyear Tire and Rubber; Pratt and Whitney; and Eaton Corporation. British Telecom has an ongoing program that encourages natural work teams to focus on quality improvements as part of their regular responsibilities. New York Life found that highly empowered teams are the best vehicle for delivering enhanced quality and service to customers. At Goodyear, corporationwide guidelines are in place to empower each division, department, work group, and individual to contribute to the continuous improvement process. At Pratt and Whitney, the term "quality fever" is used to typify the activities engaged in by employee teamwork [1]. At Eaton Corporation, worker-led teams struggle not only to get out production but also to find ways to improve quality and save money [10].

The fourth primary strategy, benchmark every major activity in the organization to ensure that it is done in the most efficient and effective way, is practiced by Ford Motor Company, Xerox, AT&T, Motorola, DuPont, General Motors, and numerous other firms [9]. After John F. Smith was appointed president of General Motors in spring 1992, one of his first acts was to mandate benchmarking in the organization before each major investment. When Ford decided on the Taurus in the early 1980s, it compiled a list of 400 features its customers found important. Using these 400 features, it found the car with the best of each one, and then modeled the new Taurus on these ideal features [13]. The Ford Taurus is an example of product benchmarking. Process benchmarking is also extensively used and will be explored in greater detail in Chapter 15, "Benchmarking."

IBM maintains a separate office to keep track of benchmarking activities. It recorded more than 500 studies over a two-year period. AT&T similarly maintains a group of 14 consultants in its benchmarking office to advise divisional managers on how and what to benchmark. It has conducted more than 120 studies during the past few years [9]. Xerox is the pioneer in benchmarking. Its first study was done in 1979, and numerous studies have followed. In one critical study, Xerox discovered that it was spending from $80 to $95 to process an order, while the company against which it benchmarked was spending only $25 to $35 [9]. Based on the above examples, benchmarking is a critical activity, and not utilizing it may cause a firm to become noncompetitive.

The fifth primary strategy, utilizing process management techniques to improve customer service and reduce cycle time, is being practiced by The New England Corporation [1]. New England discovered that one of the most promising ways to make improvements in the service business is to utilize a methodology called process management, business process improvement, or process mapping. It follows all the steps required from customer initiation until customer order delivery and eliminates steps that are ineffective, inefficient, or inflexible from the customer's perspective.

The process analysis technique (PAT) is used to establish customer requirements, analyze work flows, and make recommendations for improvement. A PAT team includes a process owner, who guides the process, a process consultant, who is trained in process management, and one or more process experts. At New England, eight PAT teams are active. It is important to link improvement efforts to the vital few measures that are essential to customer satisfaction and the overall business.

The sixth primary strategy, develop and train customer service staff to be entrepreneurial and innovate in order to find ways to improve customer service, is practiced by Cigna Property and Casualty Insurance. Cigna found that customer service is a key to survival in the competitive property and casualty insurance business. According to Cigna, the ability to adapt operations to meet the shifting needs of customers is a prerequisite for survival in the property and casualty insurance business marketplace. To be competitive, one must be entrepreneurial and innovative as a habit, and one must continually seek to improve one's ability to serve the customer [1].

The seventh primary strategy, implementing improvements so that an organization can qualify as an ISO 9000 supplier, has been practiced by ICL Plc; Johnson Controls, Inc.; and IBM Rochester, Minnesota. ICL Plc was the first customer service organization and one of the first manufacturers in the information technology industry to be registered in line with ISO 9000 international quality standards. Johnson Controls is not officially qualified for ISO 9000 quality standards but has subjected the entire organization to the requirements of the official international quality standard [1]. IBM Rochester, Minnesota qualified in December 1992 for the ISO 9000 standards [2]. (See Chapter 13 for a discussion of ISO 9000 standards.)

A summary of the seven primary improvement strategies mapped onto 17 corporations is shown in Table 2–1.

Secondary Improvement Strategies Employed by Organizations

A variety of secondary strategies are employed by companies to improve their operations and profitability, especially over the long term. The secondary strategies that firms have employed include the following:

Table 2-1
Primary Improvement Strategies Employed by Listed Corporations

	Strategy[a]						
	P1	P2	P3	P4	P5	P6	P7
Asia, Brown, Boveri		X					
AT&T				X			
Cigna						X	
DuPont				X			
Eastman Kodak		X					
Eaton Corp.	X	X	X				
Ford Motor Company	X						
General Motors				X			
Goodyear Tire		X	X				
IBM Rochester							X
ICL Plc							X
Johnson Controls							X
Motorola				X			
New England Corp.					X		
New York Life		X	X				
Pratt and Whitney			X				
Xerox Corp.				X			

[a] Primary improvement strategies are listed on p. 18.

1. Maintain continuous contact with customers; understand and anticipate their needs.
2. Develop loyal customers by not only pleasing them but by exceeding their expectations.
3. Work closely with suppliers to improve their product/service quality and productivity.
4. Utilize information and communication technology to improve customer service.
5. Develop the organization into manageable and focused units in order to improve performance.
6. Utilize concurrent or simultaneous engineering.
7. Encourage, support, and develop employee training and education programs.
8. Improve timeliness of all operation cycles (minimize all cycle times).
9. Focus on quality, productivity, and profitability.
10. Focus on quality, timeliness, and flexibility.

This list of secondary strategies includes most of the successful strategies employed by well-known *Fortune* 500 firms in their attempts to remain or become more competitive in their respective industries.

The first secondary strategy, maintaining continuous contact with customers to understand and anticipate their needs, is being utilized by British Telecom; Asia, Brown, Boveri, Inc.; New York Life Insurance; Xerox; AMP, Inc.; The New England Corporation; Johnson Controls; The Forum Corporation; Fujitsu Network Transmission Systems; Eastman Kodak; Fidelity Investments; and IBM Rochester, Minnesota.

A specific illustration includes Asia, Brown, Boveri, Inc. Customers were asked to specify their expectations in terms of improvement goals for the company's products and services. Every improvement goal that customers asked for was met, including better delivery and quality responsiveness. New York Life found that the key to quality is a strong customer focus. Firms must earn customer confidence and customer loyalty with quality performance. Xerox reorganized itself such that the operational management level is closest to the customer. Through better responsiveness to customers, quality improves and continues to improve [1].

Other examples of customer focus are Johnson Controls' circles of excellence program. Customer satisfaction was the company theme as far back as 1985, and the subject of companywide training. The Forum Corporation found that quality improvement efforts work best when top managers spend significant time with customers, listening to their needs and concerns, and then use the information gained to focus on the internal improvement process. Fidelity has done extensive research to identify the drivers of customer satisfaction and has used the research results as the basis for training all of its 1200 customer service representatives in how to respond to customer needs [1].

The second secondary strategy, developing loyal customers by not only pleasing them but by exceeding their expectations, has been utilized by Procter & Gamble; New York Life Insurance; and Johnson Controls. Exceeding expectations means doing more for the customer than what is expected under normal circumstances. This includes largely the notion of research and development, innovation, and searching for ways to expand the products or services that can be provided to enhance the customer's business. Of course, exceeding a customer's expectations is not solely an altruistic act. Procter & Gamble feels that when it pleases customers with product innovation and consistent value, it earns loyalty to its brands. New York Life feels that customer confidence and customer loyalty are built by searching for ways to enhance the services it can provide to its customers [1]. In 1987, Johnson Controls set as its corporate goal exceeding the customer's expectations. All three of these companies were not satisfied with just meeting customer expectations. They felt challenged to go that one extra step, to exceed the customer's expectations [1].

The third secondary strategy, work closely with suppliers to improve their product/service quality and productivity, is being practiced by Asia, Brown, Boveri, Inc.; AMP, Inc.; and Fujitsu Network Transmission Systems. Asia, Brown, Boveri develops improvement goals in both quality and productivity with its suppliers. These improvement goals are indirectly connected with the customer's expectations. AMP began a formal quality improvement program in 1983, including a supplier management and just-in-time manufacturing system program. This program is an important reason why AMP ranks high in overall customer satisfaction, as determined by an independent customer survey. Fujitsu

Network Transmission Systems decided early in its life that it could ill afford a large number of suppliers. What it needed was a few exceptional ones. Based on this thesis, it works very closely with its suppliers to ensure that their quality and productivity are satisfactory [1].

The fourth secondary strategy, utilizing information and communication technology to improve customer service, is practiced by VF Corporation; Holiday Inns Worldwide; and Fidelity Investments. The heart of VF's partnership with large retailers such as Wal-Mart is its market response system (MRS), which controls more than 30% of its business. MRS allows VF to maintain a 97% in-stock (in retail stores) rate versus 70% for the industry as a whole. In-store inventory can be replenished in five to seven days, thus providing significant improvement in customer service and productivity. The Holiday Inn reservation optimization (HIRO) system allows more flexibility and wider access in making reservations. The HIRO system allows maximization of hotel income, provides various options to customers, and enables the capture of reservations that are now being missed. Hence, the HIRO system improves both productivity and profitability for the firm and provides better service to the customer. Fidelity depends extensively on information technology to improve quality and customer service. According to Fidelity, in order to be successful, technology has to improve quality, cut costs, and make jobs easier and more interesting. Fidelity views itself as a learning organization staffed by service workers located in service factories linked by a high-speed fiber-optic communications network. Its competitive edge is information that it can provide in high-quality format at reasonable cost in a timely fashion. These three examples of the use of technology to improve customer service, service quality, and other customer service features will be mandatory components of all firms in the future [1].

The fifth secondary strategy, developing organizations into manageable and focused units in order to improve performance, is practiced by Chrysler; General Motors; and IBM Rochester. Chrysler found more focus by reorganizing itself into platform teams consisting of large car, small car, minivan, and Jeep/truck. Each platform team is composed of product and manufacturing engineers, planners and buyers, marketers, designers, financial analysts, and outside suppliers. Each platform team is responsible for getting its vehicles to the market. Platform teams result in better quality, lower cost, and quicker time to market [1]. General Motors is taking an approach similar to that of Chrysler. It is in the process of reducing its platforms to obtain more focus [9]. IBM is in the process of reorganizing itself into about a dozen separate organizations, each with its own focused products or services. Although in the past IBM has utilized independent business units to focus responsibility and for performance measurement, the new reorganization breaks IBM up into several essentially different and semi-independent corporations.

The sixth strategy, utilizing concurrent or simultaneous engineering, is being practiced by many corporations. A specific example of practice occurs at Pratt and Whitney [11]. One of Pratt and Whitney's vital quality initiatives is integrated product development. The concurrent engineering process pulls together employee experts in engineering, manufacturing, purchasing, and customer support at the beginning of each product life cycle. This group then works together and closely coordinates its activities until completion of the project.

The seventh secondary strategy, encourage, support, and develop employee training and education programs, is practiced by British Telecom; Johnson

Controls; and Corning. British Telecom has launched a massive new education program for its managers. It focuses on participative leadership centered on the company's key values. Its main key value is a clear focus on the customer. Johnson Controls utilizes training and implementation methodologies to make its employees thoroughly familiar with total quality control, ISO 9000 standards, and other customer focus criteria [1]. Corning has set a goal of having its employees devote up to 5% of their time to education and training programs. That much time devoted to education and training involves a major commitment by the organization to improving the quality of its workforce and the resultant services to its customers.

The eighth secondary strategy, improving timeliness of all operation cycles (also referred to as minimizing cycle times), is being practiced by many firms. It is one of the newer approaches employed to improve both quality and productivity. A specific example relates to Motorola. It has set reduction of cycle times as one of its main foci. One rudimentary illustration concerned the mail arrival rate at one of its plants. By having an employee pick up the plant's mail at the local post office, the mail arrived, on average, 36 hours earlier on the recipient's desk. Much of the mail was concerned with customer service, so the speedup in mail delivery was important in improving customer service. Numerous other benefits were obtained by reducing cycle times of activities that are notorious for unnecessary delays. Delays in activities add costs and frequently displease customers, both internal and external.

The ninth secondary strategy, focus on quality, productivity, and profitability, is being practiced by Procter & Gamble; Chrysler; General Motors; Coca-Cola; AMP, Inc.; Fujitsu Network Transmission Systems; Fidelity Investments; IBM Rochester, Minnesota; Eaton Corporation; and Ford Motor Company. Procter & Gamble found that focusing on quality creates loyal customers, drives cost out of the system, increases responsiveness to customers, and increases both the individual and collective capabilities of the organization. Coca-Cola found that when quality and image issues form the focus, volume, market share, and profits will follow. Fujitsu builds the competence of each employee to analyze, resolve, and prevent defects. Employees collectively influence costs and quality, both of which shape customer satisfaction. Fidelity Investments believes that the best-performing companies view quality not as a stand-alone process but as a vital part of a total performance triad that includes productivity and profitability [1]. Eaton Corporation found that the best way to control costs is to get employees to understand how cost savings and improved productivity can benefit them. Worker-led teams struggle to find ways to save money without negatively affecting quality [10]. Ford was able to achieve productivity improvements in a variety of ways. The three most critical ones were better labor-management relations, employee suggestions for improvement, and better engineering.

The tenth secondary strategy, focus on quality, timeliness, and flexibility, is being practiced by VF Corporation; Chrysler; General Motors; AMP, Inc.; The Forum Corporation; and IBM Rochester, Minnesota. VF Corporation, through its market response system, is able to obtain almost immediate information on the sales rates of its products, including which style, fabric, color, and size of each garment sells well or poorly. In response to this detailed market information, it can restock retailers quickly so as not to lose sales for itself or its intermediary customer, the retailer. Chrysler and General Motors were able to trim their new vehicle design and development time significantly. Through a just-in-time and logistics management program, AMP was able to improve its on-time shipments from 65% to 95%. It was also able to achieve nationwide delivery of AMP products within 3 days or less on half of its U.S. sales. Forum Corporation executives believe that quality and speed are not antithetical; they can be accomplished simultaneously [1]. IBM Rochester, the 1990 winner of the Malcolm Baldrige award, has been able to keep defect rates below six sigma limits while shipping $15 billion worth of AS/400 midrange computers per year. Their defect rates are 32 times lower than 4 years ago, and their production rate produces a computer every 12 minutes [2].

A summary of the 10 secondary improvement strategies mapped onto 24 corporations is shown in Table 2–2.

Table 2-2
Secondary Improvement Strategies Employed by Listed Corporations

	S1	S2	S3	S4	S5	S6	S7	S8	S9	S10
AMP Corp.	X	X							X	X
Asia, Brown, Boveri	X	X								
British Telecom	X						X			
Chrysler Corp.					X				X	X
Coca-Cola									X	
Corning							X			
Eastman Kodak	X									
Eaton Corp.									X	
Fidelity Investment	X			X					X	
Ford Motor Company									X	
Fujitsu Systems	X		X						X	
General Motors						X			X	X
Holiday Inns			X							
IBM Rochester	X			X					X	X
ICL Plc		X								
Johnson Controls	X	X					X			
Motorola								X		
New England Corp.	X									
New York Life	X	X								
Pratt and Whitney						X				
Procter & Gamble		X							X	
The Forum Corp.	X									X
VF Corp.				X						X
Xerox Corp.	X									

[a]Secondary improvement strategies are listed on p. 21.

QUANTIFIED IMPROVEMENTS ACHIEVED

Quantified improvements achieved by corporations are not easy to obtain. Most firms consider this information confidential and usually do not like to publish for fear of providing an advantage to their competitors. As a result, the information reported in Exhibit 2–1 is sketchy and limited. It largely consists of limited information that firms were willing to disclose. The information, therefore, is not exhaustive. It is simply a snapshot of a limited number of quantitative performance improvements that were achieved by firms as part of their total quality management programs.

One of the more noteworthy achievements is Ford's reduction in man-hours to build a vehicle from 15 to 7.25. Although this took 10 years to achieve, it is still a sterling example of productivity improvement. IBM Rochester, Minnesota's reduction in defects per million by a factor of 32 over a four-year period is worthy of note. And the ability of Chrysler and General Motors to reduce their design development times for new vehicles from 60 and 48 months to the current 33 and 34 months, respectively, is an achievement that indicates the return of competitiveness to the American automobile industry.

CONCLUSIONS

Total quality management can be described in terms of what organizations are doing and what they have been able to achieve as a result of their improvement efforts. TQM is essentially an extension of the management practices that have migrated to the West from Japan during the past decade [5, 6]. Whereas quality circles, just-in-time production, flexibility through cellular manufacturing, and focus on quality were essentially imports from Japan, the TQM concept can be viewed as more of an American creation. The fact that it is largely American in origin may explain why it has become so popular in the United States.

Reports of various organizations' TQM efforts demonstrate that quality is by no means the only focus of TQM and definitely should not be [7]. Equally important are such performance factors as productivity, timeliness, flexibility, and profitability. This is an important fact that organizations contemplating adoption of TQM should consider. Focusing on quality alone will not guarantee that productivity and profitability will also improve.

Discussion Questions

1. Describe how flexibility and quality jointly affect productivity.
2. Describe how just-in-time and quality affect competitiveness.
3. Describe how the process analysis technique works and how it is able to produce improvements.
4. Why has the TQM movement begun to focus less on quality and more on such aspects as productivity, flexibility, benchmarking, just-in-time, and customer satisfaction?
5. For each of the improvements achieved in Exhibit 2–1, identify which TQM aspect is the most prominent.

Exhibit 2-1
Summary Illustrations of Quantified Improvements Achieved

AMP. On-time shipments improved from 65% to 95%, and AMP products have nationwide availability within three days or less on 50% of AMP sales.

Asia, Brown, Boveri. Every improvement goal customers asked for—better delivery, quality responsiveness, and so on—was met.

Chrysler. New vehicles are now being developed in 33 months versus as long as 60 months 10 years ago.

Eaton. Increased sales per employee from $65,000 in 1983 to about $100,000 in 1992.

Fidelity. Handles 200,000 information calls in 4 telephone centers; 1,200 representatives handle 75,000 calls, and the balance is automated.

Ford. Use of 7.25 man-hours of labor per vehicle versus 15 man-hours in 1980; Ford Taurus bumper uses 10 parts compared to 100 parts on similar GM cars.

General Motors. New vehicles are now being developed in 34 months versus 48 months in the 1980s.

IBM Rochester. Defect rates per million are 32 times lower than four years ago and on some products exceed six sigma (3.4 defects per million).

Pratt & Whitney. Defect rate per million was cut in half; a tooling process was shortened from two months to two days; part lead times were reduced by 43%.

VF Corp. Market response system enables 97% in-stock rate for retail stores compared to 70% industry average.

NCR. Checkout terminal was designed in 22 months versus 44 months and contained 85% fewer parts than its predecessor.

AT&T. Redesign of telephone switch computer completed in 18 months versus 36 months, manufacturing defects reduced by 87%.

Deere & Co. Reduced cycle time of some of its products by 60%, saving 30% of usual development costs.

References

1. "ASQC/Fortune Quality Section." *Fortune,* October 5, 1992, insert.
2. Cauley, Leslie. "Winter Key to Success of Division." *USA Today,* January 3, 1993, B1.
3. Deming, W. Edwards. *Out of the Crisis.* Massachusetts Institute of Technology Center of Advanced Engineering Study, Cambridge, MA, 1986.
4. Feigenbaum, A. V. *Total Quality Control,* 3rd ed., revised. McGraw-Hill, New York, 1991.
5. Forker, L. B. "Quality: American, Japanese, and Soviet Perspectives." *Academy of Management Executive,* 5(4), November 1991, 63–74.
6. Goldberg, Alvin M., and C. Carl Pegels. *Quality Circles in Health Care Facilities.* Aspen Systems Corporation, 1984.
7. Hill, R. C. "When the Going Gets Rough: A Baldrige Award Winner on the Line." *Academy of Management Executive,* 7(3), August 1993, 75–79.
8. Juran, Joseph M. *Juran on Quality by Design.* The Free Press, New York, 1992.

9. Main, Jeremy. "How to Steal the Best Ideas Around." *Fortune,* October 19, 1992, 103–106.
10. O'Boyle, Thomas F. "A Manufacturer Grows Efficient by Soliciting Ideas from Employees." *Wall Street Journal,* June 5, 1992, A1.
11. Port, Otis, Zachary Schiller, and Resa W. King. "A Smarter Way to Manufacture." *Business Week,* April 30, 1990, 110–117.
12. Schonberger, Richard. "Is Strategy Strategic? Impact of Total Quality Management on Strategy." *Academy of Management Executive,* 6(3), August 1992, 80–87.
13. Templin, Neil. "A Decisive Response to Crisis Brought Ford Enhanced Productivity." *Wall Street Journal,* December 15, 1992, A1.

Source

Chapter 2 is a slightly modified version of Pegels, C. Carl, "Total Quality Management Defined in Terms of Reported Practice," *International Journal of Quality and Reliability Management,* Vol. 11, No. 5, 1994. Reprinted with permission.

Chapter three

Customer Focus and Customer Satisfaction

Outline

Introduction
Customer Focus in Japan
Customer Focus in the Travel Services Industry
Customer Focus in Health Care
Customer Focus in the Package Delivery and Financial Services Industry
Customer Focus at the Leading Retailers
Customer Focus through Value Pricing
Conclusions

Introduction

What is customer focus? What is customer satisfaction, and how can it be achieved? There is no easy answer to these questions. One commonly accepted rule is to learn who your customer is, what his or her needs are, and how he or she can be satisfied. Some people have even suggested spending a day (or a week) in the life of each one of your customers [3].

The primary rule of total quality management is to know your customer. A clear example is the Boeing 777 airliner, which will become available in 1995. It will be the first commercial airliner whose major design features originated with its primary customers, United Airlines and British Airways [9].

What are other customer focus and customer satisfaction definitions? At Motorola Inc., total customer satisfaction is stated in terms of a fundamental objective. The fundamental objective is anchored in three key issues: beliefs, goals, and initiatives. Exhibit 3–1 provides the details behind each.

Exhibit 3-1
Motorola's Three Key Issues toward Total Customer Satisfaction

A. Key beliefs—how Motorola will always act
   1. Constant respect for people
   2. Uncompromising integrity
B. Key goals—what Motorola must accomplish
   1. Increased global market share
   2. Best-in-class:
      - People
      - Marketing
      - Technology
      - Product
      - Manufacturing
      - Service
   3. Superior financial results
C. Key initiatives—how Motorola will do it
   1. Six sigma quality
   2. Total cycle-time reduction
   3. Product and manufacturing leadership
   4. Participative management within and cooperation among organizations

Separately, Motorola identifies three primary quality improvement activities in a total quality management system: continuously increasing focus on customers, upgrading operating systems and processes, and involving more and more people in the improvement process. Driving and promoting these three quality improvement activities required leadership, training of employees, and execution by problem-solving teams. By far the most critical activity is leadership—not only by top management but also by all other management levels.

How do we find out what customers like, want, or need? At Whirlpool Corporation, a standardized appliance measurement satisfaction (SAMS) survey is mailed out to 180,000 households each year asking customers to rate Whirlpool appliances on many attributes and to compare Whirlpool's appliances with competitors' appliances. If a competitor's appliance scores higher than Whirlpool's, Whirlpool wastes no time in finding out why [14].

Whirlpool's approach is based on the tenet that you must apply considerable effort to find out what customers like, dislike, want, or need in your products. In this chapter, we will review what firms in a variety of industries are doing to know their customers' needs, wants, and desires. With this information, firms can satisfy their customers so they will return again and again.

Customer Focus in Japan

The quality movement originated in Japan following extensive lecturing on quality management by two Americans, the "quality gurus," Deming and Juran. Since then, the quality movement has migrated to the United States and the rest of the Western world, and some Western-developed quality management issues have migrated to Japan. A case in point is the quality management system developed by the U.S.-based Disney firm and utilized by Tokyo's Disneyland. Disney's service quality system, which is based on extensive employee training and the use of service manuals for any conceivable problem situation, has fascinated Japanese industry. Japanese firms are flocking to Disney to observe Disney's quality management system. Japan's approach to production, design, and quality is much less documented than Western systems, so the Disney quality management system is of great interest to the Japanese. The Disney quality and operations management system has the potential to be applicable to more complex operations and service-oriented activities [6].

What makes the Disney quality and operations management system of heavy documentation especially functional and more easily deployable in the information age is the ability to put all the documentation on the laptop computer of any employee, or within reach of any employee, at relatively low cost. Computer access eliminates the need for voluminous manuals and provides easier and quicker accessibility to quality and operations management systems and procedures.

The above case illustrates one example where the Americans have "a leg up" on the Japanese in terms of quality and operations management. However, in many other areas the Japanese are still the champions of quality management and implementation.

One specific example of intensive quality management in Japan is Toto Limited, a manufacturer of bathroom fixtures. Toto started its intensive quality management programs in 1984. They organized the firm's 8200 employees into 32 focused groups in order to permeate the groups with the need and importance of total quality management. Before training its lower-level employees in the basics of TQM, Toto first sent its board members to TQM classes. The next step was to send 550 middle managers to 5-day-long courses in TQM. Each manager was required to find one quality problem and to solve that problem in one year. Toto was quite successful with the TQM training approach it used. In addition to winning Japan's prized Deming award, Toto cut inventories and lead times in half and reduced employment by 20%. Productivity soared by more than 50% and customer complaints fell by 25%. What the Toto experience illustrates is that TQM not only improves quality but also productivity [6].

One of Japan's most successful retail operations in terms of efficiency, productivity, and profitability is the 4800-store 7-Eleven chain, which specializes in food, snacks, drinks, and tobacco products. Although Japan's 7-Eleven chain started out as a franchise operation from the U.S. 7-Eleven chain, the Japanese franchiser now owns the 7-Eleven operations in both Japan and the United States. Using a sophisticated product-tracking system, 7-Eleven operates its stores very productively. It stocks only fast-moving items to minimize inventory levels. Slow-moving products are replaced with fast-moving, profitable products, causing 70% of each store's 3000 products to be replaced annually. The tracking system also monitors customer buying habits by recording sex and approximate age of each customer for each purchase made. The result is that Japan's 7-Eleven stores generate in excess of a 40% operating margin on sales of over $1.5 billion [5].

CUSTOMER FOCUS IN THE TRAVEL SERVICES INDUSTRY

The travel services industry, including airlines and hotels, is a huge industry. Although this industry has always placed the customer first in theory, in practice, the customers have not always been happy with the service they have received.

In response to this problem, Marriott Corporation decided a few years ago to put its 70,000 hotel employees through "empowerment training" [1]. The training is intended to give the employees wide latitude to step outside their normal jobs and solve guests' problems.

Toronto-based Four Seasons Hotels Inc. maintains high-quality service to its guests through a rigorous interview process for new job applicants. The new employee interview program intends to find applicants with a friendly nature and an ability to work in teams. For one new hotel opening in Los Angeles, Four Seasons interviewed 14,000 applicants for 350 jobs [1].

At Hampton Inns, guests are guaranteed satisfaction with the room and services they are provided. If they find the service unsatisfactory, their hotel bill is immediately voided. Guaranteeing satisfaction imposes an intensive discipline on all employees to ensure that all services provided by Hampton Inns are near perfection and any potential problem areas are immediately attended to.

Not all service organizations are focusing on customer satisfaction. According to estimates, only 10% of U.S. service companies in 1991 had any kind of quality program. During the 1990s, more and more service companies are expected to follow the examples set by Marriott, Four Seasons, and Hampton Inns [1].

The airline industry has always promoted its customer service. But customer satisfaction with airline service is abysmally low. The intensive competition in the airline industry and the consequent low profitability has not helped the customer service focus. Competition is increasing rapidly, particularly on international routes, and the basis of competition is frequently customer attention and service. A notable standout on customer service and satisfaction is Singapore Airlines.

Good service does not necessarily mean fancy meals and on-plane faxes and telephones. What does count in the airline industry is on-time and frequent service, a minimum number of transfers, and a reasonable amount of seating room.

Southwest Airlines is particularly popular because it provides low-cost, on-time service with frequent flights. Southwest is one of the few airlines that has remained profitable when nearly all other airlines were losing money [7].

Another airline that stands out for high-quality service is Alaska Airlines. Alaska Airlines' service can be identified by four performance measures. (1) Its food service is excellent. It spends twice as much as other airlines on meals. (2) Its planes provide more legroom than that at most other airlines.

(3) Through frequent training, its employees always provide friendly and helpful service. (4) Its flight schedules are dependable. Alaska Airlines spent considerable resources to achieve dependable flight schedules through acquisition of guidance equipment and through pilot training. These features allow its planes to take off and land safely in visibility conditions that ground other airlines [15].

CUSTOMER FOCUS IN HEALTH CARE

Health care industry interest and involvement in quality of care improvement and productivity improvement is rather sparse. However, there are indications that this condition is changing. Dr. Donald M. Berwick of the Harvard Community Health Plan and A. Blanton Godfrey of the Juran Institute ran a yearlong National Demonstration Project on Quality Improvement in Health Care. The project applied statistical quality control techniques, commonly used in industry, to health care operations and processes.

The National Demonstration Project teamed health care providers with quality experts from well-known companies such as Xerox and Hewlett-Packard to tackle a wide variety of problems in health care, such as the variability in the use of ultrasound testing, time required to transport critically ill children, reduction of time required to admit patients, time and effort required to discharge a patient, and housekeeping and food services [12].

One of the most confounding problems in health care is the variability in the performance of certain surgical procedures. In 1988, a comparison study was made between the frequency of surgical procedures performed in Syracuse and Utica, New York, two cities only 50 miles apart. The study revealed that an employee in Utica was much more likely to undergo a certain surgical procedure than an employee in Syracuse [12]. The general rule of thumb is to avoid surgery if at all possible; one wonders about the quality of health care people are receiving in Utica.

The most comprehensive study of health care quality involving patient satisfaction as well as performance quality is being implemented in Cleveland and involves a system of 30 Cleveland-area hospitals. The study is strongly supported by such well-known Cleveland companies as BP America, Parker Hannifin, Reliance Electric, and others. The intent of the study is to evaluate and then publish performance indicators for each of the 30 hospitals. Utilizers of the hospitals, including individuals, health maintenance organizations, and employee groups, can then use the information to put pressure on poorly performing hospitals to improve, or switch their business to the better-performing hospitals.

A more focused approach to improve quality of patient treatment was undertaken at Intermountain's 520-bed hospital in Salt Lake City. A study revealed that postoperative infections could be reduced if antibiotics were given to patients two hours before surgery. Intermountain used bedside computers to ensure that the antibiotic was administered two hours before the surgery. With the change to antibiotic administration, Intermountain's Salt Lake City hospital was able to reduce postoperative infection rates to 4 cases per 1000 surgical operations, compared to the national average postoperative infection rate of 20 per 1000 surgical operations [13].

The above illustrations indicate that there are pockets of activity to improve quality in the U.S. health care system. However, much more intensity and more extensive applications are required to make substantial improvements.

CUSTOMER FOCUS IN THE PACKAGE DELIVERY AND FINANCIAL SERVICES INDUSTRY

Improving quality of services is more difficult than improving the quality of products because of the temporary nature of a service. An unsatisfactory or defective product can be replaced or repaired. However, delivery of an unsatisfactory service is something that cannot be undone, so it is vital to deliver a satisfactory (or, preferably, superior) service the first time.

One way of improving quality of services is by increased spending on information technology. Especially in cases where customers prefer instant information (making reservations; buying tickets; inquiring about delivery, train, bus, or airline schedules), customers do not like to wait and definitely do not want to have to call back.

United Parcel Service, in its effort to improve information about the location of packages in its system, and also to be competitive with Federal Express and other competitors, spent as much as $1.5 billion on information technology. The UPS information system also captures signatures for delivered packages, thus enabling mail-order suppliers to send out signed delivery slips with invoices [1].

The fourth-largest credit card issuer in the United States, MBNA America Inc., has a special unit that talks to every customer who wants to drop a Visa or MasterCard, and is able to convince about half of them not to drop the credit card. As a result, MBNA keeps its credit card customers twice as long as the industry average [1].

Another example of how high-technology information services can improve customer service is USAA, a member-owned automobile insurance firm, credit card issuer, and mutual funds firm. USAA's membership consists of 2.2 million customers, most of them active or retired military officers and dependents. USAA pioneered the use of imaging systems that store documents such as insurance policies and application forms on optical disks. In the insurance business alone it scans over 40,000 pieces of mail into the system daily. Only about 5% of the paper documents are retained. USAA representatives now have virtually instant access to any document in their electronic files. This is a prime example of how investment in information technology provides USAA staff with the tools to improve customer service.

However, staff needs to be motivated to provide good service. At USAA, a system is used for rating employees on individual and group performance. Policy service representatives are scored on quality of phone calls, determined by auditors, and the number of transactions per hour. The first measure is a quality measure, and the second measure is a productivity measure [16].

Fidelity Financial Services is the nation's largest mutual funds firm, with $113 billion in assets in eight million customer accounts as of 1991. Fidelity launched a major program to obtain customer input on how it managed its interactions with its customers. In addition to focus groups, Fidelity launched the company's largest-ever client survey, in which 1330 customers rated how they perceive 70 different service attributes, from the convenience of branch locations to the aggressiveness of sales pitches. To their surprise, they found that customers prefer polite treatment ahead of investment performance and accuracy of customer account statements.

The results of the survey prompted Fidelity to institute a number of changes in its customer telephone interface operations. Productivity measures were eased. A new three-day course on phone etiquette was instituted. Efforts to humanize Fidelity became a prime objective. It was felt that more involved and happy workers pay more attention to customer feelings and needs [2].

The securities brokerage industry has lagged behind other service industries in improving its services. Charles Schwab and Company has installed an automated system that allows customers to obtain stock quotes and place orders without dealing with brokers. Using this service saves customers 10% on their transactions. Full-service brokers continue to use sales representatives to pitch their financial products to customers. The quality of these contacts often leaves much to be desired, and it behooves the full-service brokerage industry to review its customer contact practices [4].

Customer Focus at the Leading Retailers

If there is one industry where customer-firm interaction is paramount, it is retailing. The quality of interaction is frequently as important as the quality of the products that are sold. Quality in retailing is difficult to define. It consists of many components, such as low price combined with satisfactory service and wide selection, or high price with superb service.

The classic case of the retailer of the future is Home Depot, a chain of 140 giant home-improvement and hardware stores, which is still expanding rapidly and has a sales growth rate of 25% per year. Each Home Depot store stocks as many as 30,000 items for home-improvement and maintenance aficionados. The company guarantees full refunds to dissatisfied customers.

Home Depot uses extensive training programs for its salespeople, many of whom are former carpenters, electricians, and plumbers. Sales staff are encouraged to spend as much time with customers as possible and are expected to be totally familiar with everything within their area of responsibility. Customers are continuously provided with demonstrations on how to use equipment or how to install tile on a kitchen floor.

Superior information technology is no longer a luxury but a necessity for the large retailers. Bar code systems keep inventory levels to a minimum and speed reordering of fast-moving items. Wal-Mart shares its product movement information with its suppliers in order to speed up deliveries and help suppliers keep their costs down. The suppliers then pass at least part of those savings on to Wal-Mart. Because of its high-technology operations, Wal-Mart is able to keep its operating expense at 16% of sales, well below its major competitor, Kmart, whose operating expense hovers around 20%. Wal-Mart also uses satellite technology to broadcast video training classes to all its stores so that the stores can provide the training in-house. The same satellite TV system is also used to communicate with management in all stores and to introduce new products, their features, and where and how to display them [8].

At JC Penney's catalog sales division, the telephone order takers are reminded by their computers to ask customers if they need batteries whenever a battery-operated product is sold. This feature helped JC Penney attain profitable battery sales of over $1 million per year from negligible levels before [8].

At the other end of the customer dimension is Manhattan's Bergdorf-Goodman chain, where prices are way above JC Penney's, Kmart's, and Wal-Mart's. To retain its customers for its pricey merchandise, Bergdorf-Goodman offers trying-on and fitting of clothes in a customers' office, and a golf pro provides store clients with golfing tips on the store's putting green [8].

The above examples are just a few illustrations of how retailers can use technology, training, and careful employee selection to remain competitive, provide excellent service to the customer, and provide satisfaction to the customer for the products he or she purchases.

Customer Focus Through Value Pricing

What is the difference between value pricing and just cutting prices? Value pricing, by implication, means cutting prices, and lower prices usually mean lower profits (unless the lower prices dramatically increase volume and the increased volume generates higher overall aggregate profits).

One method of value pricing is to simultaneously reduce the cost of making the product. Some companies, especially high technology companies, are able to do just that. For instance, the rapid decline in prices of personal computers in the early 1990s was driven by lower production cost through improved technology and also through the lowering of distribution cost, especially by the mail-order distributors.

Value pricing, as its name implies, means offering a high quality, highly desirable product at a reasonable price. The product does not need to be cheap. But customers must feel they are getting value for their money. For instance, if BMW and Mercedes cut their prices on selected models by 30%, sophisticated customers will immediately see the value of those products.

What does not work is for a firm to claim that it is value pricing when in fact it is not. Sears claimed that it adopted value pricing in 1989. When customers started comparing Sears' prices to its competitors', they soon discovered that Sears' prices were not the lowest; as a result, Sears' value-pricing strategy failed [11]. Sears was offering lower prices than its own earlier prices but not prices lower than its competitors were offering.

Automobile companies often use value pricing to make a dramatic breakthrough in demand for a given model of automobile. By making many optional features standard equipment, manufacturers can usually generate enough savings to offer dramatic price reductions on their more expensive models, sometimes of as much as 30%.

In the personal computer (PC) industry, Apple introduced the Macintosh Classic, a stripped-down Macintosh that sold for 40% less than its predecessor. This value-pricing tactic turned out to be very successful for Apple. Sales zoomed, and Apple remained a formidable PC competitor [11].

The above illustrations show that a value-pricing tactic must be dramatic to be successful. Price cuts of 30 to 40% make customers sit up and take notice. It is clear that value pricing is not a fad; it will be around for quite a while.

Conclusions

The watchword in the 1990s has become *customer satisfaction:* find out what your customer wants, needs, likes, or prefers, or might want, might need, might like, or might prefer. Any firm not heeding this warning does so at its peril. The markets have changed. It is no longer possible to sell products that cause dissatisfaction among customers. Even low-priced products must perform a satisfactory function, must be dependable, and must satisfy the customer.

In response, many companies have developed training programs in empowerment, team formation, education, quality focus, and total quality management. Firms also focus on statistical quality programs and numerous other activities to ensure that their employees keep the customer in focus and that the final product or service fully satisfies the customer.

The ultimate beneficiary is, of course, the customer. Value to the individual is being created not just by providing a product or service but by ensuring that the customer is totally satisfied with the product or the service rendered.

The customer further benefits because companies do not stop at just satisfying customers' current needs and wants. The customer focus and customer satisfaction movement has also created an enormous awareness that, to remain competitive, companies must anticipate customers' future wants and needs. This, of course, is not entirely a new development, but the current quality and customer focus movement has brought much more attention to it.

Discussion Questions

1. Describe Motorola's key goals to achieve total customer satisfaction.
2. Describe Motorola's key initiatives to achieve total customer satisfaction.
3. In which area of total quality management are U.S. companies ahead of Japanese companies? Discuss.
4. Describe the Cleveland hospital evaluation system.
5. Describe a scenario for successful value pricing.
6. Identify five key issues of customer service in the retail industry.
7. Identify five key issues of customer service in the airline industry.
8. Visit a major department store in your area and identify what the store is doing in the area of customer focus and customer satisfaction.

References

1. Armstrong, Larry, and William C. Symonds. "Beyond 'May I Help You.'" *Business Week/Quality 1991*, 100–103.
2. Fuchsberg, Gilbert. "Gurus of Quality Are Gaining Clout." *Wall Street Journal,* January 29, 1992, B1.
3. Gouillart, F. J., and F. D. Sturdivant. "Spend a Day in the Life of Your Customers." *Harvard Business Review,* January-February 1994, 116–125.
4. Light, Larry, Leah Nathans Spiro, and Suzanne Woolley. "In High Tech They Trust." *Business Week/Quality 1991,* 120.
5. Miller, Karen Lowry. "Listening to Shoppers' Voices." *Business Week/Reinventing America 1992,* 690.
6. Neff, Robert. "No. 1—and Trying Harder," *Business Week/Quality 1991,* 20–24.

7. Oneal, Michael. "Straighten Up and Fly Right." *Business Week/Quality 1991,* 116–117.
8. Power, Christopher, and Laura Zinn. "Their Wish Is Your Command." *Business Week/Quality 1991,* 126–128.
9. Schonberger, Richard J. "Is Strategy Strategic? Impact of Total Quality Management on Strategy." *Academy of Management Executive,* 6(3), August 1992, 80–87.
10. Sherman, Stratford. "How to Prosper in the Value Decade." *Fortune,* November 30, 1992, 91–103.
11. Siler, Julia Flynn, and Susan Garland. "Sending Health Care into Rehab." *Business Week/Quality 1991,* 111.
12. Siler, Julia Flynn, and Sandra Atchison. "The Rx at Work in Utah." *Business Week/Quality 1991,* 113.
13. Solo, Sally. "How to Listen to Customers." *Fortune,* January 11, 1993, 77–79.
14. White, Joseph B. "'Value Pricing' Is Hot as Shrewd Customers Seek Low-Cost Quality." *Wall Street Journal,* March 12, 1991, A1.
15. Yang, Dori Jones. "Northern Hospitality." *Business Week/Quality 1991,* 118.
16. Zellner, Wendy. "USAA—Premium Treatment." *Business Week/Quality 1991,* 124.

Part two

Productivity and Quality Improvement through Teamwork and Training

Human Resource Management and Employee Training	4
Human Resources Enhancement through Team Utilization	5
Group Dynamics and Team Development	6
The Productivity and Quality Improvement Team	7
Team Process Leadership Roles and Functions	8

Introduction

The importance of teamwork in organizations cannot be stressed enough. There are multiple benefits to be achieved by organizations that utilize the various forms of teams. The first type of team to emerge on the world industrial scene was the quality circle. By the time it became known in the Western world, the quality circle was firmly established, and had proven itself, in Japan. Although there was a brief flurry of strong interest in and implementation of quality circles in the Western world, the concept never became firmly established and did not last long. It probably failed because of the relatively high cost of establishing and maintaining functioning quality circles. In Japan, employees met on their own time in the West, employees met on company time. Hence, there was a large disparity of cost to operate quality circles.

However, the successors of quality circles have done well. Remnants of quality circles still remain. They are now more likely to be called quality and productivity improvement teams. They are also more likely to be cross-functional, consisting of members from several functional areas. Their focus is also more likely to be productivity oriented.

A team concept that has been successfully and widely applied is the self-managed work team. Self-managed work teams improve productivity and quality because the members of the team become collectively responsible for both the quality and quantity of their work. They are responsible for their own management, thus eliminating the need for supervision, and they are frequently compensated on the basis of the quality and quantity of their output. They also frequently have some control over their team membership, thus providing the team with true management responsibility, authority, and control.

To maximize the benefits of teams, management must, of course, provide training and guidance, as well as rules and regulations. Hence, training commitment and team formation must go hand in hand. Firms that have successfully implemented both cross-functional problem solving teams and self-managed work teams know that regular training of team members is necessary for the successful functioning of the teams.

Chapter four

Human Resource Management and Employee Training

Outline

Introduction
Requirements for a More Educated and Better Trained Workforce
The Training Experts: Selected Corporations
Motorola's Foundation Is Training
The German Model for Apprenticeship Training
Conclusions

Introduction

In the mid-19th century, the United Kingdom was the dominant world power in terms of both colonial possessions and industry. The United States was number two in industry, and at the 1851 industrial exhibition in London, England, the British were amazed at American products, such as reapers and muskets, with interchangeable parts. It was called the American system of manufacture, and British industry delegations flocked to the United States to find out how the Americans were doing it. They found a highly literate workforce, as high as 95% of the free population in industrial New England. In contrast, the United Kingdom population at that time was only about 65% literate [6].

Skill levels and manufacturing techniques have changed radically since 1851, but the level of education of the workforce is still critical to the successful utilization of that workforce. The United States is currently badly lagging behind Japan, Germany, and many other industrialized countries in the area of an educated workforce.

The United States lags far behind Japan in the number of engineers per capita. And with technology changing rapidly, engineers need continual training and retraining to keep them up to date. About 10% of U.S. companies are doing an excellent job at training and retraining their workforces. But what about the other 90%? The training activities of the vast majority of U.S. firms is seriously lagging behind industrial firms in other countries [7].

In the area of training the technical manpower who do the complex technical tasks in the high-technology firms, the United States lags far behind Germany. Germany's extensive industry-driven and industry-financed apprenticeship training programs are providing it with a trained technical labor force that is superior to the U.S. labor force. To what extent is this putting the United States at a disadvantage in the global marketplace? Well, measured by international trade, the Germans far outpace the United States and Japan in exports both on an absolute and on a per capita basis.

The United States has a strong higher educational system. But is that enough to keep up with strong industrial nations such as Japan and Germany? In this chapter, we will address this problem in detail.

REQUIREMENTS FOR A MORE EDUCATED AND BETTER TRAINED WORKFORCE

The United States has one of the strongest and most comprehensive higher educational systems in the world. Unfortunately, this excellent educational system is only utilized by, and in most cases is only accessible to, about 45% of the population of college age. The other 55% of the college-age population stops their education at the high school level, and many stop well before completing high school.

Outreach programs for remedial education need to be extended to the 55% of the U.S. population who have not attended college or university. This needs to be done not when they are at college level; ideally, it should be started well before they reach this point in their lives. Those who do not qualify for college or university have no choice but to stop their education before the college level.

An article in *Business Week* [7] made four suggestions to deal with the undereducated and undertrained. The first suggestion focuses on instilling the habits of learning and working in children at a young age. Experience with the government's Head Start program has shown that every dollar spent on Head Start pays back four times in lower expenditures on public assistance, special education, and other costs. It was found that children who participate in Head Start are more likely to graduate from high school and more likely to obtain gainful employment.

The second suggestion is to pay teachers more, and perhaps transform the whole teaching process. Public school teaching at both the elementary and high school levels has been receiving considerable attention from the popular press in recent years. Suggestions have been made to switch to voucher systems, to privatize education, to use more discipline, and so on. Changes are occurring in education but probably at too slow a pace to have sufficient impact in the near future. Introduction of new technology now and in the future is promising. Computer technology will be able to make major changes in the teaching and learning process.

What is ignored by most press reports is the fact that there are numerous excellent schools in both the public and private sector. The problem, however, lies with the lower-quality schools and especially those in economically depressed urban areas. Some drastic restructuring must occur in these schools.

The third suggestion is to adopt major new incentives to train and retrain workers. The problem is who is going to pay for the incentives. If tax credits were given to industry, all training now being done without incentives would also qualify for the incentives, and the cost of such a program could skyrocket. It may be more desirable to use tuition credit for individuals to be given following successful completion of qualified training courses or programs. For instance, giving tuition credits to those without a high school diploma for passing a high school equivalency test would seem to be appropriate. Similar tuition credit incentives could be provided for reaching other levels of education.

The fourth suggestion is to tailor the workplace to the changing workforce. This suggestion includes providing incentives for more extensive child-care benefits to working mothers and working couples. Providing more flexible hours to working mothers or parents with young children would provide better performance in the workplace. Part-time work opportunities for parents of young families should be strongly supported by government legislation or incentives. A final suggestion is to consider a gradual easing into retirement instead of the current approach, which forces people from full employment status to complete retirement. Many people prior to retirement are at a high skill level, and losing them is frequently costly to the firm.

THE TRAINING EXPERTS: SELECTED CORPORATIONS

Training of employees on a year-round basis is becoming the practice at some companies. Most of these companies do not consider their training expenditures as expenses but rather as investments in their human resources.

At Federal Express, every one of the company's 40,000 employees who is in customer contact takes a computer-based exam at least once per year. The exam identifies areas of weakness in employees, and, on the basis of the exam scores, remedial training is prescribed. The computer keeps track of all exam scores, and performance on exams is part of the annual review process. Federal Express keeps a record of customer complaints; the skill level of employees has been shown to be inversely related to the number of customer complaints.

At Federal Express, all employees also attend two TQM programs called "Quality Advantage" and "Quality Action Team." These programs teach the employees the basics of quality management and quality team development [1].

General Electric's aircraft engine division uses training as a tool for survival in a declining aircraft engine market. Training is provided by line managers and hourly employees instead of by outside consultants to cut costs. Classes are relatively short and are usually held in close proximity to the employee's workplace. Employees are also encouraged to take courses outside their regular work hours to upgrade their skills and education.

Solectron of Milpitas, California, sends employees to training programs for as long as 110 hours per year. Solectron assembles printed circuits and other highly technical components. Because of rapidly changing technology and rapid growth, training is a must for companies like Solectron. Training is provided by Solectron's own employees and by outsiders.

One company widely known for its extensive training programs is Corning of Corning, New York. At Corning's Ceramics plant in Erwin, employees involved in the manufacture of Celcor, a special ceramic, must be certified as Celcor specialists. The training program that enables one to become a Celcor specialist usually takes two years, during which time the employee spends an average of one day per week in training, on the job or in the classroom. Once certified, employees receive a 20% raise. The results of Corning's training program are impressive. Productivity has increased and defects have declined by 38% in one year.

The U.S. Army is also heavily involved in training. Most of the army's heavy equipment, from rocket launchers to tanks, is high technology and requires constant training and retraining. All recruits have at least a high school education and receive intensive technical training to maintain and operate the new high-technology equipment.

The above examples are selected illustrations of training and education programs in successful organizations. These organizations are, of course, not successful only because of their training, but the training programs certainly contribute to their ongoing success [4].

Table 4–1 gives a summary of the number of hours employees in a selected group of companies spent in training per year and also the percent of payroll each company spent on training their employees.

Motorola's Foundation is Training

Motorola is one of America's leading corporations in the quest for innovation in high-technology products. Its products are produced virtually defect free and respond to customers' wants and needs.

Motorola started out, in 1920, as a car radio manufacturer, got into television set production during the post–World War II years, and today is one of the leaders in high-technology electronic and computer products. In the first year

Table 4–1

Training Intensity of Selected Companies

Company	Number of Employees	Average Training Hours per Employee per Year	Percent of Payroll Spent in 1992 on Training
Federal Express	93,000	27	4.5
Solectron	3,500	95	3.0
Corning	14,000 (domestic)	92	3.0
Motorola	107,000	36	3.6

Source: Adapted from Henkoff, Ronald. "Companies That Train Best." *Fortune,* March 22, 1993, 62–75.

of the Malcolm Baldrige National Quality Awards (1988), Motorola was one of the three winners.

Motorola has reached its present level of success not by chance but by a carefully planned approach. As the central focus of its quality plans it adopted the six sigma quality level as a goal it wanted to achieve by 1992. Although it did not quite achieve this goal, it came very close.

Setting a goal by itself is not enough; a carefully designed approach is necessary. Motorola studied what the quality experts such as Deming, Juran, Crosby, and Ishikawa proposed. It selected what it deemed were their good points and implemented those points where feasible. For instance, it rejected Ishikawa's idea that the customer be defined as the next person who receives what you have done on the job. Motorola decided there is only one customer: the person who buys and uses your product. He or she is the one to whom all efforts should be devoted.

The one suggestion that Motorola took to heart was Deming's idea about training. Training, according to Deming, should also include education. Training applies to specific skills and should be offered to those employees needing them. But employees also need to be educated, and education never ends.

In response to Deming's ideas, Motorola set up its own university in Schaumburg, Illinois. It is located in an 88,000-square-foot building and is Motorola's training and education headquarters. Training also occurs at plant and foreign locations. But every Motorola employee receives a minimum of 40 hours of training or education per year, equivalent to at least 2% of his or her work time.

The type of training Motorola employees receive is not necessarily highly technical. Training involves the reinforcement of routine practices and procedures that are critical and important to ensuring quality production and high productivity.

Training is also required of employees at all levels in the organization to ensure that the material covered by lower-level employees will be accepted by their superiors. For instance, coverage of such routine techniques as Pareto charts, control charts, and process diagramming is taught to all levels of employees to ensure that these procedures are accepted at all levels of the organization.

Motorola's budget for training exceeds $60 million per year for the actual training activities plus an equivalent amount for salaries paid to employees while they are being trained. Is Motorola spending too much or too little? An independent study made in the 1980s showed that for every dollar invested in training, Motorola received a $30 return [1]. This huge return is questionable, and if true is not likely to continue forever. However, training employees is an investment that pays for itself, and it can provide substantial dividends to the firm [3].

THE GERMAN MODEL FOR APPRENTICESHIP TRAINING

Each year, German companies spend about $18 billion to train the country's 1.8 million apprentices, or about $10,000 per apprentice. Another $18 billion is spent by German industry on retraining their existing workforce [8]. U.S. industrial firms spend about $30 billion in total training cost, but the training is largely restricted to the 10% of companies that are heavily involved in training programs. Also, much of U.S. training goes to additional training for already-trained professionals. The U.S. government spends about $18 billion on training, but most of it goes to disadvantaged potential workers or to dislocated workers, and not to those on the job who need upgrading of their skills.

Close to 70% of German youth pass through apprenticeship programs in a variety of technical industries, such as metalworking, electronics, and computer hardware and software, and in such nontechnical industries as sales, hairstyling, clerical work, transportation, and maintenance. The remaining 30% of German youth go on to college or university.

The interesting part of Germany's apprenticeship system is that on-the-job training is almost entirely funded by industry. Apprentices also spend one to two days a week in class, where they are taught the basic courses necessary for their technical careers.

Not all apprentices stay with the firms where they do their apprenticeship training, but many do. However, since there is an enormous pool of qualified talent, mobility is not a problem or a deterrent to Germany's apprenticeship system.

In contrast, the U.S. population is notoriously undertrained and undereducated. About 56% of young people in the United States have no college education. They are at a severe disadvantage in finding a suitable job; there are too many of them for the limited number of jobs for which no skill or low skills are required [2].

The United States has a large undereducated and undertrained workforce, which may hinder it in competing in the global marketplace of the future. About 20 million U.S. workers need remedial or additional education in reading, writing, arithmetic, basic mathematics, and general subjects. Who will pay for this education and training is an important question. There appears to be an urgent need for both the government and industry to cooperatively attack this serious problem.

Could a German apprenticeship program be developed in the United States? Even if it could be started on a small scale, the benefits would be visible soon and would provide incentives for other firms to join it. Again, there is need for a cooperative industry-government project.

Conclusions

In this chapter, we have addressed the problem of human resource management, particularly as it relates to employee training and retraining. We first looked at the requirements for a more educated and better trained workforce. The key part related to how the approximately 55% of youth without ability or interest in college work can be trained to make them employable in the workforce of the future.

Next we looked at those progressive corporations that are viewed as the training experts. Unfortunately, most of the training in U.S. industry is done by only 10% of the more progressive firms.

A special section was devoted to Motorola's performance, which is attributed to its high-intensity training programs and its focus on defect-free performance and customer satisfaction.

Finally, we described the German apprenticeship system, a system that is often viewed as the cause of Germany's ability to be the world's largest exporter of high-technology and high-quality products.

In all the above programs it is clear that the training programs of these companies aim to empower the individual employee so that he or she can become a greater contributor to the organization. With employee empowerment, the firm is able to tap the creative and intellectual energy of each employee in the organization [5].

Discussion Questions

1. In which areas of education and training is the United States at a disadvantage with Germany?
2. In which areas of education and training is the United States at a disadvantage with Japan?
3. In which area of education is the United States superior to other developed countries?
4. Motorola trains all levels of its employees in the same productivity and quality techniques. Why does Motorola follow this policy?
5. Why has U.S. industry not adopted the German apprenticeship system?
6. Discuss why the German apprenticeship system may be a potential drag on the Germany economy.
7. Develop an incentive scheme for employees to further their education outside the firm in part-time education programs.
8. It has been reported that newly hired employees at automobile assembly plants have a much higher average level of education than employees who have worked in the same plants for 10 years or more. Is this a good development? Discuss and explain your rationale.
9. Does overeducation of employees lead to higher productivity or to lower productivity? Discuss and explain your rationale.
10. What impact does level of education have on employee mobility? Discuss and explain your reasoning.

References

1. Blackburn, R. "Total Quality and Human Resources Management." *Academy of Management Executive,* 7(3), August 1993, 49–59.
2. Berstein, Aaron, Richard Brandt, Barbara Carlson, and Karen Padley. "Teaching Business How to Train." *Business Week/Reinventing America 1992,* 82–90.
3. Dobyns, Lloyd, and Clare Crawford-Mason. "How Motorola Saved Itself." *American Machinist,* April 1992, 54–76.
4. Henkoff, Ronald. "Companies That Train Best." *Fortune,* March 22, 1993, 62–75.
5. Kiernan, M. J. "The New Strategic Architecture: Learning to Compete in the Twenty First Century." *Academy of Management Executive,* 7(1), February 1993, 7–21.
6. Nussbaum, Bruce. "Needed Human Capital." *Business Week,* September 19, 1988, 100–103.
7. Pennar, Karen. "It's Time to Put Our Money Where Our Future Is." *Business Week,* September 19, 1988, 140–141.
8. Schares, Gail E. "Experts in Overalls." *Business Week/Reinventing America 1992,* 90.

Chapter *five*

Human Resources Enhancement through Team Utilization

Outline

Introduction
Japan's Participative Management Style
The European Nissan Plant
The Western View of Workers
Japanese and American Management Views
Effective Employee Development
The Japanese Management Style
Labor versus Capital
Conclusions

Introduction

Productivity and quality improvement teams—productivity improvement teams, in briefer terms—are a means of improving quality and productivity, applying work simplification methods, and containing costs. It is often through a direct impact on employee morale and attitude that indirect benefits—such as higher-quality work, more efficient and effective output, and cost savings—are generated.

When quality circles (now commonly called productivity improvement teams in the United States) were implemented in Japan in 1962, the morale of the Japanese worker was not considered a problem. Most Japanese workers were employed in a highly participative and cooperative environment. In addition, they had virtually guaranteed lifetime jobs with substantial benefits. The motivation for productivity improvement team implementation was not worker morale improvement but rather the quality and productivity problem facing Japan at that time. Japanese industry was forced to export to survive and grow. Yet it still shouldered the pre–World War II reputation of shoddy merchandise. To overcome that reputation, Japanese industry leaders realized that they had to manufacture products for export that were superior in performance and quality to competing products in the importing countries. To attain that superior quality, Japanese industry had to do something beyond the routine inspection and statistical quality control of products. To meet this challenge, a Japanese engineer from the Toyota automobile organization developed and implemented the productivity improvement concept.

Because productivity improvement teams also have the potential for employee morale improvement, they are particularly fitting for the U.S. environment. Low morale is usually not the fault of employees but rather of the organizational structure in which management and employees must function. Productivity improvement teams have the potential to change the traditional American organizational structure and thus improve morale, motivation, and dedication to the objectives of the organization.

Especially in those cases where firms must restructure their operations, such as in downsizing, plant closings, and other organizational restructuring operations, the maintenance of employee morale is critical. Several studies have shown that following organizational restructuring, surviving employees become narrow-minded, self-absorbed, and risk-averse. As morale drops, productivity declines and employees distrust management [2, 3]. In such a situation productivity improvement teams and strong management support for them can alleviate the inevitable drop in employee morale.

JAPAN'S PARTICIPATIVE MANAGEMENT STYLE

Japan is recognized as a country with a culture in which both child and adult have considerable respect for elders and, especially, for older parents. In such a society, one would thus expect a strong hierarchical authority relationship to develop in an organizational structure. Surprisingly, the opposite is true. Although new and young employees are still subservient to older employees who serve as mentors, after they pass through a lengthy apprentice and training program they become full-fledged employees of the organization and are considered equals.

The result is that the Japanese organizational structure emerges as participative, as less authoritarian and hierarchical than the American organizational structure. In the Japanese structure, everyone is in charge, never just one person. If we in the West enter an organization, office, store, school, factory, or even a hospital, we know that a designated person is responsible for the entire organization. In contrast, the Japanese feel that no one person is capable of being totally in charge, of carrying such an enormous burden. Because Americans feel uneasy in an organization that does not have a single authority figure, when visiting Japanese organizations they initially receive the impression of disorganization; only after studying the system for a while do they realize that things function smoothly.

To illustrate the Japanese structural style, in a visit to a Japanese industrial plant by the author, it was virtually impossible to deduce who was in charge.

Introductions were without titles; only names were used. In retrospect, however, there was one clue. The person with the highest rank in a group of Japanese people will virtually always be the oldest male, and that was true in this case. The oldest man in the group of five was the plant manager, the two younger men were his assistants, and the two women were the secretaries from the reception area. Although all five people were clearly responsible members of the organization, sharing responsibility for the welcoming of the visitors, it is doubtful if their official status in the organization was as equal as their observed responsibilities.

The European Nissan Plant

The classic story of how the Nissan automobile corporation selected the location of their European automobile plant is must reading for anyone in the Western world who is satisfied with the status quo in employer-management relations.

In the late 1970s and early 1980s, Nissan began searching for an appropriate location for an automobile manufacturing plant to serve the European common market. The Japanese are very concerned about labor relations in the foreign countries where they establish manufacturing plants, so it came as a great surprise to many when Nissan announced that their automobile assembly plant would be built in Great Britain. The British automobile industry during the late 1970s had been beset with labor problems for years, with frequent plant shutdowns. How could Nissan management decide to build an automobile plant in Great Britain?

In reality, Nissan's plan to build the plant in Great Britain had been extensively researched. The fact that the British speak English undoubtedly helped, because the Japanese usually have reasonable ability in English, whereas if they had located in a non-English-speaking country, they would have had to communicate in an unfamiliar language. Nissan had also studied extensively the experience of other Japanese firms that had established plants in Great Britain, and they had found that those firms had all managed to establish excellent labor-management relations by using the Japanese model of equal responsibility and equal treatment. Nissan was therefore confident that it would be able to operate efficiently and effectively in Great Britain, without the debilitating strikes and slowdowns that plagued British industry.

Why were Japanese managers more adept at employee-management relations than their British counterparts? The reason was to be found in employee treatment. At Nissan's British plant there is one cafeteria and one parking lot for all employees, and washroom facilities are accessible to all. At a comparable British automobile plant, different cafeteria levels existed for blue-collar workers, for lower-level management, for middle management, and for higher-level management. Chief executives were served in the dining room. Similarly, parking was determined by a person's status level in the organization, with blue-collar workers assigned parking spaces farthest away. At one British facility there were seven levels of washrooms!

The point of this story is that employees will behave in relation to the way they are treated by their organization. In the Western world, we may be living with a status quo that may never have been right, but today it is more outdated than ever. Today, employees have more education and greater expectations regarding job satisfaction, acceptable work environments, and recognition for their work contributions. It is in these areas that we can gain from the Japanese experience.

THE WESTERN VIEW OF WORKERS

The U.S. Department of Health, Education and Welfare (HEW), a forerunner of the present Department of Health and Human Services (HHS), reported in a study the following complaints about management by American workers: (1) management failed to listen to them when they made suggestions for productivity improvements; (2) management demonstrated little respect for their intelligence; and (3) management viewed the workers as being incapable of thinking creatively about their jobs.

These complaints argue strongly for the implementation of productivity improvement teams that provide employees an opportunity to participate in managerial activities. The productivity improvement teams also provide management the opportunity to show employees that it respects their intelligence and believes that they are able to think creatively about their jobs. Yet a one-time commitment to productivity improvement teams is not sufficient. An ongoing management commitment, in the form of acceptance of productivity improvement team recommendations, is needed to avoid these kinds of employee complaints.

JAPANESE AND AMERICAN MANAGEMENT VIEWS

There are significant differences between Japanese and American employment practices. In our society, there is a history of an a priori adverse relationship between worker and management that is expressed in strong and active unionism on the part of the workers and in little management concern for the workers' welfare. Historically, U.S. management stresses guidance rather than worker incentives or initiatives; it typically adopts the view that workers have one responsibility and management another. This results in little opportunity for mutual cooperation to reach a common goal.

This approach has reinforced an authoritarian supervisory style in which nonsupervisory employees perform routine structured work and are not allowed to help solve organizational problems. However, when productivity or quality sags, pressures are created for changes in these culturally embedded managerial practices. Productivity improvement teams provide an important vehicle for such changes. And many firms have adopted changes extensively.

In contrast to the historical practices of the American employer, the Japanese manager aims to develop the skills of the employees fully, through on-the-job or classroom training and by attaching new and young employees to older employees who can serve as mentors in the organization.

The improvement of the employee as a human being is another important goal of the Japanese employer. The employee is viewed not as a specialist but as a person with an enormous range of capabilities that the Japanese employer recognizes and attempts to channel into productive activities for all concerned.

Employees need to be viewed as resources that can yield economic returns, and trained employees are investments by the firm. With this view, it is clearly feasible and justifiable to devote considerable financial resources to employee development.

In this context, productivity improvement teams can be viewed as a potential resource. The training of employees to participate in productivity improvement teams is an investment not only in the individuals but also in the productivity improvement teams, as a group resource that will ultimately provide economic gains.

EFFECTIVE EMPLOYEE DEVELOPMENT

Employee development should aim to build confidence among the employees and at the management level, to ensure that available resources will produce measurable changes. The Japanese approach to employee development places great responsibility on the employees because they are part of management, and as such are taking responsibility for their immediate environment. They do not use narrow job descriptions that confine an employee's responsibility to a few structured tasks. Instead, they give the Japanese employee broad responsibilities, as illustrated by the fact that the secretarial staff in the reception office of a Japanese manufacturing plant felt as much responsibility for the welfare of the visitors as the plant manager. The Japanese approach to building confidence in workers is an important aspect of their assuming responsibility and encourages their participation in problem identification and resolution.

The Japanese thereby also instill a sense of competition among divisions and departments. However, within departments, competition among employees is perceived as counterproductive to fostering cooperation among them. Because the employees are taught the importance of both cooperation and responsibility in decision-making activities, any competition among them is subordinated to the need for cooperative and consensus decision making. An employee who competes with others, without considering the value of being part of the team, will not succeed in the Japanese environment.

A Japanese employee assumes responsibility for correcting a problem in someone else's job or responsibility area. It is understood that such intervention is to be expected and is desirable. Indeed, in most settings, several employees check each other's work to ensure that the work produced by all of them is problem free. The result is a built-in system of quality control that is applied during a process rather than at the end.

To attain this, the Japanese have, in effect, replaced the boss-subordinate relationship with an equal-to-equal relationship. Every employee, in essence, functions as a supervisor, thereby increasing worker satisfaction through responsibility. Employees feel proud of the products or services their organization produces because they know they are an essential part of the organization.

Another seemingly small, yet significant, aspect of the Japanese management approach is the insistence on good housekeeping and on being as precise as possible at all levels of the organization with regard to the products or services being produced. In the case of job descriptions, preciseness is replaced by comprehensiveness.

The Japanese approach to employee development is viewed by many as culturally dependent. Yet the same approach can be applied in the American workplace. In the present Western setting, employees are supposed to stay in their slots, as defined by job descriptions. This concept is not the employee's idea; it is the organizational structure that defines that role. If employees interfere in other areas, they will very quickly be told to stop. Clearly, the Western organization that can apply even a modicum of Japanese methods of utilizing their employees to the fullest will achieve a substantial competitive edge.

THE JAPANESE MANAGEMENT STYLE

There are six major components of the Japanese management style:

1. Worker participation
2. Stable employment
3. Strong insistence in quality
4. Motivation by quality of product
5. Worker opinions
6. Insistence on a neat and clean work environment

Worker participation serves multiple purposes. It builds worker confidence, expands worker abilities, and adds value to the organization. It also trains employees in the kind of cooperative teamwork that is necessary to ensure quality and efficiency in skills and on-the-job training in supervisory and managerial concepts.

Worker participation is especially required in identifying and solving problems. The productivity improvement team is, of course, a vehicle for these activities, but individuals can be involved also. Japanese firms place much more emphasis on employee suggestion plans than do American firms. Basadur [1] reports that of 10 well-known Japanese firms surveyed, the median number of suggestions per employee per year is about 64, or more than one per week per employee. The comparable figure for U.S. firms is 2.3 suggestions per person per year. To be sure, not all suggestions are viable, but one would expect the net yield of useful suggestions to be a lot higher in Japan than in the United States.

Basadur [1] even suggests that the more emphasis is placed on problem finding, the easier it is to solve the problem and implement the solution. The basis behind his idea is the commonly accepted fact that people involved in finding, defining, and solving a problem will be more enthusiastic in implementing the solution to the problem they worked on.

Stable employment is also a condition for attaining worker participation, cooperation, and commitment. In the Japanese system, lifetime employment is quite common. The employees know that they will be employed as long as the organization is operational and thus are motivated to aid collectively in the functioning of the organization.

The achievement of superior quality in Japanese products is mandatory because of Japan's dependence on world export markets. The insistence on quality and productivity is pervasive not only in export industries but also in service and government industries. Because the Japanese also compete in local markets, the need to maintain a good competitive reputation in export markets has produced a pervasive and sophisticated system of built-in quality and productivity control.

Finally, there is the issue of a neat and clean environment. It is an axiom in Japanese companies (and in Japanese-managed American plants) that good housekeeping is important not only to the organization but also to the employee. The result is that the typical Japanese workplace is both well organized and spotless.

Labor Versus Capital

Although some American corporations are what economists call labor intensive, many others are able to substitute capital for labor. By developing new machinery and equipment, those firms are able to produce the same amount with fewer people. American farming is a good example. A small fraction of the American workforce is now able to feed a large portion of the world, compared with 100 years ago, when the majority of American workers were employed in agriculture. The same is happening in the manufacturing industry. Automation and robotization are gradually eliminating the need for large numbers of blue-collar workers. Japan already has a machine plant that is staffed only by machines and robots; the only people employed are those in maintenance, who are called by machines when their services are required. There are thus obvious advantages in being able to switch from a labor-intensive to a capital-intensive way of producing things. Machines and robots do not need rest periods, vacations, incentives, motivation, or morale boosters; there are no problems with absenteeism, turnover, or union negotiations. Clearly, the substitution of capital for labor has many attractive advantages.

In short, the management of a labor-intensive corporation must realize that, if it is to become more efficient and effective, it must do so through its existing mode of operation. Therefore, to gain efficiencies, existing human resources must be utilized more effectively. The productivity improvement team approach has proven itself to be a highly effective way of maximizing human resource development.

Conclusions

There are several reasons why teamwork is considered increasingly important in many firms. The first major movement to utilize teams did so for the purpose of improving quality and solving problems in the organization. The teams were called quality circles and originated in Japan. They flourished for a while in the United States, largely in California, during the 1980s. Some quality circles survived; others were renamed and frequently reoriented to focus not only on quality but on productivity problems.

The current focus on teams is for the purpose of self-management of employees, thus flattening the organization and providing participation by employees in the management of their and their fellow team members' work activities. Thus the idea of self-managing work teams was born, and it has flourished since then with outstanding success.

Also important has been the evolution of cross-functional teams. These teams are usually at a somewhat higher level than self-managing work teams. They also function frequently more like traditional quality circles, because they usually focus their activities on problem areas that need resolution.

Thus, self-managing work teams, problem-solving teams, and cross-functional teams all serve to improve the activities of the firm, while at the same time providing more work satisfaction to the employees through more active participation in critical activities of the organization.

Discussion Questions

1. Discuss the motivation for productivity improvement team development in Japan.
2. Why did Nissan decide to locate their European automobile assembly plant in Great Britain?
3. To what extent have Western employers adopted the Japanese practice of equal treatment, including parking and other perquisites for all employees?
4. Develop the argument that productivity improvement teams can be viewed as a resource to the organization.
5. Discuss the idea that competitiveness and cooperation can exist side by side in a work organization, and can benefit the organization if energies are properly utilized.

References

1. Basadur, M. "Managing Creativity: A Japanese Model." *Academy of Management Executive,* 6(2), May 1992, 29–42.
2. Brockner, J. "The Effects of Work Layoffs on Survivors: Research, Theory and Practice," in B. M. Shaw and L. L. Cummings (eds.), *Research in Organizational Behavior,* Vol. 10, pp. 213–255. JAI Press, Greenwich, CT, 1988.
3. Rice, D., and C. Dreilinger. "After the Downsizing." *Training and Development,* May 1991, 41–44.

Chapter six

Group Dynamics and Team Development

Outline

Introduction
Historical Background of Group Dynamics
Span of Control of Small Work Groups
Size of Small Work Groups
Leadership Style of Small Work Groups
Group Structure
Pitfalls of Team Utilization
Three Types of Teams
Conclusions

Introduction

The productivity improvement or work team experience is not a radical departure from the everyday experiences of the team members. People do not exist in isolation; they work together, play together, and live together. Some of us spend more time than others in small groups, but it would be difficult to lead a normal life without being a member of one or more small groups.

The most common small group is the family. Normally, even those who live alone still consider themselves part of some family. Children belong to larger groups as they enter school; outside of school they usually belong to smaller groups, such as a sports team or a neighborhood group of friends.

In part of their work time, working adults function in groups. Committee sessions, other meetings, and just doing one's daily routine tasks all involve group activities. People frequently are part of a team at work. In their spare time, these people belong to other groups, such as bowling leagues, social clubs, golf foursomes, tennis clubs, and exercise clubs.

In short, as part of the maturation process, people learn to adapt themselves to the small group environment. They learn the give-and-take necessary to function in small groups. They become so accustomed to groups that, if deprived of group interaction, they feel a loss. The retirement shock can be at least partially explained by individuals being deprived of their small group interactions. A societal trend toward even greater group interaction is illustrated by car pools, increasing attendance at sporting events, condominium living, and food co-ops.

The small group is thus a natural and important part of the maintenance of one's mental health, happiness, and satisfaction. There is, of course, the possibility of group overload, sometimes resulting in stress. Clearly, some can deal with more group interaction; others cannot. Yet group interaction is an important part of daily living, and it can be enjoyable if the group task is pertinent to each member of the group.

The purpose of the productivity improvement team is to discuss problems that are of interest to the participating individuals because they are related to their everyday work activities. The team members are generally volunteers; they have an interest in problem identification and problem solving, and it is assumed that they enjoy participating in a group activity. Yet, although most employees need the therapeutic benefits of group activity, some of them have a greater need than others for group affiliations. The voluntary aspect of productivity improvement team participation among the workers is thus a primary consideration. Indeed, many competent and industrious employees may choose not to participate.

An entirely different situation exists among self-directed work teams. In the work team case, all members must be willing and able to participate. Anyone unable to work cooperatively with others in a work team concept must not be asked to participate in such work teams. Alternative work should be found for those employees.

In any event, once the participants of a productivity improvement team or a work team begin to achieve common goals, the principles of group dynamics will play an important role.

Historical Background of Group Dynamics

In a general sense, group dynamics is concerned with the ways groups are organized and managed and how they behave. Cartwright and Zander [2] identify three views of group dynamics. The first encompasses leadership, participation of members in decision making, and the gains obtained by society, the organizations, or the individual participants. The second view of group dynamics portrays it as a set of techniques or processes, such as role playing, discussion sessions, observation and feedback of group process, and group decision making. This interpretation has been employed widely in training programs designed to improve skills in human relations and in the management of conferences and committees. The third view of group dynamics is of a field of inquiry dedicated to achieving knowledge about the nature of groups, about the laws of their development, and about their interrelations with individuals, other groups, and larger institutions.

This last view is the one that is held by most academicians and researchers. Its advantage is that it is able to shed light on how groups actually behave, with the potential of improving their functioning. However, with respect to practical application of the group dynamics concept, the other views cannot be ignored.

Organizational management has reason to be particularly concerned with the functioning of small groups. After all, organizations are essentially collections of overlapping teams; they depend to a considerable extent on the efficient and effective coordination of those teams to achieve their goals.

Surprisingly, until Frederick Taylor's work around the turn of the century, there were few studies or theories regarding the management of individuals or groups. Taylor's work was primarily related to individuals—how they could be more efficiently utilized by providing them with the proper tools and training.

The first major studies of work groups were the Hawthorne studies of Elton Mayo at the Western Electric plant in Chicago in the 1930s [8, 10]. An earlier study by Follett [4] had some theoretical implications, but they did not receive much attention until the Hawthorne studies were developed. The Hawthorne effort began in 1927 as a series of studies of individual workers to determine the relationship between working conditions and the incidence of fatigue. The results revealed a considerable number of group characteristics that had not been anticipated.

One result of the Hawthorne studies is the discovery of a phenomenon now known as the Hawthorne effect. When human subjects are being observed as part of a study, their behavior is going to be different than if they were not being observed. This difference in behavior is known as the Hawthorne effect. For instance, human subjects being observed as part of a productivity study may either work faster or slower, more steady or less steady than humans not being observed, depending on what the human subjects believe the study results are going to be used for.

Because of these unanticipated results, Mayo and his associates placed much greater emphasis on the social organization of the work group, including the social relationship between supervisor and workers; on the informal standards governing the behavior of work group members; and on the attitudes of the workers functioning in the groups.

Barnard's *The Functions of the Executive,* published in 1938, was heavily influenced by the Hawthorne studies and pointed out the importance of human needs and social processes [1]. Barnard's view was that, because large organizations are social institutions, the individual worker cannot be studied in isolation from fellow workers and managers.

By the end of the 1930s, Kurt Lewin had begun to use the term *group dynamics* to describe the study of small groups [7]. Considerable research on small groups was now beginning to provide empirical documentation of some of the untested theories that had evolved previously. Following World War II, a rapid expansion of empirical research created a considerable body of knowledge about the dynamics of small groups.

Finally, in the early 1960s, the quality circle and later the productivity improvement team emerged as a model to which many of the earlier empirical research results could be applied. More significantly, the proliferation of work teams provided a new large population of small groups on which small group theories could be tested.

SPAN OF CONTROL OF SMALL WORK GROUPS

The span of control of a supervisor is related to the number of employees who report to the supervisor. Graicunas [5], applying mathematical theory, found that, as the span of control increased, the number of personal relationships within the immediate work unit of the supervisor increased geometrically. He expressed this relationship with the formula $R = N(2^{N-1} + N - 1)$, where R is the number of personal relationships and N is the span of control or the number of subordinates.

If the geometric model proposed by Graicunas is applied to a team of up to 12 members, plus the leader, the number of personal relationships as a function of group size can be obtained, as shown in Table 6–1. Note that a team with 10 members (9 members plus the leader) will have nearly 2400 personal relationships. A team with 13 members (12 members plus the leader) will have nearly 25,000 personal relationships.

Stieglitz [11] has described an analytical approach developed by the Lockheed Missile and Space Company to determine the span of control of their managers. Based on experience and classical theory, Lockheed concluded that seven factors should be considered when determining the span of control:

1. Similarity of function
2. Geographic contiguity
3. Complexity of functions
4. Direction and control
5. Coordination

Table 6–1
Personal Relationships as a Function of Team Size

Number of Productivity Improvement Team Members	Number of Personal Relationships
1	1
2	6
3	18
4	44
5	100
6	222
7	490
8	1,080
9	2,376
10	5,210
11	11,374
12	24,708

Note: Team members do not include group leader.

6. Planning
7. Organizational assistance

The span of control is concerned mainly with the amount of direction given by a supervisor or manager to workers' activities. In a team, the leader provides leadership, but as little direction as possible. The whole idea of a productivity improvement team (exemplified by brainstorming) is the self-motivation of its volunteer members to propel the team onward. In other words, the team requires self-direction, self-motivation, and self-guidance. Beyond that, the fact that the structure and process of the team are accepted by the members provides a basis for exerting considerable control over the activities of the team. Finally, the usual presence of the team facilitator adds an additional element of control and support to both the leader and the members.

SIZE OF SMALL WORK GROUPS

Although the typical size of a productivity improvement team or work team is independent of size, there are teams with as few as 2 and as many as 12 members. However, if a team is too large, many of its members may become marginal contributors to the team. Although most activities are sufficiently structured to ensure the participation of all members, the same is not true of all of the team's problem-solving, problem-analysis, and work activities. Therefore, it may be desirable, especially during the initial stages of team implementation, to keep the membership to a lower level.

Behavioral research has shown that cohesiveness is easier to maintain in smaller groups [6]. In large groups, there is a tendency for subgroups to form, which breaks down cohesiveness. This suggests the desirability of splitting a team into two smaller groups when it becomes too large. An additional cost would arise from the need to train another leader and the extension of support to the second team by a facilitator. On the other hand, the productive output of a team is relatively independent of team size. Hence, breaking up a team into two teams has the potential of doubling the output.

Large teams are warranted when they have as their sole purpose the improvement of morale, cooperation, or motivation. In such instances, the larger team will probably attain the same result as a smaller team, but at a lower cost. In this age of employee empowerment and work enrichment, it is not difficult to imagine that the management of an organization would want to make a commitment to problem solving or work teams with the sole objective of improving morale and cooperation without gaining the additional benefits that the team could provide.

LEADERSHIP STYLE OF SMALL WORK GROUPS

The team leader is in many respects more of a moderator and coordinator than a leader. However, leadership does impose considerable responsibilities, as indicated by relevant theory and research.

At one time, it was believed that the success of any group activity depended solely on the leader. However, recent research has disproved this belief. The effectiveness of a group is dependent not only on the leader; it is highly dependent on the group members, on their interactions, and on the interactions of the group members and the leader.

Leadership behavior may be classified by four behavioral types: (1) autocratic, (2) supportive or participative, (3) instrumental, and (4) champion. An autocratic style would probably inhibit team member participation and thus is the least desirable for team operation. If a work group with an autocratic supervisor decides to volunteer as a productivity improvement team, rather than name the supervisor as leader, the leader may have to be selected from one of the more senior members of the work group, or perhaps the assistant supervisor could serve as team leader.

Unlike autocratic leaders, participative or consultative leaders encourage suggestions from group members and attempt to create a climate of open exchange. Using cooperative strategies, the participative leader encourages member initiatives and feels comfortable with the team concept of total participation.

Instrumental leaders are good at planning, organizing, controlling, and coordinating activities. They are typically more task oriented than people oriented. Instrumental leaders attempt to accomplish organizational objectives by providing guidance and structure to the activities of group members. Thus, the instrumental leader may, in certain circumstances, make an excellent team leader. However, such a leader will not necessarily be able to develop the social climate for an open and nonthreatening team environment. What is needed in addition is the ability of the members to generate their own emotional and social needs and requirements.

The leader as champion is a combination of the instrumental leader, the supportive or consultative leader, and the goal-oriented leader. This type of leader will be able to foster member interaction and member participation and set the social climate in which productive and satisfying work can be accomplished. Success with such a leader is almost ensured. Unfortunately, champion leaders are rare.

Group Structure

Each group member has a position and status that is determined by how that member is perceived by others in the group. The position each group member occupies in the group will be determined by the combined perceptions of all other group members.

In most productivity improvement or work teams, the members have the same or similar rank. However, their status may vary considerably and will help to determine their influence on other members of the group. In turn, the influence of the leader, the only person of possibly differing rank in the group, will be determined to a great extent by the degree to which that leader is held in esteem by the group members.

There are two types of group structures: formal and informal. The formal structure is the one imposed by management. The informal structure evolves over time as group members determine how much esteem each member deserves, regardless of their position in the formal structure. Because creativity and problem-solving ability are best nurtured in a relaxed environment, informal group structure is clearly more relevant than formal group structure to the team process.

In nonteam work activities, employees are expected to behave within the confines of the formal group structure established by management. In the productivity improvement or work team environment, team members are told that they are now viewed as equals, that their expertise and creativity are needed to help solve problems and perform the specified work assignments. The group structure in the team environment must therefore be quite different from that in the nonteam work environment. If it is not, the team members will view their assignments under the old management structure, and the benefits of team participation will be lost.

Though initially the team may be more homogeneous than other groups, as it matures, it will develop its own structure. Some members will be more proficient or more active on certain projects and will probably rise in status. Others will be verbal contributors and will establish a different niche in the group structure. Finally, the weak participants will probably drop out, either on their own or because of pressure from other team members or management.

Pitfalls of Team Utilization

Not every experiment with teams has worked as well as the original intent or expectation. Because teamwork and group activities develop into another form of organizational structure, with all the pitfalls inherent in organizational bureaucracy, problems may develop.

At General Electric, under the direction of CEO Jack Welch, quality circles were replaced in 1989 with what G.E. called a Work-Out program. The quality circle or productivity team concept had not worked well at G.E. because it was felt that many upper and middle managers were actively resistant to new ideas such as those embodied in the problem-solving team approach [9].

The Work-Out program brought managers and workers together in large forums organized for airing new ideas, the more radical the better. The frequency and duration of the Work-Out meetings were flexible and according to the perceived needs of a particular operation, plant, office, or division. The open forum setting of the Work-Out meetings forced reluctant managers to face up to pressures for change. Managers were also expected to give on-the-spot responses to employee suggestions. More technically oriented suggestions clearly had to be explored through a more detailed analysis and evaluation.

So, one may ask, how is G.E.'s Work-Out program different from the more traditional productivity improvement team? It appears to be more costly because of the large numbers of employees that become involved. Also, will employees be intimidated by the large number of people, including their superiors, at the meetings? On the positive side, the Work-Out program meetings do involve all levels of local management directly.

In the long run, because of the high cost of employee time, the frequency and duration of Work-Out meetings will probably diminish. But then, what works for one organization does not necessarily work for another.

The moral of this scenario is that not every organizational development works for every firm. Management must be selective in what it decides to adopt from the huge menu of productivity and quality improvement approaches.

Three Types of Teams

Over time, three types of teams have evolved in organizations on the basis of their membership and their function: vertical teams, horizontal teams, and interorganizational teams [3].

The vertical team is composed of members who reside at various hierarchical levels in the organization. The team may be cross-functional or made up of members from one department. Many productivity improvement teams made up of members from one department who hold different positions can be considered as vertical teams.

The horizontal team is most likely cross-functional, with members from several departments, such as operations, maintenance, logistics, quality, and engineering. The horizontal team could also be a work team in a department, with every member holding the same rank and responsibility.

The interorganizational team is made up of members from the firm plus outsiders from suppliers, service organizations, or customers. The team's function is to ensure orderly coordination of all activities that not only involve members of the firm but also outside members.

Conclusions

Productivity improvement teams and work teams are essentially small groups whose activities are coordinated by a designated or chosen leader and involve group dynamics. The decision to establish a productivity improvement team or work team therefore should be made in the light of available theory and research on the nature of leadership and the effects of group dynamics.

The span of control and size of the team will have an important bearing on the team's performance and effectiveness. The style of leadership is also important. A leader with an autocratic style will be less effective than a leader with a participative or instrumental style. Ideally, a strong supervisory training program should accompany a productivity improvement team or work team effort to help develop the champion type of leader.

Finally, an informal group structure has been found to be more conducive to productivity improvement team or work team achievement than a formal group structure. Indeed, any team is likely to create its own informal group structure as it develops over time.

Discussion Questions

1. Describe why team members may enjoy participating in the group discussion process fostered by quality and productivity improvement teams.
2. Describe the Hawthorne effect.
3. Why should an individual employee not be studied in isolation?
4. What influences the desirable span of control in a work situation?
5. Productive output of a team is relatively independent of team size. What size of quality and productivity team would you recommend?

6. What type of leader will foster the most productive output of a quality and productivity improvement team?
7. Describe the four behavioral leadership types.
8. G.E.'s Work-Out program was adopted in place of productivity improvement teams. Which of the two modes of eliciting employees' suggestions will survive longer? Explain your rationale.
9. Describe the difference between vertical teams and horizontal teams.
10. Describe why interorganizational teams are important.

References

1. Barnard, C. I. *The Functions of the Executive.* Harvard University Press, Cambridge, MA, 1938.
2. Cartwright, D., and A. Zander. *Group Dynamics—Research and Theory,* 2nd ed. Row, Peterson, Evanston, IL, 1960.
3. Dean, J. W., Jr., and J. R. Evans. *Total Quality Management, Organization and Strategy,* pp. 17–18. West Publishing, Minneapolis, MN, 1994.
4. Follett, M. P. *Creative Experience.* Longmans, Green, New York, 1924.
5. Graicunas, V. A. "Relationship in Organization," in L. Gulick and L. Urwick (eds.), *Papers on the Sciences of Administration.* New York Institute of Public Administration, 1937.
6. Hare, A. P. *Handbook of Small Group Research.* Free Press, New York, 1962.
7. Lewin, K. *Field Theory in Social Science.* Harper, New York, 1951.
8. Mayo, E. *The Human Problems of an Industrial Civilization.* Macmillan, New York, 1983.
9. Nohria, N., and J. D. Berkley. "Whatever Happened to the Take-Charge Manager?" *Harvard Business Review,* January-February 1994, 128–137.
10. Roathlisberger, F. J., and W. J. Dickson. *Management and the Worker.* Harvard University Press, Cambridge, MA, 1939.
11. Stieglitz, J. "Optimizing Span of Control." *Management Record,* 24(9), September 1962, 111–115.

Chapter seven

The Productivity and Quality Improvement Team

Outline

Introduction
Objectives of Productivity Improvement Teams
Training of Team Members and Facilitators
Establishment of Productivity Improvement Teams
Implementation of Productivity Improvement Teams
Success Factors
Cross-Functional Teams
Conclusions

Introduction

The basic premise of the productivity and quality improvement team process is that nobody knows more about the requirements and problems of a job than the people directly responsible for getting the job done. Given this premise, it is not surprising that the productivity improvement team movement has expanded rapidly, first in Japan, and now in the United States. At first, teams were established mainly in manufacturing; today, they are being introduced increasingly in service-oriented organizations, including health care, transportation, and other services.

In their most elementary form, productivity and quality improvement teams are trained, organized, and structured groups of 3 to 10 employees who share common interests and problems and meet regularly, usually once a week for an hour or longer. These groups identify problems, find the causes of the problems, develop solutions, and then propose the solutions to management in a formal presentation. If the proposal is accepted by management, the solution is implemented. Because the solution was suggested by the employees who were directly involved with the problem, the implementation is usually ensured. The productivity improvement team then continues on to identify, analyze, and solve other problems.

Team leaders should receive training in group dynamics and team techniques. They are usually the supervisors or leaders of the team members. Continuous communication needs to be maintained with supervisors who are not part of the team.

Notwithstanding their obvious benefits, many American organizations that adopt productivity improvement teams expect too much too soon. Consulting groups that market team training activities have a tendency to make claims of savings that are not always attainable. Also, management is not always aware of the start-up costs associated with productivity improvement teams. In fact, a productivity improvement team must be viewed as a long-term investment, as a permanent way of managing, with continuous, not necessarily rapid returns. ■

Objectives of Productivity Improvement Teams

As the name implies, productivity and quality improvement is the major objective of productivity improvement teams. Quality improvements contribute directly or indirectly to productivity improvements and vice versa. Thus, these teams might be accurately referred to as productivity improvement teams. Another important objective of productivity improvement teams is the improvement of communications, especially in a hierarchical organization. Beyond these general objectives, productivity improvement teams have a great many positive applications whose results may be difficult to document in explicit terms:

- Enhancement of the quality of work
- Cost containment
- Employee involvement
- Employee motivation
- Management-employee communications
- Supervisor-employee cooperation
- Development of problem-solving skills
- Safety awareness
- Leadership training

An added benefit of a well-functioning productivity improvement team in an organization is the good feeling that is created among the participating employees. The fact that management recognizes the employees' skills and willingness to identify and solve problems is a powerful motivating force for the employees, because such recognition addresses a basic human need: the need for self-accomplishment. Moreover, through their participation in problem solving, the employees acquire a feeling of control over the work they are doing. They are thereby given the opportunity to improve not only the quality and productivity of their work but also the quality of their work lives.

Training of Team Members and Facilitators

To achieve these objectives, management must be willing to make the requisite commitment of resources to the training of team facilitators, leaders, and members. A facilitator is an expert who attends productivity improvement team meetings and serves as a resource person to ensure that the members expedite the quality and productivity improvement process. Productivity improvement team leaders are usually unit department heads or supervisors. They should receive training in group dynamics and productivity improvement team techniques. They must realize that, as productivity improvement team leaders, they function in a different role from that of manager. As leaders, they must provide leadership to the principal productivity improvement team activity—the generation of ideas for operational improvements and the elimination of problems. Yet the leader must also be able to act as a peer in the problem-solving process, because all recommendations of the productivity improvement team must be based on group consensus.

Member training can be accomplished during the regular weekly meetings. Several meetings, or equivalent parts of the initial meetings held to deal with selected problems, should be devoted to training. The training should continue during subsequent meetings, as the productivity improvement team members gradually become accustomed to the process of identifying a problem, searching for its causes, finding a solution, and presenting the solution to management.

Establishment of Productivity Improvement Teams

An organization that wants to establish productivity improvement teams must first gain an understanding of their nature and requirements. The first step is to introduce management to the concept of productivity improvement teams. This can be done by having the managers attend productivity improvement team workshops. A workshop organized by someone with improvement team experience is recommended. The organization may then decide to utilize staff members trained in productivity improvement team development. In this way, many management staff members can be exposed simultaneously to the concept of productivity improvement teams. Alternatively, symposiums organized by local associations or groups may be used to introduce the concept of productivity improvement teams to the management staff.

Implementation of Productivity Improvement Teams

Following the education phase, management must decide whether to proceed with the implementation of productivity improvement teams in the particular setting. Although advocates of productivity improvement teams sometimes claim that they are immediately cost-effective, in fact, in the short run, especially during the implementation phase, the costs are likely to exceed the benefits. Management thus must be willing to make an initial investment without the expectation of immediate benefits.

Once the decision has been made to implement a productivity improvement team, management must decide on ways of training the team's facilitators and leaders. A team facilitator is a staff specialist who coordinates and guides the activities of the team. A properly trained facilitator can also provide training courses for team leaders and members.

The persons chosen for the facilitator training program can begin implementing the productivity improvement team program immediately upon completion of their training. Alternatively, to tailor the training more closely to institutional needs and to gain maximum understanding of the team goals and process, a consultant could be brought in-house to provide initial leader/facilitator training.

Productivity improvement team members do not require the in-depth training needed for facilitators and leaders. Team members cannot be taken away from their jobs for extended periods of time. It is therefore imperative that their training sessions, though brief, be spread out over a sufficiently long period of time. Assuming that a team meets once a week for an hour, the minimum initial training period will consist of several weekly sessions. Because of the extended training period, one must not expect recommendations from the productivity improvement team members during the first three months. However, implicit benefits will usually still be ensured through higher productivity and superior quality as a result of improved communication flow.

Having decided on its training needs, management must now determine what strategy to follow in establishing the productivity improvement team process. If an organization is small and the number of potential productivity improvement teams is limited, management may decide to train only one productivity improvement team facilitator to perform both leader and member training. However, a productivity improvement team training program should normally not be dependent on just one individual. It is advisable to train two productivity improvement team facilitators; if only one is needed, each can be used on a half-time basis, with the rest of that person's time devoted to other productive activities. Facilitators typically come from management, engineering, or employee development programs. Probably the most significant characteristic to look for in a facilitator is the ability to communicate with all types of employees and to establish a feeling of mutual trust with them. With properly trained facilitators, courses can then be offered to train department heads and supervisors to act as team leaders. The training of both leaders and members must be thorough, and their access to the facilitators should not be impeded.

After the leaders are trained, the process of forming the productivity improvement teams can begin. It is wise to plan for a gradual growth rate. For example, it is better to begin with two well-functioning productivity improvement teams than ten weakly performing ones. Then more productivity improvement teams can be added every three to six months. Whenever a productivity improvement team meets, especially in the initial phases, the team facilitator should be present to aid new leaders and members in productive problem solving.

In the work setting, the kind of participative management philosophy required for a productivity improvement team's continued success may be difficult to apply throughout the organization. In such cases, it is strongly suggested that management use a highly structured format and move slowly during implementation. The structure of the implementation procedure may at times appear to be too rigid. Still, the structure is based on past implementations and should be given firm management support.

Management must also be sure that the productivity improvement team facilitator is well qualified and is not overloaded. Finally, it is important that upper and middle management remain informed at all times as a basis for their continuing support of the program.

If management follows this kind of strategy and is willing to wait for results, it can be assured of a successful productivity improvement team program. There have, of course, been productivity improvement team failures, but the majority of these were the result of improper preparation and inadequate training of the team participants. Finally, it must be remembered that a productivity improvement team program is not an activity that proceeds on its own; productivity improvement teams need nurturing, supervision, and a visible commitment by management in order to be productive and to generate dividends for the organization.

Success Factors

A number of preconditions of success for productivity improvement teams in an organization have been identified. These preconditions are based on the Japanese model, but they can be readily applied to the American environment.

The first precondition is that candidates for productivity improvement team membership be reasonably well educated, to the extent that they are able to learn basic data collection and analysis techniques. However, productivity improvement teams have also worked quite well in departments where the educational level is substantially lower than in the professions. The role of the facilitator is of course of increased importance in teams of minimally educated employees. In such cases, training related to data collection and analysis must be a continuous process.

The second precondition is that management must trust its employees with cost, output, and quality data that in some instances may be considered confidential. Management must also provide rapid responses to all suggestions for improvement that emanate from productivity improvement teams. No response is worse than a negative response. If the administration cannot support a proposal made by a productivity improvement team, it should let the team members know quickly so that they can move on to another project. A management decision not to implement a recommendation should be supported by a reason for that decision. If team members perceive through feedback from management that their activities are not supported or that management believes there are no problems to resolve, the effectiveness of the productivity improvement team will quickly dissipate.

The third precondition is that the team members must be comfortable with each other in a group and be willing to work together cooperatively to resolve problems. If there is too much internal competitiveness and individualism, there are bound to be problems. Some experts maintain that the productivity improvement teams themselves can serve as vehicles for fostering cooperation and ameliorating internal competitiveness. In any event, internal competitiveness or lack of cooperation among an organization's employees should not by itself deter management from establishing a productivity improvement team if there is sufficient interest in the idea among the employees.

A final, but important, point to consider is that, if an organization decides to adopt productivity improvement teams, it must be willing to nurture and revitalize them continuously. As noted, management must provide rapid and positive feedback to the productivity improvement teams. At times, even such feedback, by itself, may not be sufficient to sustain interest and provide recognition. Additional training sessions may be required to enhance the abilities of the productivity improvement team members. In short, management must be ready to reinvest some of the benefits or savings that teams provide in further development of the team members.

Cross-Functional Teams

So far much of our discussion and description has been focused on the productivity improvement team usually functioning at the operations level. There are, however, many other team concepts utilized in organizations. One of these is the tactical business team (TBT) used by Allegheny Ludlum Steel.

Allegheny organized one TBT for each of its six product groups, and delegated responsibility for managing each business to the respective TBT. The six product groups consisted of stainless plate, stainless sheet, stainless standard strip, stainless customized strip, silicon, and high-tech alloys.

Each TBT was headed by Marketing and included the appropriate plant manager and representatives from technical services and production control. The TBT was held responsible for performance measures under its direct control such as sales, conversion costs, variances, and the use of working capital and equipment.

Longer-range decisions, such as capital acquisitions, new product development, and other strategic decisions, involved each TBT but were not within its realm of responsibility or decision [1].

Another example of the cross-functional team is the one utilized by Lehrer McGovern Bovis Inc. (LMB), a construction firm. The completion of a building or other project requires three phases: the design phase, the bid phase, and the construction phase. The sequential nature of the three phases tended to lengthen the time to complete a project from concept to completion. As a result, some construction firms proposed design-build methods of construction, avoiding the bid phase and thus reducing overall time to completion of the project.

LMB was largely in the construction management field and was thus focused on the build phase of each project. LMB utilized project teams to manage each project. Project teams consisted of experienced construction managers who collectively made all decisions related to the project. Each project team was supported by specialists in the various technical and support areas. Overall, LMB's management attributed much of LMB's success to the project management team approach [2].

Conclusions

Quality circles, or productivity improvement teams, have not been as successful in the United States as in Japan because of two reasons. The first reason is the cost-benefit relationship. In Japan, problem-solving team members typically meet on their own time, and as a result the actual operating cost of these problem-solving teams is low. In the United States, team members typically meet on company time, and as a result they are quite costly to the firm, in terms of lost production and higher operating cost. The second reason is that the educational level of lower-level employees is usually lower in the United States than in Japan. As a result, it is difficult to train U.S. employees to utilize the problem-solving tools typically used by problem-solving teams.

The one area where problem solving activities have been successful is in cross-functional teams. Cross-functional team members are usually at a high organizational level, and are usually also better educated. As a result, they are in a better position to use problem-solving tools and techniques.

Continuous improvements is now the aim of most progressive firms. One excellent way to maintain continuous improvement is to have employees identify and solve problems. Because of this, we can expect a revival of the problem-solving team approach in the future.

Discussion Questions

1. Describe the leadership requirements of a team leader.
2. Describe the requirements for a facilitator of a quality and productivity improvement team.
3. Develop a set of criteria that should be satisfied before a quality and productivity team can make a recommendation to management.
4. Develop a training budget for implementation of five quality and productivity improvement teams, including use of a half-time facilitator, training of one facilitator, five team leaders, and 35 team members.
5. How long will the implementation phase of question 4 take before it is fully completed?
6. Describe several factors for successful team implementation.
7. Why are cross-functional teams important for coordination?
8. Allegheny Ludlum's tactical business team is essentially a senior management team. Discuss the differences in management teams and lower-level employee teams. Will either one be more or less successful?

References

1. March, A. "Allegheny Ludlum Steel Corporation," in D. A. Garvin (ed.), *Operations Strategy*, p. 286. Prentice Hall, Englewood Cliffs, NJ, 1992.
2. Simpson, J. "Lehrer McGovern Bovis, Inc.," in D. A. Garvin (ed.), *Operations Strategy*, pp. 404–405. Prentice Hall, Englewood Cliffs, NJ, 1992.

Chapter eight

Team Process Leadership Roles and Functions

Outline

Introduction
Leadership Roles
Stages of Team Development
The Polite Stage of Team Development
The Why-Are-We-Here Stage of Team Development
The Struggle-for-Power Stage of Team Development
The Productive Stage of Team Development
The Team Spirit
Conclusions

Introduction

The unique dynamics and objectives of a productivity improvement or work team require close attention to the leadership styles, interpersonal communications, and management techniques involved in the group process. The fact that team meeting times and meeting frequencies are limited makes it mandatory that leaders plan and conduct productive sessions that stay on a steady course leading to a successful and timely completion of projects. Both leaders and facilitators must learn to mesh the skills and personalities of the team members in such a way that the team becomes a cohesive unit with a sense of purpose and a spirit of unity. Indeed, the creation of a team that works efficiently and cooperatively is a prerequisite for mastering team process techniques.

Team leadership is often different from the kind of leadership that managers are accustomed to exercising and to which employees are trained to respond. Supervisors who serve as team leaders must shed the autocratic aspects of their roles; they must help the team rather than boss it. Teams work best when they can pool the creative energies of all members. In such groups, the members view themselves as equals in the decision-making process, and the leader creates the environment and directs the process that fosters full participation. Thus, a careful selection of supervisors to lead the initial teams provides a solid foundation for the program and facilitates the development of models for future team leaders. Department heads are a primary source for quickly identifying potential team leaders among first-level supervisors who are already employing techniques of participative management with their staffs. In contrast, managers and supervisors with more autocratic tendencies may first need to view teams in other areas, attend management presentations, and become better acquainted with the advantages of employee involvement before they can qualify as team leaders.

Leadership roles

The group process in a team is concerned with two main functions or roles. The first is to attend to the task to be accomplished; the second is to focus on the needs of the group in order to maintain an effective team. These functional roles of task and maintenance, which are examined during leader/facilitator training, may be contrasted with nonfunctional behavior, which tends to make teams weak and inefficient. As an example of the latter type of behavior, leaders and members involved in the resolution of high-priority problems often produce situations of tension or conflict. Thus, although the immediate task in a team is to solve particular problems, the long-term goal is to improve working relationships.

To aid the team in its team-building and problem-solving efforts, the following roles should be reviewed during training:

1. Task roles
   - *Initiating.* Suggesting new ideas, alternative problem definitions, or other approaches to data collection; clarifying and setting interim goals.
   - *Regulating.* Influencing the direction and pace of the process, requesting more information, summarizing.
   - *Informing.* Delivering information and opinions to the group.
   - *Supporting.* Encouraging members to give opinions, voicing group feelings, using humor to relieve tension, creating a comfortable emotional climate.
   - *Evaluating.* Testing for group consensus, drawing together the activities of members or subgroups, noting the group process.
2. Maintenance roles
   - *Encouraging.* Being friendly, praising members and their ideas, accepting all contributions.
   - *Gatekeeping.* Making it possible for all members to participate.
   - *Standard setting.* Keeping within the team charter.
   - *Following.* Going along with group decisions, serving as an audience for group discussions.
3. Task and maintenance roles
   - *Testing for consensus.* Tentatively asking for group opinions to determine proximity to consensus, sending up trial balloons to test group feelings.
   - *Diagnosing.* Determining the sources of difficulty and appropriate steps to take.
   - *Mediating.* Harmonizing, conciliating member differences.

A group is strengthened to work more efficiently if its leaders and members are aware of the roles required of them. Leaders should be given the opportunity to observe a demonstration of each of these roles and to practice them during their training.

Stages of Team Development

Some teams are composed of members from a common work area, whereas others include workers from various similar areas. Whatever its composition, the team's team-building efforts and team activities will vary as it passes through successive stages of development. Team leaders and facilitators need to know which stage of development the team has reached in order to move it further in its evolution as a productive group working cooperatively and efficiently.

The Polite Stage of Team Development

In their initial meetings, team members are generally cautious, discuss innocuous topics, and are careful not to offend anyone. Sometimes, even coworkers who have worked together for years hesitate to participate. In this polite stage, the members really do not know one another, some members are new, and the presence of the leader or facilitator may be inhibiting. This initial phase is unavoidable; its positive aspect is that it allows the team members to become accustomed to working together in an entirely new way. However, it is best to refrain from pushing or criticizing team members at this stage; to do so might increase their feelings of being scrutinized, and thus prolong the stage.

The Why-Are-We-Here Stage of Team Development

The why-are-we-here stage of team development finds members asking themselves and each other just how much they really want to be team members. Until they apply the process to resolve a problem, they cannot be certain of what the process is or whether the techniques make sense and can be applied to problems in their work area. Leaders and facilitators can guide the group through this phase by explaining clearly how the team fits into the organization. Citing examples of how the team process has been used successfully to make changes can also help to reassure new members.

The Struggle-for-Power Stage of Team Development

The third stage of development involves a struggle for power. Every work group has a formal power structure as well as an informal pecking order. Each member brings sensitivity, his or her reputation, and experience to the team. Thereafter, as the group establishes team roles for each member, subtle bids for power develop, based on the members' work-area roles. During the ensuing struggle for power, there is likely to be increased tension, the formation of cliques, and difficulty in reaching decisions. Over time, however, the team's informal authority relations become settled, and a fairly standard set of roles is established, with designated leaders for various types of activities.

The Productive Stage of Team Development

Once the team has become committed to a set of goals and has established a fairly stable authority structure, it enters its productive phase. Each member feels accepted by the team, contributes without fear of criticism, and risks offering ideas that might be rejected. Arguments occur in an atmosphere of trust and acceptance. As the productive stage progresses, the team usually develops a feeling of great closeness and establishes a kinship that reaches back into the workplace. It takes a team weeks, or even months, to achieve a truly productive stage. Leaders and facilitators should be aware that a team does not start out as a close-knit, decision-making unit—it develops into one [2].

The team process is designed for maximum participation. It provides opportunities for members to improve their interpersonal skills, learn more about themselves, and experiment with new roles and behaviors. For members who are unaccustomed to such self-disclosure, the process can be frightening and demanding. Thus, defense mechanisms and avoidance behavior are often displayed and interfere with individual and group growth. Leaders and facilitators who recognize such "fight-or-flight" responses in members can not only address them but, in many cases, prevent their recurrence.

Some manifestations of a fight defense are a cynical attitude about the process and the other members, competition with the leader or facilitator, and interrogation of other members in a cross-examination style. In contrast, flight defenses are most frequently used to avoid honest involvement in the group process. For example, through intellectualization, members may deal with their emotions in an objective or diagnostic manner but avoid gut-level feelings. Thus, a team involved in a worthwhile project can be detoured by evasive, dime-store psychology, resulting in drawn-out discussions of irrelevant social and general behavior issues. Similarly, through generalization, negative impersonal statements may be applied to the team as a whole. "Everybody is so uptight" usually translates as "I'm very uptight." In another type of flight response, consistently silent members may be passively learning, but they are not developing interpersonally. The ultimate flight response is withdrawal, manifested in a range from boredom to actual physical removal from the team.

THE TEAM SPIRIT

In order to move forward effectively through a team's developmental stages, strike a balance between task and maintenance functions, and address defense mechanisms, the team leader and facilitator must act as a member of the team. During meetings, the facilitator keeps a low profile, monitors the process, and acts as a resource. The leader thus must furnish the critical elements that are necessary for an effective meeting. If the leader displays energy and enthusiasm toward the task, the team will adopt similar behavior. Conversely, a leader who opens meetings in a meek manner and with a blasé attitude will likely experience poor attendance, nonparticipation, and a group tendency to slip away from the topic.

Behind the scenes, facilitators and leaders must work together to ensure productive meetings. Together they must plan an agenda for each meeting and post it in the work area. It is far easier to stay on task when every member knows exactly what is to be accomplished during the meeting hour. After each meeting, the facilitator provides feedback on the team process and its group dynamics to the leader. Here, the facilitator should be straightforward and honest, noting both positive and negative aspects of the meeting. As an observer, the facilitator is in a position to judge whether or not the members understood the techniques and to determine which members were frustrated or confused and how productive the meeting was overall. Many facilitators use a leader evaluation checklist as a basis for follow-up sessions. However, if there is a good rapport between the leader and the facilitator, an informal constructive feedback discussion is probably more productive.

The challenge of managing a team is in keeping diverse individuals working together. Although the members share similar work, they usually differ in experience, education, age, and background. Leaders and facilitators thus need to gain expertise in conducting effective meetings through training in the group dynamic skills of listening, handling differences of opinion, and preventing and correcting interaction problems.

Members invest time and energy in teams. The organization invests money and provides resources. Leaders and facilitators are custodians of those resources, and they fulfill their roles by moving the teams toward specific goals and their members toward personal satisfaction.

Conclusions

One of the big benefits of team membership is the feeling among team members that their contributions to the team, and ultimately to the organization, are important and are appreciated. This is part of the employee empowerment process. The objective of empowerment is to utilize the creative and intellectual energy of all employees in the organization, not just management [1].

It is therefore imperative that team leaders keep in mind that to keep creativity flowing, individual members must be treated as equals on the team. Team leaders must avoid becoming supervisors and not fall back into the old hierarchical organizational format.

Discussion Questions

1. How is team leadership different from supervisory leadership?
2. Describe the five task roles of a problem-solving team.
3. Describe the four maintenance roles of a problem-solving team.
4. Describe the polite stage of team development.
5. Describe the why-are-we-here stage of team development.

6. Describe the struggle-for-power stage of team development.
7. Describe the productive stage of team development.
8. How can team spirit be maintained in a problem-solving team?

References

1. Kiernan, M. J. "The New Strategic Architecture: Learning to Compete in the Twenty First Century." *Academy of Management Executive,* 7(1), February 1993, 7–21.
2. Miles, Matthew. *Learning to Work in Groups.* Teachers College Press, New York, 1981.

Part three

Quality and Productivity Improvement and Control Techniques

Brainstorming, Data Analysis, and Charting	9
Cause and Effect Diagrams and Pareto Analysis	10
Statistical Control Charting	11
Quality Function Deployment	12

Introduction

Total quality management requires changes in ways of thinking, managing, and organizing. It also requires total utilization of all the talents of all the employees in the organization. Once that has been accomplished or is in the implementation phase, there must be extensive education and training.

In this section, we address a variety of techniques in which employees can be trained. These techniques then provide the means for employees to implement a variety of total quality management concepts.

The first chapter addresses brainstorming, data analysis, and flow-process charting, which provide the basis for problem identification and the initial problem diagnosis. The second chapter covers cause and effect diagrams and Pareto analysis, which provide the means for analyzing a specific problem or problems in detail.

Statistical control charting is a means of controlling a process. If the process deviates from its intended function, the statistical control chart will signal the user before too much damage is incurred. In the fourth chapter, the rather complex approach to quality function deployment is described, explored, and illustrated. It may be considered a more advanced technique. In the final chapter of this section we cover process control and ISO 9000 standards. ISO 9000 standards are the first global standards employed to control and standardize processes in firms that operate in the international environment.

Chapter nine

Brainstorming, Data Analysis, and Charting

Outline

Brainstorming
Use of Affinity Charts as an Alternative to Brainstorming
Data Gathering, Tabulation, and Bar Diagrams
Histograms
Presentation Techniques
Flow-Process Charting
Recording Entries
Application of the Flow-Process Analysis Chart
A Proposed-Method Flow-Process Analysis Chart
Conclusions

Introduction

This chapter describes and discusses some of the more common techniques used in problem solving. These techniques will be, in most instances, new to the problem-solving team. It is therefore important that the team members be well trained in their use and applications.

The four operational steps in the team process are as follows:

1. Problem identification
2. Problem selection
3. Problem analysis
4. Recommendation to management

Each of these operational steps requires the use of one or more of the following techniques:

- Brainstorming
- Affinity charting
- Data gathering, tabulation, and bar diagrams
- Interrelationship diagrams

- Histograms
- Pareto analysis
- Cause and effect diagrams
- Presentation techniques
- Flow-process charting

These techniques can be applied at each of the four operational steps, depending on the problem under analysis. For example, data gathering may be necessary to verify the problem and, again, to confirm the cause.

Below we examine some of the techniques and provide examples to illustrate each. (Two of the techniques, Pareto analysis and cause and effect diagrams, are discussed in later chapters.)

BRAINSTORMING

Brainstorming is a form of group thinking. It is a process that produces ideas that are greater than the sum of the ideas contributed by the individual members of the group. To gain the greatest synergistic effect—that is, to produce a group output that is greater than the sum of the individual outputs—adherence to several rules is advisable.

First, criticism of others' ideas should not be allowed. The purpose of brainstorming is to generate ideas, with one idea leading to another. In fact, a nonoperational idea may very well lead to an operational one. Criticism inhibits this kind of creative thinking and interrupts momentum.

Next, team members should be encouraged to forget how a certain job or task is done so that they will feel unencumbered and be able to generate new ideas. It is important to generate as many ideas as possible, from which the good ideas can later be extracted.

Brainstorming can be applied to problems, causes, or solutions. In each case, the sessions should include all members. Although the members will vary in the number of ideas or solutions they put forth, it is imperative that each member have an equal opportunity to participate. The members give one idea in turn; if they do not have one, they say "pass" for that particular round.

The team leader or an assigned member should record every idea that is suggested, regardless of its value. The recording should be visible to all members, by the use of such devices as a flip chart, a blackboard, or an overhead projector. The members can thereby constantly review the ideas that have been suggested, and those ideas can then become triggers for other ideas.

Following completion of the brainstorming session, the complete record of all ideas contributed should be made available to the team members. They can then refer back to it for evaluation before the next meeting. Supplemented with information from other sources, members can prioritize the ideas and select one based on group consensus [2].

Brainstorming is an important activity because it identifies problems. The Japanese experience with continuous improvement activities has shown that the problem-finding phase of brainstorming is very important because it identifies new and useful problems to be solved. The problem-solving phase develops new, useful, and imaginative solutions. Solution implementation follows the problem-finding and the problem-solution phases. The group that finds and solves a problem is involved in the solution to the problem and usually will implement the solution quickly. The Japanese have found that the more emphasis is placed on problem finding, the less time and effort is required for implementation of the solution [1].

Use of Affinity Charts as an Alternative to Brainstorming

One of the problems with brainstorming is that it produces many ideas, problems, questions, and suggested solutions, but in a somewhat disorganized format. To be sure, a good note taker at a brainstorming session will organize all that is generated at the session. But how is the generated material to be organized, and who is going to do the organizing? Typically, the group leader or possibly the note taker organizes the generated information and then submits it to the group members at a later date.

An alternative to traditional brainstorming is brainstorming with the use of affinity charts. When affinity charts are used, the participants also generate the ideas, questions, and problems, but they do so silently and in written form. The ideas are usually written on large post-it notes, which are then stuck on a wall for everyone to see. In order to have some focus prior to the start of the silent process, participants will usually agree on a question, problem, or idea that then becomes the focus. As participants stick their respective notes on the wall, it becomes everyone's responsibility to organize the notes in an orderly and related fashion. In other words, common responses, ideas, and suggestions will become clustered together. All of this takes place in silence. At some point the group must, of course, reach a point where the silent process is terminated, and another question is addressed. However, silence should not be broken until each group member is ready. Exhibit 9–1 shows the steps in the affinity chart process.

How does the affinity chart process produce results superior to traditional brainstorming? Typically, the affinity chart process takes more time. But it produces better-organized results, which can be used in subsequent planning processes and/or strategic plans. The affinity chart does, however, have limitations. It does not work well when the group is too large. It may be desirable to break up larger groups into smaller subgroups. The simple physical space required to allow all group participants to view the notes posted by others limits the number of participants to about six or seven. Brainstorming, on the other hand, can be used with larger groups of participants.

Upon completion of the affinity chart process, the participants can and should develop an interrelationship diagram. This process is not done silently; it is done in an open discussion, with everyone who was previously involved in the affinity chart process participating. The process is described in Exhibit 9–2.

The objective of the interrelationship diagram development process is to put more order in the results generated by the silent affinity chart process. A productive affinity chart process will produce numerous post-it notes, which will then be organized into topics headed up by topic titles. How does each one

Exhibit 9-1
Guidelines for Affinity Chart Process

1. *Agree on a topic.* Come to an agreement on the question, problem, or idea to be addressed. Do not discuss or clarify the chosen topic so that participants will not be biased.
2. *Brainstorm.* Brainstorm in silence. Each participant writes responses on large post-it notes, and sticks them on wall. Responses should be as brief as possible, consisting of noun, verb, and a few other words. You may want to limit responses to 10 words.
3. *Announce response (optional).* In somewhat larger groups it may be desirable for each participant to announce his or her response before sticking it on the wall. In smaller groups, total silence may be more desirable.
4. *Response to responses.* Participants can, will, and should respond to their fellow participants' responses. These responses should then be posted next to the response being responded to.
5. *Organize responses in groups.* Based on relationships between responses, group them together. Everyone should participate in this without obstruction. Remain silent. Try to attain consensus. Add other responses if deemed necessary.
6. *Summarize.* Head up each group of responses with a topic title. Titles should be concise. Then organize the responses under each title in a logical, useful order.

of these topic titles relate to the other topic titles? That is the question the interrelationship diagram is intended to solve.

Following completion of a satisfactory interrelationship diagram, the results can be used for future planning or for help in implementation of a solution or a plan.

Exhibit 9-2
Guidelines for Interrelationship Diagrams

Objective: To draw logical connections among the responses generated by an affinity chart process exercise.

1. *Brainstorm.* Take output of affinity chart process and verbally discuss each group of responses. Expand ideas contained on post-its to strengthen the original input.
2. *Identify each group.* Label each topic title card with an alphabetic character for future identification.
3. *Identify relationships among topics.* Determine which topic titles are related, including the direction of the relationships. Develop a diagram with alphabetic topic identifiers and arrows to show how they are related.
4. *Build interrelationship diagram.* Continue guideline 3 until all topic titles appear on the diagram. They may not all be related into a completely connected diagram. However, too many subdiagrams may be an indication of fuzzy thinking. If this happens, return to guideline 1 and repeat the process.

DATA GATHERING, TABULATION, AND BAR DIAGRAMS

In one team, in an effort to reduce hotel guest complaints, the team collected the records of 200 hotel guest complaints and organized them by cause (some complaints were made for more than one reason). This information was recorded on the hotel guest complaint records.

Table 9–1 presents a summary of the reasons for the 200 hotel guest complaints. If there was more than one reason for a complaint, only the primary reason was recorded. For each hotel guest complaint category, the percentage of all complaints for that category was also recorded.

The tabulated information on hotel guest complaints was then transferred to a vertical bar diagram, as shown in Figure 9–1. Bar diagrams show tabular data in graphical form and make the data easier to interpret. They also show relative magnitudes more clearly. Note that the major source of complaints in our example is food service.

Histograms

If, in our example, we take the hotel customer complaint data and record all causes of hotel customer complaints, not just the major causes, the generated data can be shown in tabular form, as in Table 9–2, and in histogram format, as in Figure 9–2. Note that the histogram shows the dominant cause to be food service, followed by the two next most common causes, room service and housekeeping. Two minor causes, front desk and environment, are also shown.

Presentation Techniques

A well-functioning team will make recommendations for method improvements, productivity enhancements, and process changes to raise performance levels. Many of the proposed changes will exceed the team's span of control and will accordingly be presented to management for approval and implementation. Thus, team members must develop techniques to communicate their proposed changes to management. These techniques involve oral presentations,

Table 9–1
Tabular Array of Major Hotel Guest Complaints by Cause

Cause of Complaint	Number of Complaints	Percent of Total Complaints
Room service	52	26
Food service	68	34
Front desk	24	12
Housekeeping	36	18
Environment	20	10
Total	200	100

Figure 9-1
Bar Chart of Major Hotel Guest Complaints by Cause

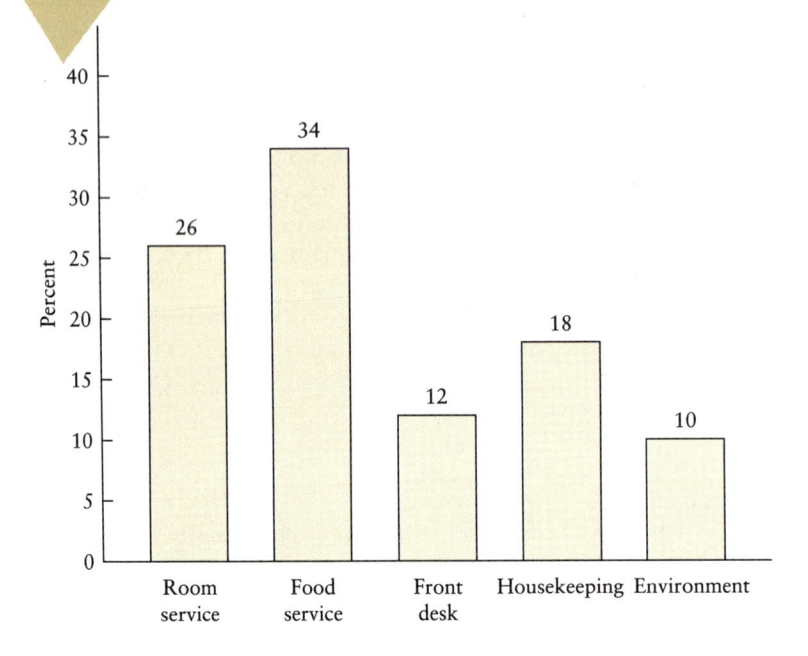

but they may also involve the preparation of written reports to supplement the oral presentation.

Presentation techniques include summary writing, preparation of tabular data, graphical presentation of data, tabular comparisons of present and proposed methods, use of overhead projectors, use of blackboards, and concise oral communication.

Although the team leader may have had prior training in presentation techniques, the responsibility for the presentation cannot rest on the leader alone. All members should be strongly encouraged to participate.

Table 9-2
Tabular Array of All Hotel Guest Complaints by Cause

Cause of Complaint	Number of Complaints	Percent of Total Complaints
Room service	65	26
Food service	85	34
Front desk	30	12
Housekeeping	45	18
Environment	25	10
Total	250	100

Figure 9–2
Histogram of All Hotel Guest Complaints by Cause

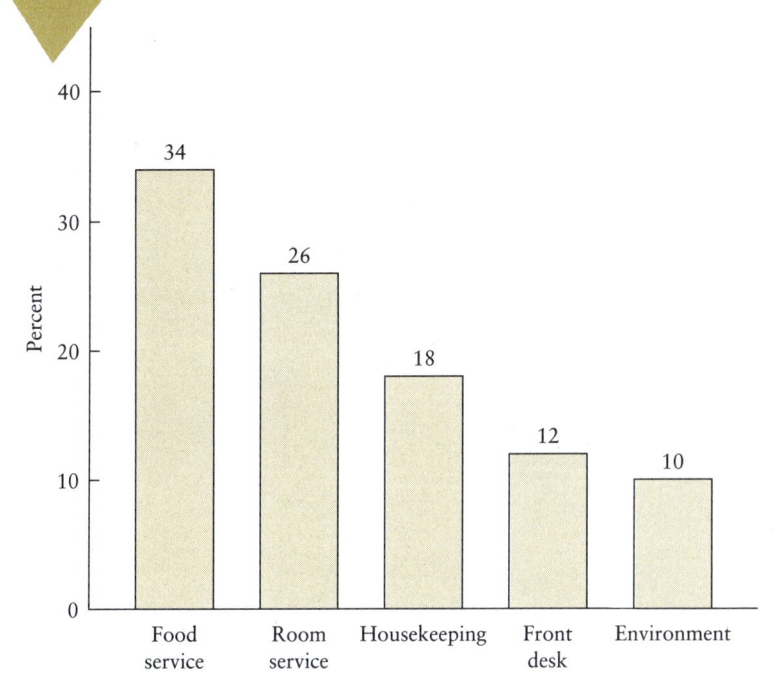

[Bar chart showing percent of complaints by cause:
- Food service: 34
- Room service: 26
- Housekeeping: 18
- Front desk: 12
- Environment: 10]

Clearly, a presentation by a group of maintenance or housekeeping employees will not be as sophisticated as one by a group of engineers. Yet management presentations are often the only opportunity for employees to communicate directly with management. The participating employees may be initially nervous but, after several presentations, they are likely to relax and become enthusiastic about sharing their findings. In such cases, managers find the team presentations most gratifying. To ensure that the presentations are professional, clear, convincing, and complete, the team members should be provided with secretarial support and graphics services to prepare presentations. Team members should be taught communications and presentation skills.

FLOW-PROCESS CHARTING

Flow-process charting and diagrams are excellent tools for determining how the step-by-step details of a job are being performed. In such areas as the office and the laboratory, flow-process charts can aid in detecting the causes of delays. The technique is also applicable to paperwork in clerical operations.

The flow-process chart portrays graphically an entire process. It is a map that enables one to picture the entire process, much as a geographic map aids a navigator. It is a means of organizing facts in such a way as to ensure a minimum of errors in judgment and to reduce the possibilities of leaving out steps [2, 3]. A typical flow-process chart is shown in Figure 9–3. It depicts the task of completing a form. A blank flow-process analysis chart form is shown in Table 9–3.

Figure 9–3
A Typical Flow-Process Chart—Completing a Form

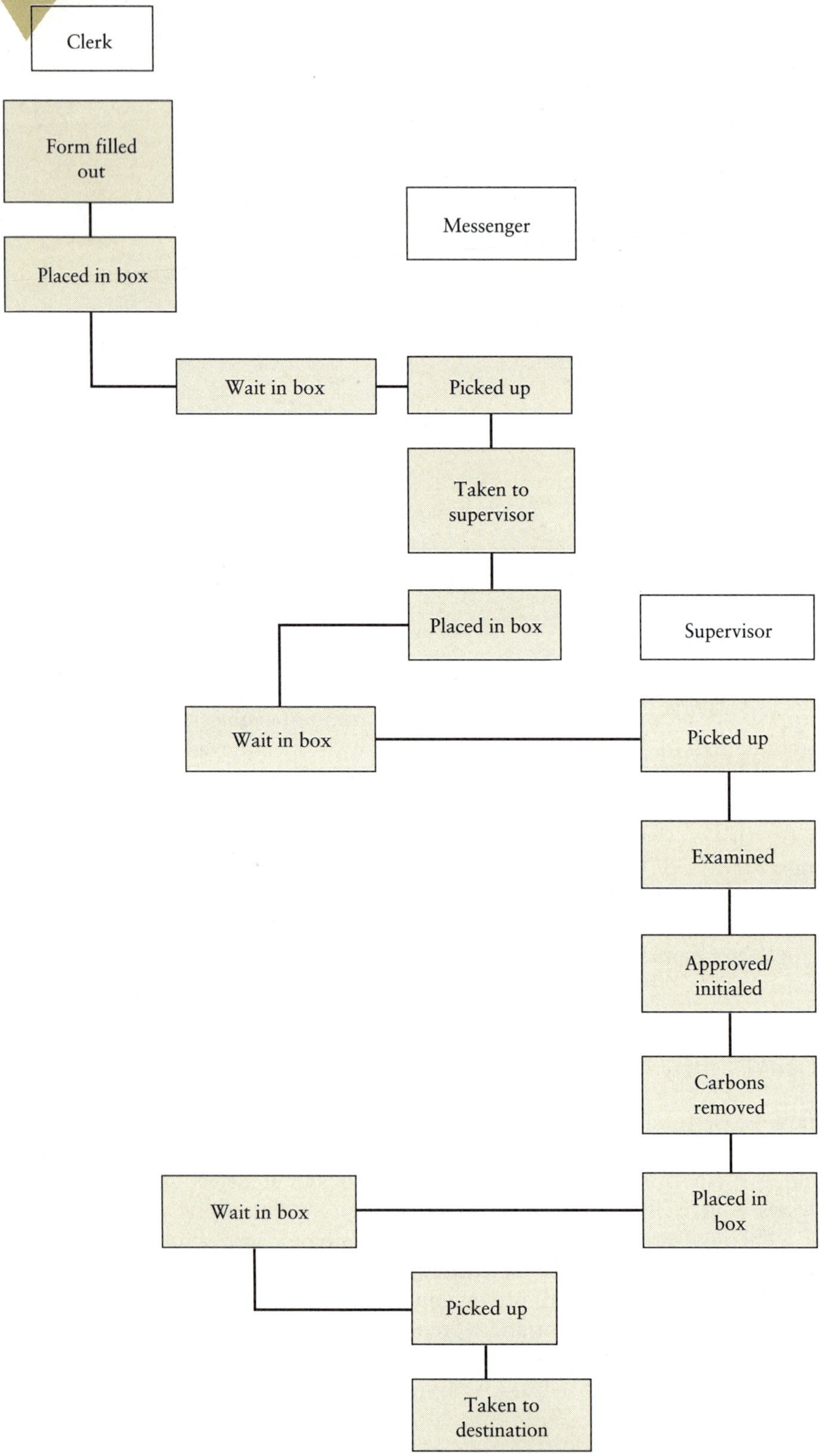

Clerk

Form filled out → Placed in box → Wait in box

Messenger

Picked up → Taken to supervisor → Placed in box → Wait in box → Picked up

Supervisor

Examined → Approved/initialed → Carbons removed → Placed in box → Wait in box → Picked up → Taken to destination

Table 9-3
Flow-Process Analysis Chart Form

Task Description:							
Element Number	Element Description	Operation	Inspection	Transport	Delay	Storage	Notes
		○	□	→	D	▽	
		○	□	→	D	▽	
		○	□	→	D	▽	
		○	□	→	D	▽	
		○	□	→	D	▽	
		○	□	→	D	▽	
		○	□	→	D	▽	
		○	□	→	D	▽	
		○	□	→	D	▽	
		○	□	→	D	▽	
		○	□	→	D	▽	
		○	□	→	D	▽	
		○	□	→	D	▽	
		○	□	→	D	▽	
		○	□	→	D	▽	

Recording Entries

After the task has been selected, it is described at the top of the chart. The next step is to select the element of that task to be followed. The element could be an employee, a supply item, a production part, or a paper form. Each entry recorded on the chart must be something that has happened to that element.

The next step is to decide a starting and ending point for the process. There will be surprising detail, even in a short process, so each portion of the process should be examined. A brief description of each element should be recorded for the selected task, noting each step. If the element is a production part or supply item, every time there is a move, a wait, a procedure check, or an inspection, it should be recorded exactly the way it happens, even if it should have been done differently. A separate line should be used for each element, adding extra pages if necessary.

Each element should then be categorized by one of five symbols. These symbols simplify the task of analyzing the element; they make it easier to summarize the process and to portray graphically the results when submitting a recommendation for approval. The five symbols on the flow-process chart represent the following occurrences:

1. *Operation.* An element is intentionally changed, receives a treatment, or undergoes a procedure; an element is prepared for another operation or for transportation, inspection, or storage; information is communicated, for example, by a phone call, letter, memo, or teletype message.
2. *Inspection.* Something is checked or verified against a predetermined standard. Inspections are specialized operations that ensure the quality of a service, procedure, or treatment. Because of the importance of quality, inspections are categorized as separate operations. Examples of inspections are checking a requisition for completeness and checking a production part against the specification.
3. *Transportation.* An element is moved or moves from one place to another (except when such movements are a part of an operation or inspection).
4. *Delay.* A waiting period occurs, as when a supply item is waiting to be picked up, a customer order is waiting for delivery, or a production part is waiting for inspection.
5. *Storage.* An element, such as a production part, is kept and protected against unauthorized removal.

Application of the Flow-Process Analysis Chart

The next step is to identify the "do" occurrences. These involve physical changes in an element—for example, when a supply item is being utilized. The identification is accomplished by shading each symbol that represents a do occurrence.

Next, each element on a chart is challenged. A note column is provided on the chart for checking all the possibilities that come to mind as a result for challenging questions. Improvement from such questioning usually results from eliminating or reducing "make-ready" and "put-away" occurrences because they add to the time but not to the end results. On a commonsense basis, however, the most logical way of dealing with make-ready and put-away occurrences is to question the do occurrences. This is because make-ready and put-away depend on do occurrences. Thus, the elimination of a do occurrence (or a combination of do occurrences) will automatically eliminate the make-ready and put-away occurrences on which the do occurrence depends.

In this way, each symbol that has been shaded is checked, in the order of its occurrence, against the possibilities that arise from the question challenges, and relevant comments on each are entered in the note column for future reference. As noted, changes in do occurrences may require changes in make-ready and put-away occurrences.

A Proposed-Method Flow-Process Analysis Chart

After completing the above changes, a proposed-method flow-process chart can be made directly from the information recorded on the original analysis chart. Each element is copied on the new chart, except for those that have

Table 9-4
A Flow-Process Analysis Chart for the Task of Completing a Form

Flow-Process Chart

Task Description: Form completion

Element Number	Element Description	Operation	Inspection	Transport	Delay	Storage	Notes
1	Filled out by clerk	●	☐	→	D	▽	
2	Placed in OUT box	○	☐	→	D	▽	
3	Wait in box	○	☐	→	D	▽	
4	Picked up by messenger	○	☐	→	D	▽	
5	Sent to supervisor	○	☐	→	D	▽	
6	Placed in IN box	○	☐	→	D	▽	
7	Wait in box	○	☐	→	D	▽	
8	Picked up by supervisor	○	☐	→	D	▽	
9	Examined	○	☐	→	D	▽	
10	Initialed for approval	●	☐	→	D	▽	
11	Placed in OUT box	○	☐	→	D	▽	
12	Wait in box	○	☐	→	D	▽	
13	Picked up by messenger	○	☐	→	D	▽	
14	Sent to clerk	○	☐	→	D	▽	
15	Placed in IN box	○	☐	→	D	▽	
16	Wait in box	○	☐	→	D	▽	
17	Picked up by messenger	○	☐	→	D	▽	
18	Examined for signature	○	☐	→	D	▽	
19	Carbons removed	●	☐	→	D	▽	
20	Placed in OUT box	○	☐	→	D	▽	
21	Wait in box	○	☐	→	D	▽	
22	Picked up by messenger	○	☐	→	D	▽	
23	Sent to destination	○	☐	→	D	▽	

been eliminated. The symbols are again applied, as before, with new distances and estimated times if available.

The resulting proposed-method flow-process analysis chart can then serve as an instruction sheet for trying out a proposed improvement in a pilot run or for training new employees in its presentations to help explain proposed changes that require management approval.

Tables 9–4, 9–5, and 9–6 illustrate the use of a flow-process analysis chart as applied to the task of completing a form. Table 9–4 shows the elements used in the current method of completing the form, Table 9–5 shows an improved version of the method, and Table 9–6 illustrates a further improvement. The reader should review each chart in the light of the procedures discussed above and follow each element change in the process.

Table 9–5

Flow-Process Analysis Chart for the Task of Completing a Form: First Improvement

Flow-Process Chart

Task Description: Form completion

Element Number	Element Description	Operation	Inspection	Transport	Delay	Storage	Notes
1	Filled out by clerk	●	□	→	D	▽	
2	Placed in OUT box	○	□	→	D	▽	
3	Wait in box	○	□	→	D	▽	
4	Picked up by messenger	○	□	→	D	▽	
5	Sent to supervisor	○	□	→	D	▽	
6	Placed in IN box	○	□	→	D	▽	
7	Wait in box	○	□	→	D	▽	
8	Picked up by supervisor	○	□	→	D	▽	
9	Examined	○	□	→	D	▽	
10	Initialed for approval	●	□	→	D	▽	
11	Carbons removed	●	□	→	D	▽	
12	Placed in OUT box	○	□	→	D	▽	
13	Wait in box	○	□	→	D	▽	
14	Picked up	○	□	→	D	▽	
15	Sent to destination	○	□	→	D	▽	

Table 9-6

Flow-Process Analysis Chart for the Task of Completing a Form: Second Improvement

	Flow-Process Chart						
Task Description: Form completion							
Element Number	Element Description	Operation	Inspection	Transport	Delay	Storage	Notes
1	Filled out by clerk	●	☐	→	D	▽	
2	Examined	○	☐	→	D	▽	
3	Carbons removed	●	☐	→	D	▽	
4	Placed in OUT box	○	☐	→	D	▽	
5	Wait in box	○	☐	→	D	▽	
6	Picked up by messenger	○	☐	→	D	▽	
7	Sent to destination	○	☐	→	D	▽	
		○	☐	→	D	▽	
		○	☐	→	D	▽	
		○	☐	→	D	▽	
		○	☐	→	D	▽	
		○	☐	→	D	▽	
		○	☐	→	D	▽	
		○	☐	→	D	▽	
		○	☐	→	D	▽	

CONCLUSIONS

In this chapter we covered two categories of techniques: problem-identifying techniques and problem-solving techniques. Problem-identifying techniques consist of brainstorming, affinity charts, and interrelationship diagrams. Problem-solving techniques consist of data analysis using bar graphs, histograms and tabular arrays, and process analysis techniques using process charting.

Problem-identifying techniques are expanding because many firms have discovered that not much problem solving can occur until you know what the real problems are. How to identify the real problems has, therefore, become an area of focus for many progressive organizations. The three techniques described in this chapter provide an important approach to problem identification.

Problem-solving techniques are not revolutionary. To be sure, the personal computer and its ability to provide graphs of all varieties is proving to be increasingly helpful. However, the process analysis technique, although it has been around for a long time, is still only sparingly used.

Discussion Questions

1. What are the common techniques used by productivity improvement teams in analyzing and solving operations problems?
2. Describe brainstorming.
3. Describe how affinity charting is used.
4. Describe why interrelationship diagrams are important.
5. When is the use of affinity charts preferred to open brainstorming?
6. What do presentation techniques consist of?
7. Describe flow-process charting.
8. What are the five symbols used in flow-process charting?
9. How does the flow-process chart differ from the flow-process analysis chart?

References

1. Basadur, M. "Managing Creativity: A Japanese Model." *Academy of Management Executive,* 6(2), May 1992, 29–42.
2. Goldberg, A. M., and C. C. Pegels. *Quality Circles in Health Care Facilities*, pp. 108–109, 123–129. Aspen Systems Corporation, Rockville, MD, 1984.
3. Stevenson, W. J. *Production/Operations Management,* 3rd ed., pp. 401–403. Irwin, Homewood, IL, 1990.

Chapter ten

Cause and Effect Diagrams and Pareto Analysis

Outline

Introduction
Examples of Cause and Effect Diagrams
Expanded Cause and Effect Diagram
Staged Cause and Effect Diagram
Pareto Analysis: A Problem Analysis Technique
Principles and Applications of Pareto Analysis
Conclusions

Introduction

Next to brainstorming, the cause and effect diagram is probably the technique used most often. The cause and effect diagram is often called the fish-bone diagram because, in its final form, it resembles a fish bone, with the head representing the effect (problem) and the fins and tail bones representing the major causes. The diagram is usually confined to four or five major causes so as not to complicate the analysis of the problem. However, if more in-depth analysis is required, all causes can be shown on the diagram. To facilitate identification of causes for a cause and effect diagram, ideas are often classified in the following categories: materials, machines, personnel, methods, environment, and measurement.

Examples of Cause and Effect Diagrams

Figure 10–1 shows a cause and effect diagram with five major causes shown on the tail and fins of the diagram. In this case, the effect or problem is a hotel guest complaint. The major causes of the complaint are room service, food service, housekeeping service, front desk, and environmental conditions.

The simple type of cause and effect diagram shown in Figure 10–1 is useful for some kinds of problem solving, but its usefulness is limited. It merely shows

Figure 10-1
Cause and Effect Diagram of Hotel Guest Complaints

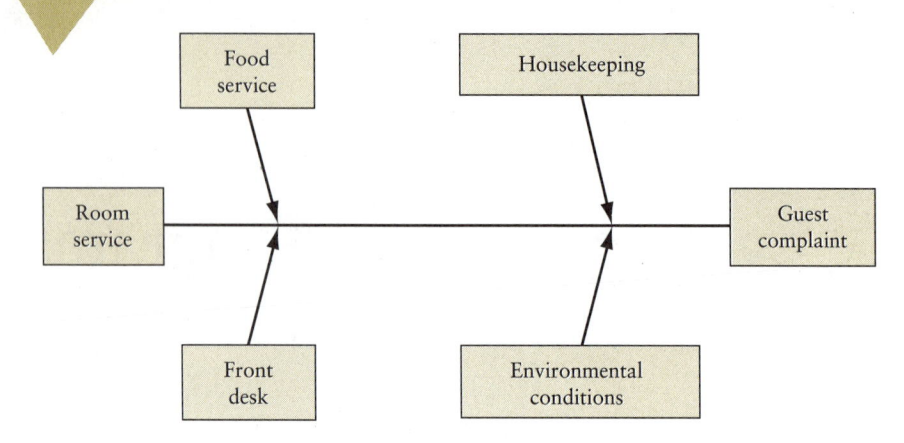

how the major causes relate (as indicated by the arrows) to the effect (in this case, hotel guest complaints).

Expanded Cause and Effect Diagram

The cause and effect diagram can be expanded to become a more useful vehicle by eliciting and recording the minor causes that combine to contribute to the major causes. Ideas for the minor causes can be generated by the problem-solving team in a brainstorming session. Figure 10-2 shows the expanded cause and effect diagram in which the minor causes have been added by the problem-solving team to provide additional information for problem analysis.

Figure 10-2
Staged Cause and Effect Diagrams of Food Service Complaints

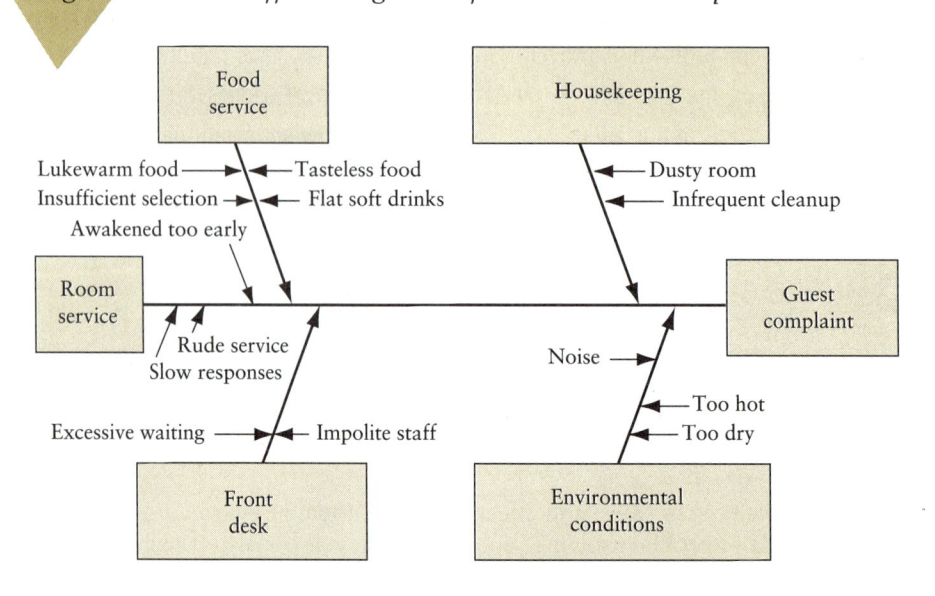

CAUSE AND EFFECT DIAGRAMS AND PARETO ANALYSIS

As in brainstorming, the problem-solving team should participate in the development of this more comprehensive cause and effect diagram. The greater the number of causes listed, the more information there will be for problem resolution. Again, the problem-solving team should be discouraged from criticizing contributions made by their fellow problem-solving team members while creating the fish-bone diagram.

If the diagram becomes too crowded, it may be necessary to break up the single problem into two or more problems with their own cause and effect diagrams. An example of two separate but related cause and effect diagrams is shown in Figure 10–3.

Figure 10–3
Separated Cause and Effect Diagrams of Related Hotel Guest Complaints

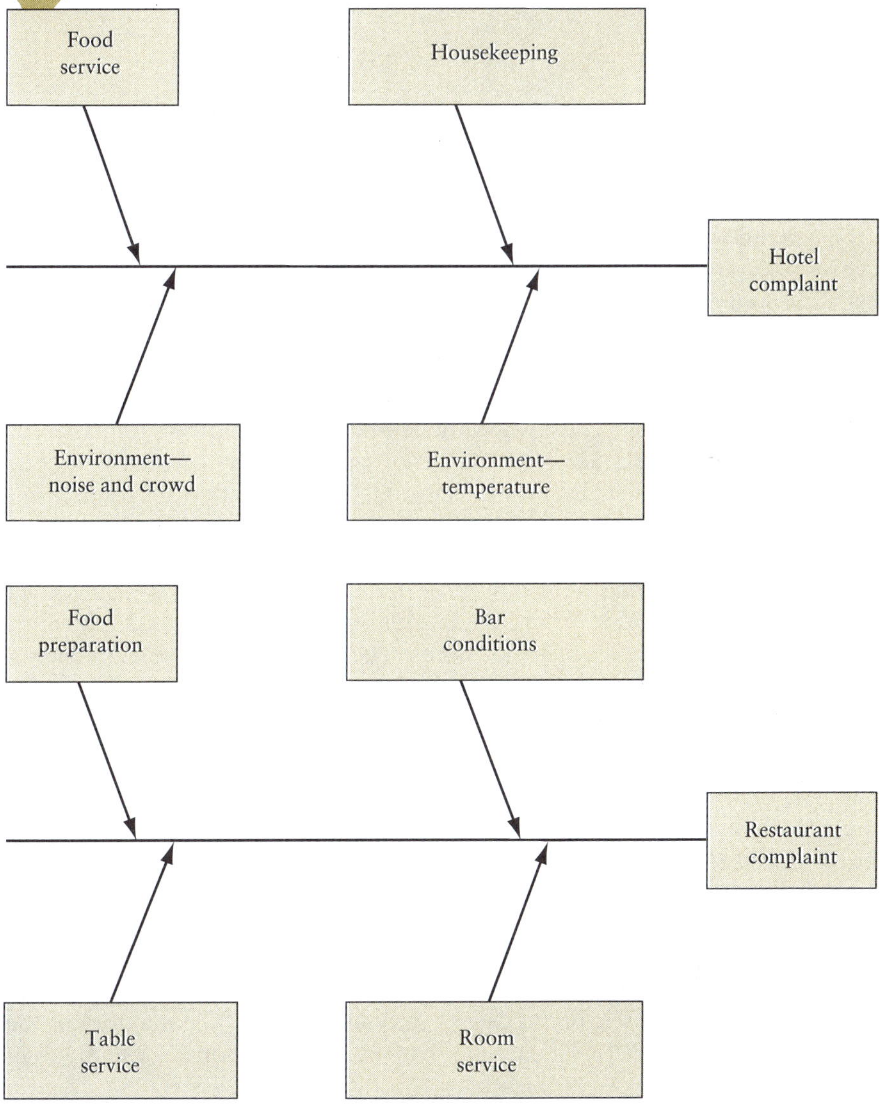

Figure 10-4
Staged Cause and Effect Diagram of Food Service Complaints

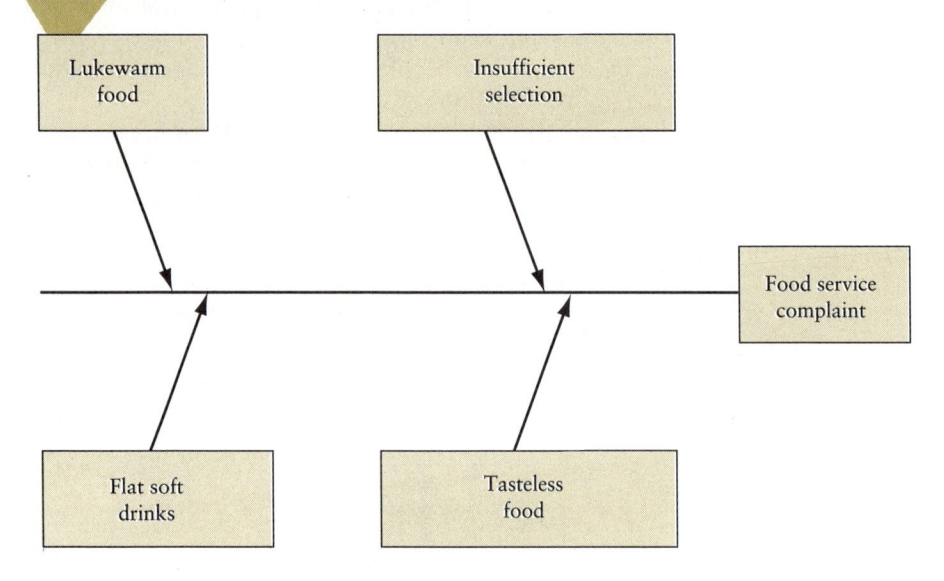

Staged Cause and Effect Diagram

If the expanded or separated cause and effect diagrams become too busy, it may be necessary and desirable to take one of the major causes and construct a new cause and effect diagram using that cause as the new problem. For example, if food service complaints are the problem, or effect, the causes of the complaints might include lukewarm food, insufficient selection, tasteless food, and flat soft drinks, as shown in Figure 10–4. For each of these four causes, one can find the cause, or reason. Thus, when an identified problem grows too large for a single cause and effect diagram, the major causes on the original fish-bone diagram can be used as effects on supplemental cause and effect diagrams.

Cause and effect diagrams are a useful technique in problem solving. After sufficient information has been recorded, the major causes of a problem can be isolated by brainstorming, then circled on the diagram. The causes must then be prioritized and verified. Each major cause so identified is then addressed until, at some point, the problem has been reduced substantially or eliminated.

PARETO ANALYSIS: A PROBLEM ANALYSIS TECHNIQUE

Pareto analysis is based on the work of Vilfredo Pareto, an Italian economist. Pareto had, at the turn of the century, discovered that a few families controlled much of Italy's wealth. Thus, Pareto analysis became a method for separating the "vital few" from the "trivial many." The technique was introduced to the Japanese by the quality control expert J. M. Juran. While troubleshooting in the quality control field, Juran had discovered that, for any quality problem that had numerous causes, only a few of the causes created the majority of the problem occurrences. Pareto analysis thus became an important technique in the quality movement.

Pareto analysis identifies all causes of a problem and then lists them by order of importance according to a quantitative criterion. The technique is particularly useful in prioritizing the major causes of a problem in a cause and effect diagram in order to decide which are primary [1, 2]. In the example below we have used the number of causes as the quantitative measure. However, cost can also be used, and frequently is, in applying Pareto analysis.

Principles and Applications of Pareto Analysis

Pareto analysis uses a modified histogram, called a Pareto diagram, to identify the major causes of a problem. To illustrate, when a department has frequent staff overload problems, a question immediately arises as to the causes. An easy solution to the problem is to add more staff, but this may not always be feasible or in accordance with cost containment objectives. Thus, at one particular firm, it was decided to keep track of overload problem occurrences. Each day an overload occurred, the cause of the problem would be identified. The four causes found were (1) higher than normal work load, thus creating more work than the department staff could handle effectively; (2) special cases requiring more than normal staff time; (3) a high absentee rate, forcing more work on the remaining employees than they could comfortably handle; and (4) one or more vacant lines, creating an effect similar to absenteeism. On some days, more than one of these causes created the overload problem. For those days, only the major cause of the problem was listed.

The survey of the overload problem in this firm was continued for 100 consecutive workdays. In this period, it was found that during 40 days there was no overload problem. In the remaining 60 days, 18 days had a higher than normal work load, causing an overload; 12 days had special cases that caused an overload; 6 days had vacant staff lines leading to an overload; and 24 days had high absenteeism, creating an overload problem. The frequency of occurrences (days) of the causes is shown on the histogram in Figure 10–5. If the causes are added and combined with the number of days that had no overload problem, we arrive at 100 days, the length of the survey.

Note that the histogram shows the frequencies of occurrences of the causes as well as the frequency of the days in which no overload problem occurred. Because, in this case, we are not interested in those days on which no problem occurred, we have redrawn the histogram in Figure 10–6 to show only the frequency of overload causes.

Based on the Figure 10–6 histogram, we can derive a Pareto diagram. As noted earlier, a Pareto diagram is essentially a redrawn histogram that shows the most important cause to the left and the remaining causes in order of importance to the right. Figure 10–7 shows the first part of the Pareto diagram, or the partial Pareto diagram. Note that the most important cause of the overload is absenteeism, followed by high workload, special cases, and vacant lines.

The Pareto diagram is completed in Figure 10–8 by the addition of the cumulative percent of the four causes. Note that 90% of all instances of overload are the result of absenteeism, high workload, and special cases, and that the category "all causes" includes absenteeism, high workload, special cases, and vacant lines. The cumulative line expresses, in percentage form, the degree to which overstaffing could be alleviated if the causes of the problem were eliminated.

Figure 10-5
Histogram of Overload Causes, Including No Overload Frequency

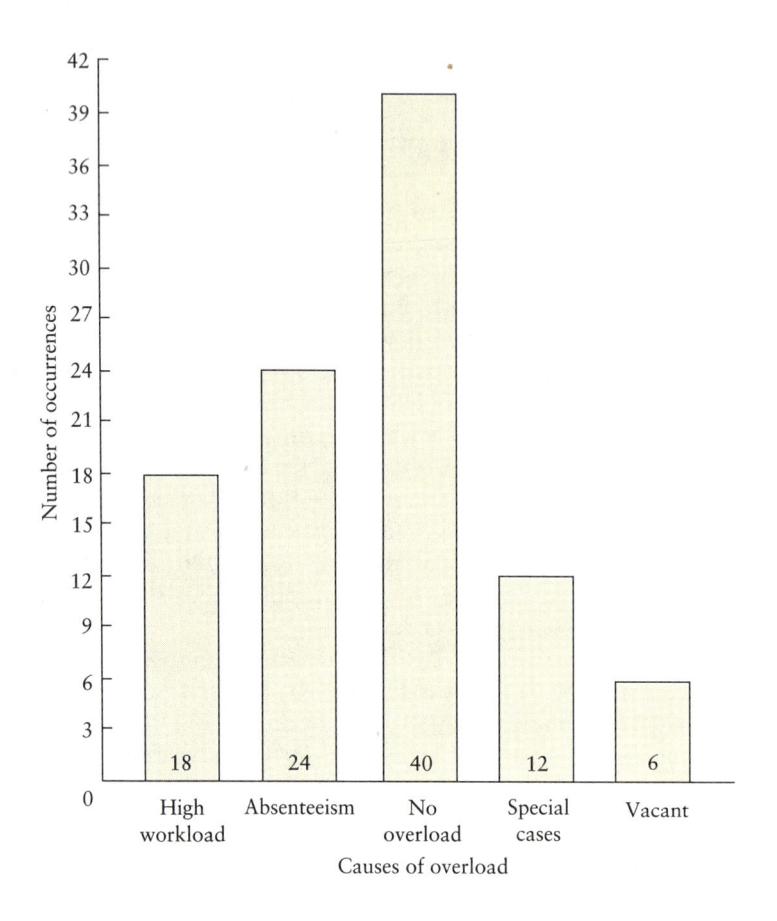

[Histogram: High workload 18, Absenteeism 24, No overload 40, Special cases 12, Vacant 6. Y-axis: Number of occurrences. X-axis: Causes of overload.]

One logical suggestion that could be derived from the Pareto diagram would be to concentrate on solving the absenteeism problem first. Because absenteeism is responsible for more than a third of the overstaffing problem, a reduction in its rate would have a substantial positive effect.

In applying Pareto analysis to the overload problem, it was assumed that on each day only one major cause could be assigned. This may be a reasonable assumption in most situations. However, in some cases, the assumption may not be valid and must be rejected or adjusted to fit the reality. For example, it is quite possible that, on any given day, overload could be caused by both absenteeism and a high workload, or by a vacant line and special cases, or, for that matter, by all four.

Let us assume that, on the basis of a 100-day census, it was found that the problem of overload occurred on 60 days and that it could be attributed to absenteeism on 30 days, to a high workload on 24 days, to special cases on 15 days, and to a vacant line on 6 days. Because it is now assumed that more than one cause may be responsible for the problem, the sum of the frequencies of the causes of the problem exceeds 60, the number of days on which overload problems occurred.

CAUSE AND EFFECT DIAGRAMS AND PARETO ANALYSIS

Figure 10-6
Histogram of Overload Causes Only

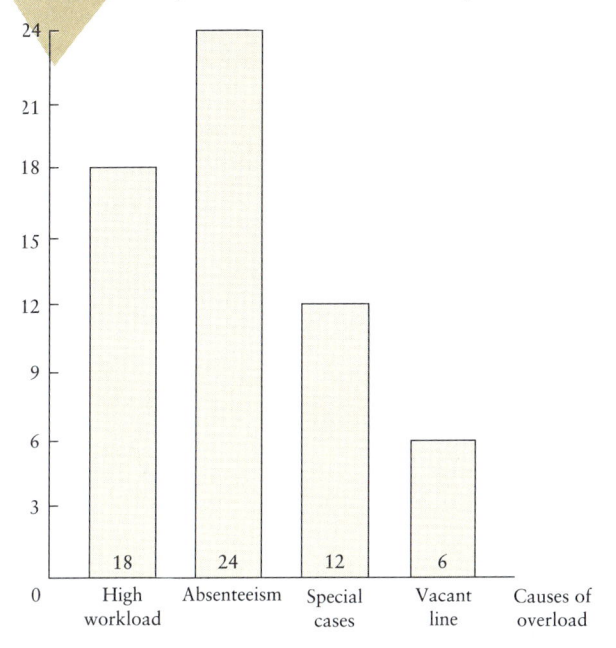

Cause	Count
High workload	18
Absenteeism	24
Special cases	12
Vacant line	6

Figure 10-7
Partial Pareto Diagram of Overload Cases

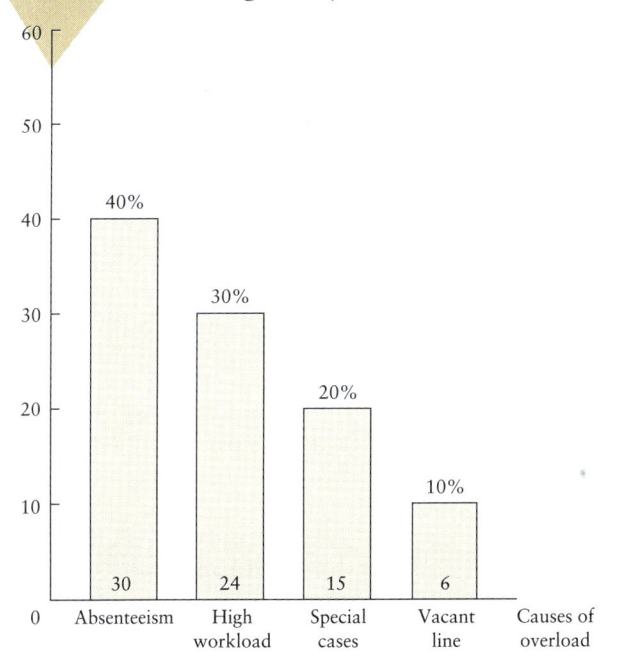

Cause	Count	Percent
Absenteeism	30	40%
High workload	24	30%
Special cases	15	20%
Vacant line	6	10%

Note: Number of causes is shown in each column.

Figure 10-8
Complete Pareto Diagram of Overload Cases

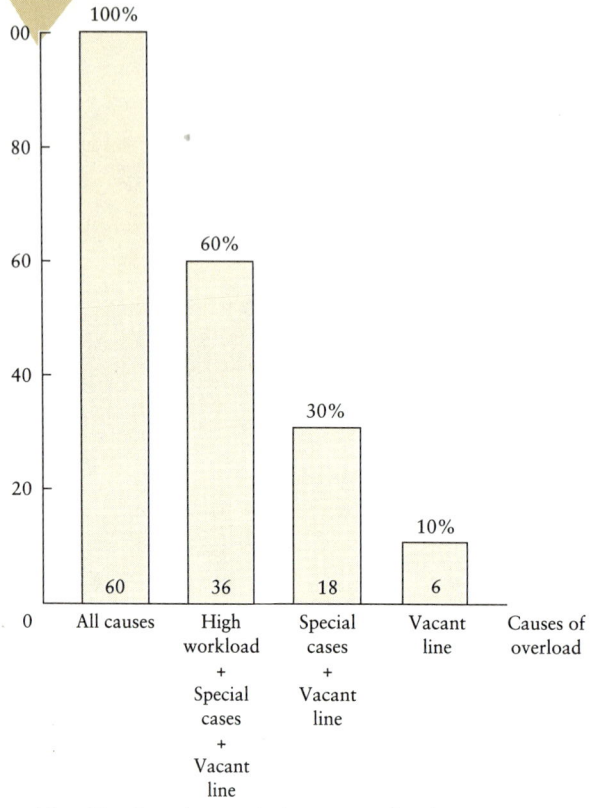

	All causes	High workload + Special cases + Vacant line	Special cases + Vacant line	Vacant line
%	100%	60%	30%	10%
Number	60	36	18	6

Causes of overload

Note: Number of causes is shown in each column.

Figure 10–9 shows the Pareto diagram of the overload problem in this case. Note that the cumulative frequency of causes numbers 75, occurring over the 60-day period. Again, the most serious cause is absenteeism. If it were resolved, 40% of the causes of overload would be eliminated. Even if it could be reduced by half, a more likely possibility, the relief of the overload problem would be substantial.

Pareto analysis is a useful technique for isolating and identifying the major causes of a problem. The Pareto diagram graphically identifies the causes, ranking them so that the major causes are revealed.

The Pareto diagram can also be used as a control tool to show how improvements have occurred as a result of the resolution of identified problems. "Before" and "after" Pareto diagrams can show the reduction in the frequency of causes contributing to the problem.

The key word in Pareto analysis is not "Pareto" but "analysis." Before the problem-solving team can make recommendations, the problem and its causes must be well understood. Through Pareto analysis, the problem-solving team becomes thoroughly familiar with the problem and its causes and is able to make appropriate recommendations for its solution.

Figure 10-9
Variation of Pareto Diagram for a Staffing Problem

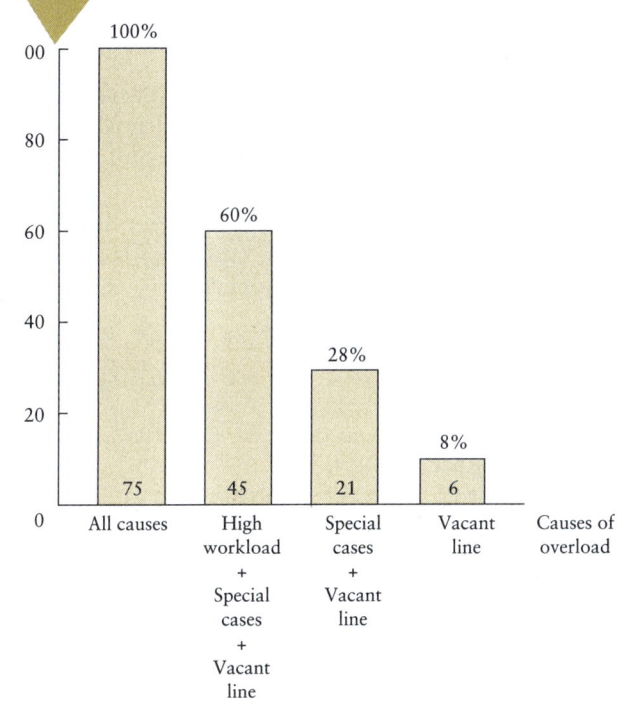

	All causes	High workload + Special cases + Vacant line	Special cases + Vacant line	Vacant line	Causes of overload
	100%	60%	28%	8%	
	75	45	21	6	

Note: Number of causes is shown in each column.

Conclusions

Cause and effect diagrams, also known as fish-bone diagrams, are probably the best-known and most widely used problem-analysis and problem-solving tools used by individuals and problem-solving teams. They allow a problem to be broken down into several categories. The problem solver can then focus on each category separately.

Pareto analysis also enjoys wide popularity. It allows a ranking procedure of the causes of a problem. By discovering what the major causes are, the problem solver can focus his or her energies on those causes that will provide the largest return.

Both techniques described and illustrated in this chapter have become widely known because of their extensive use by Japanese quality circles. Considering the successes achieved by Japanese quality circles, it behooves problem solvers to use these techniques whenever possible.

Discussion Questions

1. Develop a simple cause and effect diagram for an airline passenger complaint about foul air in an airplane cabin.
2. Expand the airline passenger complaint diagram analysis by adding at least one cause to each complaint source.
3. Develop a Pareto diagram for complaints about an automobile consisting of the following categories: ride, interior comfort, handling, road noise, fuel consumption, and reliability. The six complaints had incidences of 8, 6, 10, 12, 16, and 14, respectively.
4. The automobile manufacturer ranked the six complaints by the following respective importance weights: .30, .15, .10, .15, .15, and .15. Develop a revised Pareto chart on the weighted values of each complaint.

References

1. Goldberg, A. M., and C. C. Pegels. *Quality Circles in Health Care Facilities*, pp. 113–132. Aspen Systems Corporation, Rockville, MD, 1984.
2. Thompson, P. C. *Quality Circles—How to Make Them Work in America*, p. 105. American Management Association, New York, 1982.

Chapter eleven

Statistical Control Charting

Outline

Introduction
Control Charting
Averages Control Chart
Other Types of Control Charts
Proportion Control Charts
Error Control Charts
What Is a Process Variation?
Decision Rules for Process Variation Control
Motorola's Six Sigma Challenge
Conclusions

Introduction

Statistical control charting is a methodological tool to control and maintain quality, performance, acceptability, output, package weight, or any similar standard set by an organization in the manufacture of products or the provision of services. Normally, quality, operating, and performance standards are maintained through measurement or performance evaluation of the product or service against predetermined standards and specifications. However, measurement and performance evaluation can be expensive and time-consuming, adding considerably to the cost of the product or service. Therefore, to maintain adequate performance and product or service quality, organizations use statistical sampling techniques. In particular, statistical sampling is widely used in operations and quality control. Service providers constantly monitor the quality of their services against standards they develop themselves or standards set by the government or trade organizations. Product manufacturers similarly monitor the products produced against engineering specifications [1, 2, 4].

Statistical sampling is a low-cost way to obtain measurement information about a process producing a large volume of output, without incurring a large cost for measuring each unit of output separately. By randomly selecting a statistical sample of the output, measurement information can be derived at a relatively low cost.

Control Charting

Statistical control charting involves the charting of statistics on a chart in such a way that deviations from a standard can be quickly observed and action can be taken to correct the undesirable deviations. Although there are several types of statistics that can be controlled with a control chart, we will first illustrate the control of an average, or $\bar{x}$ statistic, on a control chart. For the average or $\bar{x}$ control chart the statistics recorded are the averages ($\bar{x}$) and ranges (R) of specified quantitative measures, such as those representing waiting times, the quality level of a product, the chemical measures of a product, or the verification of a laboratory testing procedure. Averages and ranges from several observations are calculated to obtain sample average and sample range statistics.

Control charting enables one to determine if a standard measure is being attained or if a process is being properly controlled. For example, a random sample of fixed size is drawn from the output of a service process, and those sample measurements are then used to determine the statistic to be charted. Through such sampling, control costs can be kept low while still ensuring adherence to performance standards.

Averages Control Chart

Assume that management wants to keep statistical control on the response times to customer telephone inquiries. Let us assume that, historically, the average response time is 46 minutes; that is, $\bar{x} = 46$. From analysis of the response times, it has been found that the response time is distributed with a standard deviation $S_x = 0.4$ minutes. The response times are unchanged as long as the average, $\bar{x}$, and the sample standard deviation, $S_{\bar{x}}$, remain unchanged. By drawing a random sample of nine response times, we can obtain nine random observations of the response times, shown as sample 1 in Table 11–1. Averaging the nine observations enables us to calculate the average response time, identified as $\bar{x}$, of the sample. The $\bar{x}$ value can be considered as a random value drawn out of a normal distribution with mean $\bar{x}$ and a standard deviation $S_{\bar{x}}$ by the formula $S_{\bar{x}} = S_x/\sqrt{n}$, where n is the sample size of nine observations or measurements. In our example, therefore, $S_{\bar{x}} = 0.4/3 = 0.1333$ minutes.

Let us further assume that management allows a 0.3% chance—three standard deviations from the average—that $\bar{x}$ will fall outside of the control limits if the response times remain unchanged. The average response time is 46 minutes, so the upper control limit (UCL) will be $46 + 3(.133) = 46.4$ minutes, and the lower control limit (LCL) will be $46 - 0.4 = 45.6$ minutes. Table 11–1 shows the observations, sample means, and sample ranges of five samples of the response times to customer inquiries. From the raw data, the averages for the five samples are calculated as 46.00, 45.77, 45.89, 46.11, and 46.33 minutes.

The upper chart in Figure 11–1 is the control chart for the statistical control of $\bar{x}$ for the response process. The five plotted values of $\bar{x}$ indicate the trend, make the chart easier to read, and show that all five values of $\bar{x}$ fall within the control limits.

A process such as customer response times may be said to be under control as long as the average, $\bar{x}$, and the standard deviation, $S_{\bar{x}}$, of the observations remain unchanged. As noted, process control charts can be used to control the average. Using a similar approach, we can also calculate the standard

STATISTICAL CONTROL CHARTING

Table 11–1
Sample of Response Times to Customer Inquiries

Sample Observation Number	Sample 1	Sample 2	Sample 3	Sample 4	Sample 5
1	46	45	45	45	46
2	45	48	45	45	46
3	46	47	45	46	46
4	46	46	45	47	46
5	47	45	46	48	47
6	46	46	47	47	47
7	48	46	47	46	47
8	45	45	47	45	46
9	45	44	46	46	46
Sample total	414	412	413	415	417
Sample mean	46.00	45.77	45.89	46.11	46.33
Sample range	3	4	2	3	1

Note: Response times are in minutes; the sample size (n) is 9.

deviations of each sample and plot them so that extreme variations within the sample are identified. However, to avoid having to calculate the standard deviation of each sample, a widely used substitute method can be employed. The substitute method is the range chart, which plots the range of each sample. This chart is often preferred because the range of values in a sample is much easier to determine than the standard deviation. For samples of size 10 or less, it is at least as accurate as the standard deviation control chart.

The ranges of the customer response time samples are shown at the bottom of Table 11–1. These values were calculated by subtracting the lowest observed value from the highest observed value in each sample. For example, the lowest response time in sample 1 is 45 minutes, and the longest response time is 48 minutes, generating a range of 3 minutes.

To construct a statistical control chart for the range R, we specify the upper control limits to be $\bar{R} + 3S_R$ and the lower control limit to be $\bar{R} - 3S_R$. R is the range observed in a sample of size n, and the average value of the range R is determined by a large number of sample observations. S_R is the standard deviation of the range, as determined from observations of a large number of samples. The use of three standard deviations in either direction of $\bar{R}$ on the control chart ensures that there will be only an approximately 0.3% chance that the observations will fall outside that range if the process is out of control.

To avoid having to calculate S_R, we can calculate the upper and lower control limits more simply by using the multipliers in Table 11–2. For example, for a sample with $\bar{n} = 9$, the lower control limit is $0.18\bar{R}$ and the upper control limit is $= 1.82\bar{R}$.

Figure 11-1

Average ($\bar{x}$) and Range (R) Control Charts for Customer Response Times

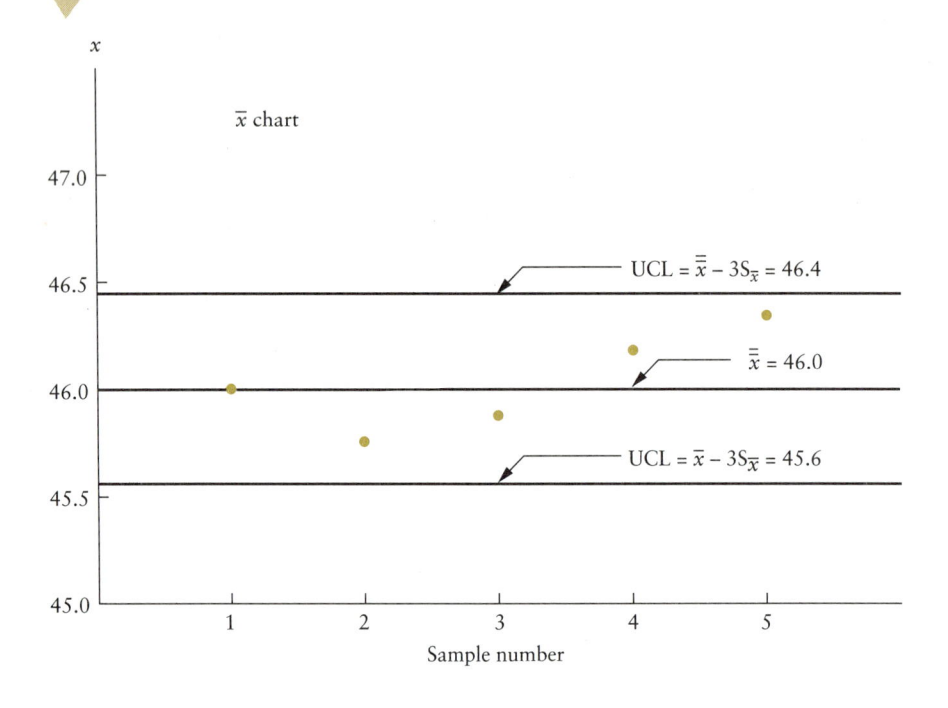

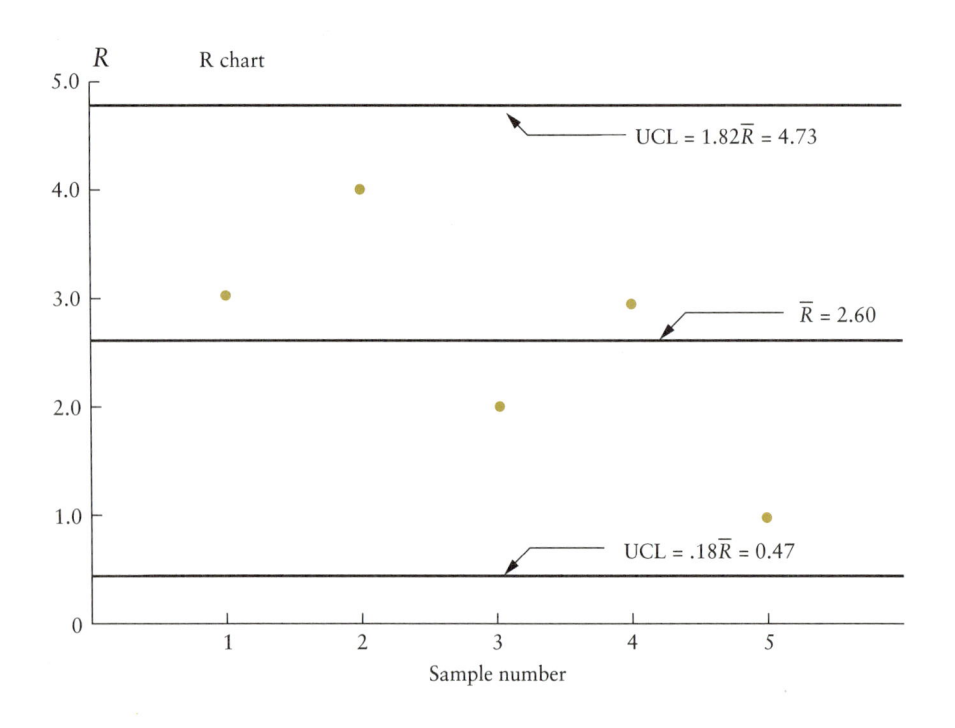

$\bar{x}$ chart

UCL = $\bar{\bar{x}} - 3S_{\bar{x}} = 46.4$

$\bar{\bar{x}} = 46.0$

UCL = $\bar{\bar{x}} - 3S_{\bar{x}} = 45.6$

Sample number

R chart

UCL = $1.82\bar{R} = 4.73$

$\bar{R} = 2.60$

UCL = $.18\bar{R} = 0.47$

Sample number

STATISTICAL CONTROL CHARTING

Table 11-2
Multipliers for Calculating Lower and Upper Control Limits of Ranges for Three Standard Deviations

	Multipliers	
Sample Size	Lower Control Limit, L	Upper Control Limit, U
2	0	3.27
3	0	2.57
4	0	2.28
5	0	2.11
6	0	2.00
7	.08	1.92
8	.14	1.86
9	.18	1.82
10	.22	1.78
11	.26	1.74
12	.28	1.72
13	.31	1.69
14	.33	1.67
15	.35	1.65
16	.36	1.64
17	.38	1.62
18	.39	1.60
19	.40	1.60
20	.41	1.59

Note: If average of range is $\overline{R}$, the upper control limit (UCL) = $U\overline{R}$ and the lower control limit (LCL) = $L\overline{R}$.

If we assume that we already know that the average range $\overline{R}$ in the customer response time process is 2.60, we can develop a control chart for R and plot the observed values of R of the five samples as shown on the lower chart of Figure 11–1. Note that all five values of R fall within the control limits.

OTHER TYPES OF CONTROL CHARTS

The basis and underlying theory of the statistical control chart to control sample means was presented and illustrated above. The process that the sample mean control chart controls must generate dimensional outputs for which sample means can be generated based on the random sample drawn from the process. The above illustration used response times to customer inquiries, but we also could apply the sample mean control chart to the weight of a package, the diameter of a shaft, the length of a bushing, or the width of a roll of paper.

We will extend the control chart to other dimensions of a process that needs to be controlled. We will first present the proportion control chart, which measures the proportion of a sample with unacceptable or unusual attributes. We then follow it up with the error control chart, which measures the number of unacceptable or unusual attributes of a unit or item. Both of these control charts are based on the same statistical sampling principles used for the sample mean control chart.

The proportion control chart takes samples of a specified size n and then evaluates each of the n observations (or pieces) and determines the proportion (p) that is unacceptable or unusual. This proportion (p) is then charted on a proportion control chart.

The error control chart takes a random sample of size 1, the unit or item, of the output of a process and then evaluates the one unit of output and counts how many unsatisfactory or unusual attributes (errors) there are in the one unit of output. The number (c) of errors is then charted on an error control chart. An example will make this clearer. Suppose a full-length column of narrative in a newspaper is the unit output. The evaluator will check the spelling, punctuation, or grammatical errors and add them up. The number of errors is then identified by the symbol c. The symbol c can take on values of $c = 1, 2, 3, 4$, and so on.

Next we present a routinized way to identify for any statistical control chart how to determine if a process is under control or if it is out of control and deviating from its specifications, even if the recorded sample values generated by the process are still within the upper and lower control limits. This problem identification approach is not necessarily optimal, but it has a statistical basis and is used by at least one large firm, Motorola.

Finally, we present what Motorola calls its "six sigma challenge." Although the six sigma challenge is not a statistical control charting approach, its foundation is related to statistical control principles. It provides a challenge, imposed by Motorola on itself, to improve quality levels to near perfection.

Proportion Control Charts

Control of proportions occurs when we want to control a process in order to ensure that a certain percentage or fraction is maintained after the process is stabilized. Examples where this occurs could be in the case of absenteeism (percent absent), accepted admissions to a program (percent accepted), and number of unacceptable units produced (percent defects). In these situations there is some approximate standard percent that is viewed as normal. Deviations from that standard need to be identified quickly and routinely, and then investigated to determine why the standard is not being maintained. In cases where a process is changeable, we may not necessarily want to maintain the process, but improve it. For instance, in the case of defects, we want to reduce the mean value that is produced by the process; in the case of yield generated by a process, we want to increase it. In most cases, however, the concern of control charts is the maintenance of a mean generated by the process.

STATISTICAL CONTROL CHARTING

Controlling the above percentage—nearly always the proportion measured is a decimal between 0 and 1—is accomplished with the proportion control chart. Instead of controlling the sample mean ($\bar{x}$), we now control the sample proportion, defined as p. It is called a sample proportion because it is based on a random sample drawn from a population, or rather from an ongoing process. For instance, if we obtain a daily absentee rate, the daily rate is essentially a sample from the ongoing process, which generates a daily sample absentee rate. To be sure, this daily sample of absenteeism is not random, and although randomness is desirable, it can be violated, as in this case, without violating the underlying assumptions and the validity of the procedure.

From the sample proportions, p, generated over an extended period of time we can determine the average proportion, $\bar{p}$. The average proportion is defined as

$$\bar{p} = \frac{1}{m}\sum_{i=1}^{m} p_i$$

where m is the number of samples drawn with their respective sample means, p_i.

Next, we can determine the sample standard deviation, S_p. It is defined as

$$S_p = \sqrt{\frac{\bar{p}(1-\bar{p})}{n}}$$

where n is the sample size of each sample drawn.

We can now calculate the upper control limit (UCL) and lower control limit (LCL) of the proportion control chart. They are defined as

$$\text{UCL} = \bar{p} + z\,S_p$$

and

$$\text{LCL} = \bar{p} + z\,S_p$$

where UCL is the upper control limit, LCL is the lower control limit, and z is the number of sample standard deviations (sigmas) the control limits are removed from the average proportion. Most control charts use a value for z equal to either 2 or 3. For a z-value of 2, 94.5% of the sample means will fall within the upper and lower control limits. For a z-value of 3, 99.7% of the sample means will fall within the control limits. This completes our discussion of the concepts underlying the proportion control chart; we will illustrate it with the following example.

Suppose we have taken 12 samples of size 100 for controlling the absentee rate of a small organization. The absentee rate, p, as well as the actual absentees are listed in Table 11–3. Observe that the absentee rate ranges from 1 absentee to as many as 11 absentees. The average absentee rate is 6.5 absentees per day, producing a proportion average $\bar{p} = 0.065$.

The standard deviation is determined by the formula

$$S_p = \sqrt{\frac{\bar{p}(1-\bar{p})}{n}} = \sqrt{\frac{.065(.935)}{100}} = 0.02465$$

We can now determine the upper control limit and lower control limit on the basis of $z = 3$ standard deviations. Then,

$$\text{UCL} = \bar{p} + 3S_p = 0.065 + 3(0.02465)$$
$$= 0.065 + 0.074 = 0.139$$

Table 11-3
Absentee Rates and Proportions

Day (j)	Number of Absentees	Proportion of Absentees (P_i)
1	5	.05
2	7	.07
3	4	.04
4	8	.08
5	2	.02
6	11	.11
7	4	.04
8	3	.03
9	6	.06
10	9	.09
11	1	.01
12	5	.05
Total	65	$\bar{p}$ = .065

Note: Sample size, n, is 100.

and

$$\text{LCL} = \bar{p} - 3S_p = 0.065 - 3(0.02465)$$
$$= 0.065 - 0.074 = -0.011$$

The lower control limit cannot be less than zero, so we set it equal to zero. The upper control limit is 0.139. Reviewing our original data, we can observe that all 12 proportions of absentees fall within the upper and lower control limits of the proportion control chart, as depicted in Figure 11–2.

Error Control Charts

Control of errors occurs when we want to maintain control of a certain number of errors, mistakes, or occurrences generated by a defined process or situation. The chart used for this control procedure is the error control chart, or c-chart.

Examples of error generating processes abound. For instance, the number of spelling or grammar errors occurring on one page of a newspaper or book is a good example. The range of errors occurring ranges from zero to an unbounded number. Another example is the number of burglaries reported in a police district over a daily or weekly period, or the number of traffic deaths per day or week in a city or county. All of these illustrations are examples of errors or occurrences, which can be controlled on an error control chart. What all of the above illustrations have in common is that they can range from zero to a

STATISTICAL CONTROL CHARTING

Figure 11–2
Proportion Control Chart for Absentees

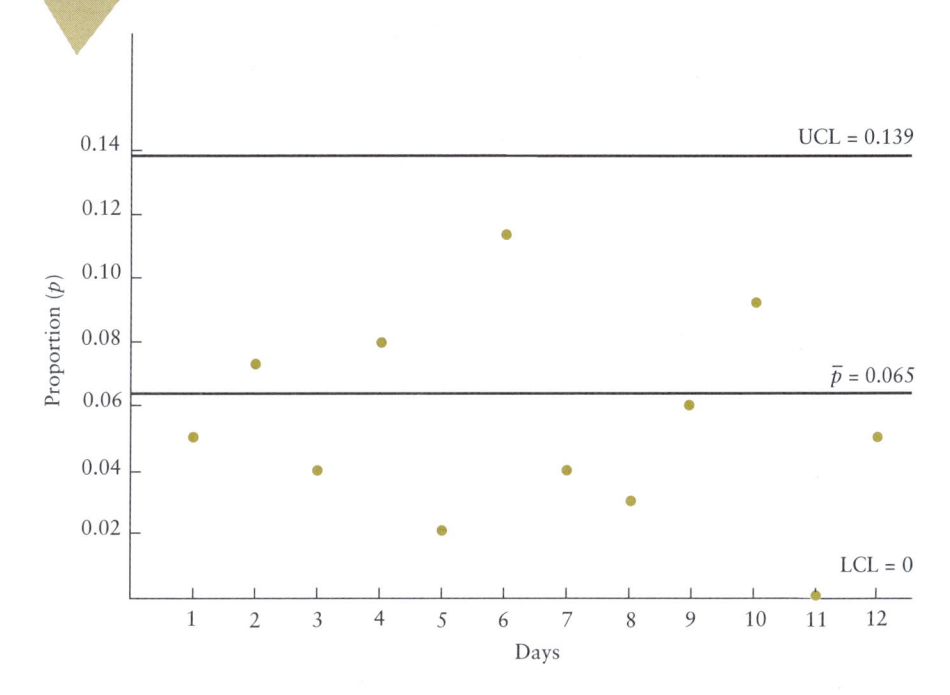

large number and that they are generated by a recurring process. The error control chart tracks the errors and is able to identify when and if the process has changed or is changing.

The number of errors for each occurrence or each sample is identified by the symbol c. There is no sample size in this case because we simply count the number of errors generated by the process. The process that produces the number of errors, c, is, however, considered a random process.

If we collect the number of errors, c, over a period of time we can determine the average number of errors, $\bar{c}$, generated by the process. It is found with the formula

$$\bar{c} = \frac{1}{m}\sum_{i=1}^{m} c_i$$

where m is the number of samples (observations) used to determine the average number of errors.

The sample standard deviation used in the error control chart is proportional to the average number of errors. It can be found by the formula

$$S_c = \sqrt{\bar{c}}$$

We can now proceed to determine the upper control limit and the lower control limit for the error control chart with the following formulas:

$$\text{UCL} = \bar{c} + zS_c \quad \text{and} \quad \text{LCL} = \bar{c} - zS_c$$

where z is the number of standard deviations (sigmas) from the average number of errors, c.

Table 11-4
Monthly Traffic Death Rates in Erie County

Month (c)	Traffic Death Rate (c_i)
1	9
2	11
3	12
4	7
5	6
6	11
7	15
8	16
9	13
10	10
11	7
12	13
Total	120
Average	$\bar{c} = 10$

To illustrate this, suppose we take 12 observations of traffic deaths in Erie County. Each observation covers a period of 1 month, so the 12 observations cover a full year. The actual observations and the average error rate, c, are listed in Table 11-4. Note that the monthly death rates range from 6 to 16 and produce an average monthly death rate, c, of 10.

The standard deviation is determined by the formula

$$S_c = \sqrt{\bar{c}} = \sqrt{10} = 3.162$$

We can now determine the upper control limit and lower control limit on the basis of $z = 3$ standard deviations by the formulas

$$\text{UCL} = \bar{c} + 3S_c = 10 + 3(3.162) = 19.486$$

and

$$\text{LCL} = \bar{c} - 3S_c = 10 - 3(3.162) = 0.514$$

The lower control limit is 0.514 and the upper control limit is 19.486. Reviewing our original data, we note that all observations fall within the upper and lower control limits, as depicted in Figure 11-3.

Figure 11-3
Error Control Chart for Monthly Traffic Deaths

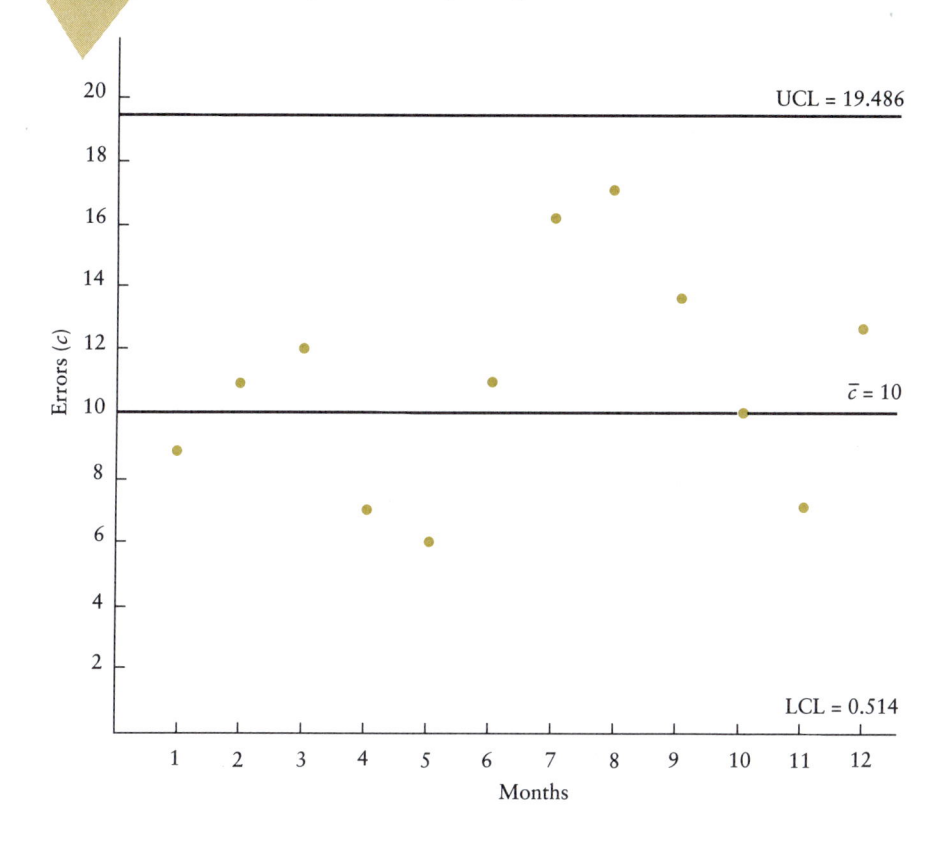

UCL = 19.486
$\bar{c}$ = 10
LCL = 0.514

WHAT IS A PROCESS VARIATION?

Process variations can be attributed to two fairly general sources. Using Motorola's [1] terminology, the two general sources are called common and special causes. Common causes produce deviations that are inherent in the process and cannot be reduced without changing the process itself. The process change may involve modification of the machinery, changing tooling, or changing methods employed in the process. It could conceivably even involve changing the design of the product. Common causes determine the capability of the process, and any basic improvements in process capability can be achieved only by reducing or eliminating the deleterious effects of common causes. The efforts and costs involved in eliminating common causes can be substantial.

Special causes, on the other hand, result from deviations in external conditions, and external conditions are generally controlled. Examples of special causes are operator training and experience and variations in temperature, humidity, and other aspects of the ambient environment. Variations in raw material can also result in special causes. A process, therefore, cannot be considered to be under control until special causes have been eliminated or at least minimized. The primary function of statistical process control is the detection and elimination of special causes.

Decision Rules for Process Variation Control

Statistical process control at Motorola [3] uses a set of decision rules to determine whether a process is in control or if the process has changed. The tool used is the process control chart. These rules are by no means exhaustive or optimal. The rules are useful to Motorola and may also work for others.

To apply the decision rules, the process control chart is divided into three zones, zones A, B, and C. Zone A covers ±1 standard deviation (sigma) from the process mean or centerline. Zone B represents the area between ±2 sigma and ±1 sigma from the process mean or centerline. Zone 3 represents the area between ±3 sigma and ±2 sigma from the process mean or centerline. Figure 11–4 illustrates the three zones as well as the respective areas measured in terms of percentage of area under the standard normal curve.

The following list describes each of the decision rules. The decision rules determine when the process appears to have changed and corrective action needs to be taken.

Decision rule 1. One point outside the three sigma limits, as shown in Figure 11–4.

Decision rule 2. Two out of three consecutive points more than two sigma from the centerline, as shown in Figure 11–5.

Figure 11-4

Statistical Control Chart, Decision Rule 1: One Point Outside Control Limit

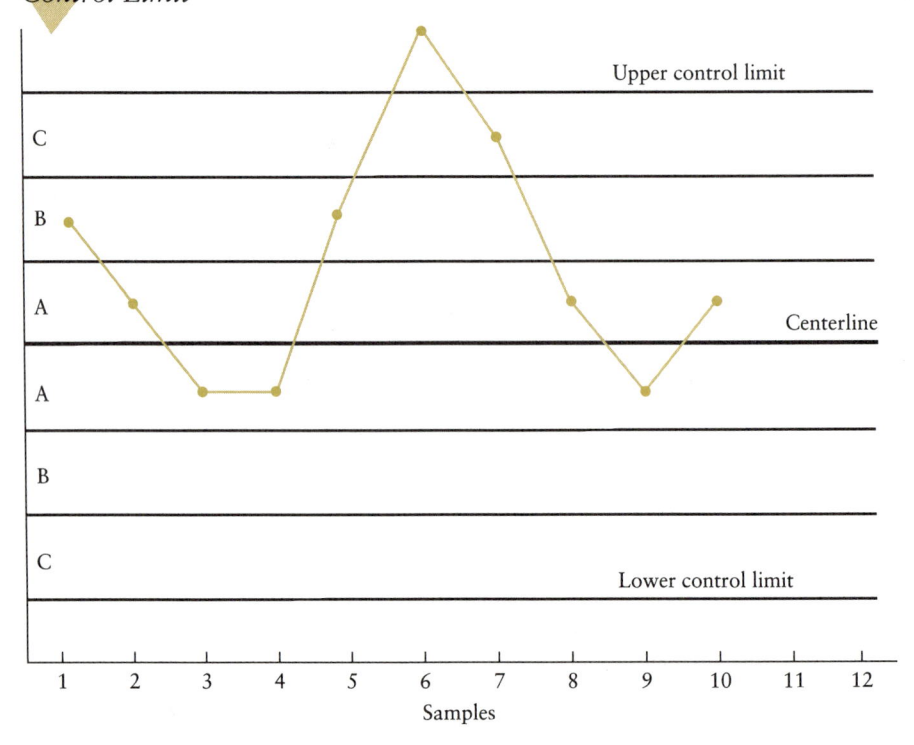

STATISTICAL CONTROL CHARTING

Figure 11-5

Statistical Control Chart, Decision Rule 2: Two Out of Three Consecutive Points More than Two Sigma from Centerline

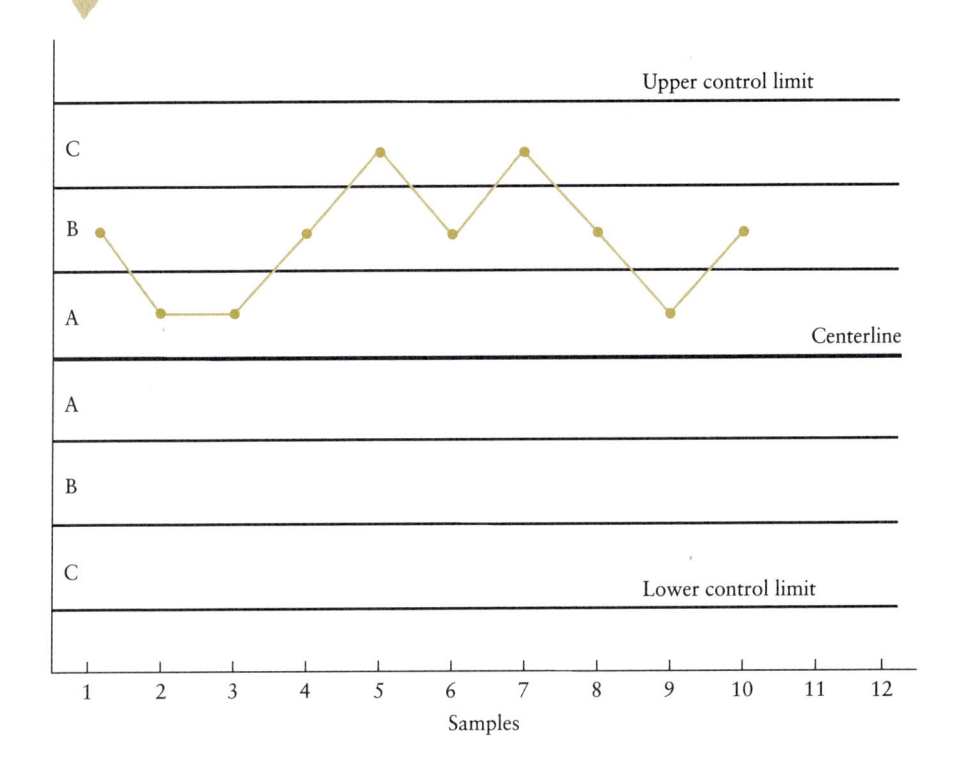

Decision rule 3. Four out of five consecutive points more than one sigma from the centerline, as shown in Figure 11–6.

Decision rule 4. Seven consecutive points above the centerline, as shown in Figure 11–7.

Decision rule 5. Seven consecutive points below the centerline, as shown in Figure 11–8.

Decision rule 6. Seven consecutive points trending up, as shown in Figure 11–9.

Decision rule 7. Seven consecutive points trending down, as shown in Figure 11–10.

The next two rules are based on the premise that about two-thirds of the observations fall within ±1 sigma from the previous mean. The process, therefore, will be deemed to have changed if one of the following occurs:

Decision rule 8. Only 1 out of 10 consecutive points is located within ± sigma from the centerline, as shown in Figure 11–11.

Decision rule 9. Nine out of ten consecutive points are located within ± sigma from the centerline, as shown in Figure 11–12.

Figure 11-6

Statistical Control Chart, Decision Rule 3: Four Out of Five Consecutive Points More than One Sigma from Centerline

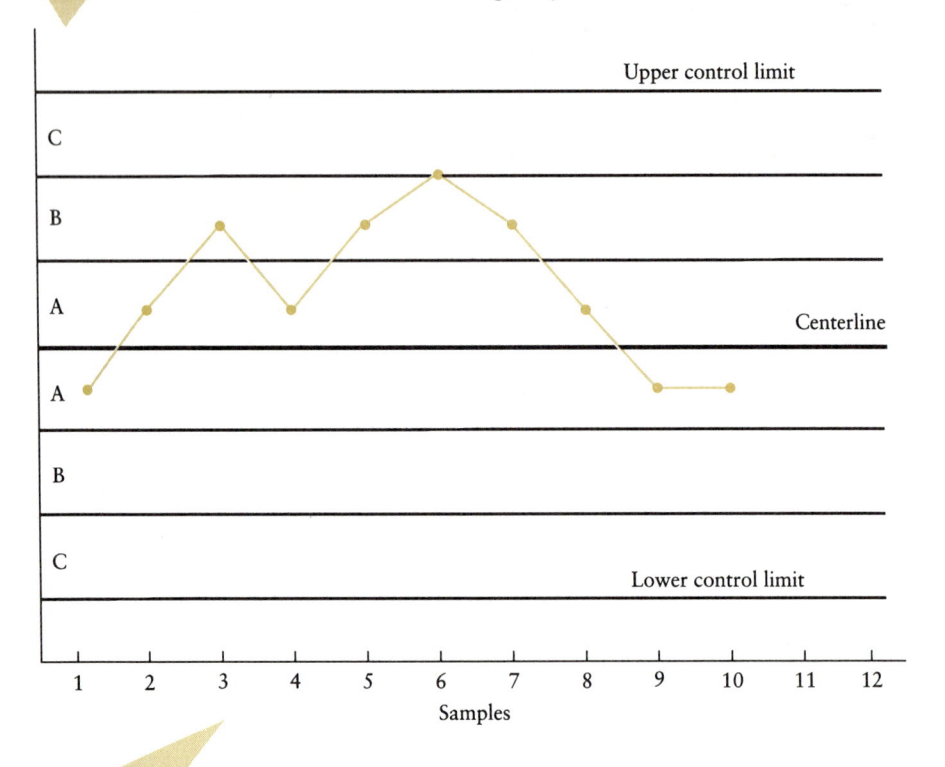

Figure 11-7

Statistical Control Chart, Decision Rule 4: Seven Consecutive Points Above Centerline

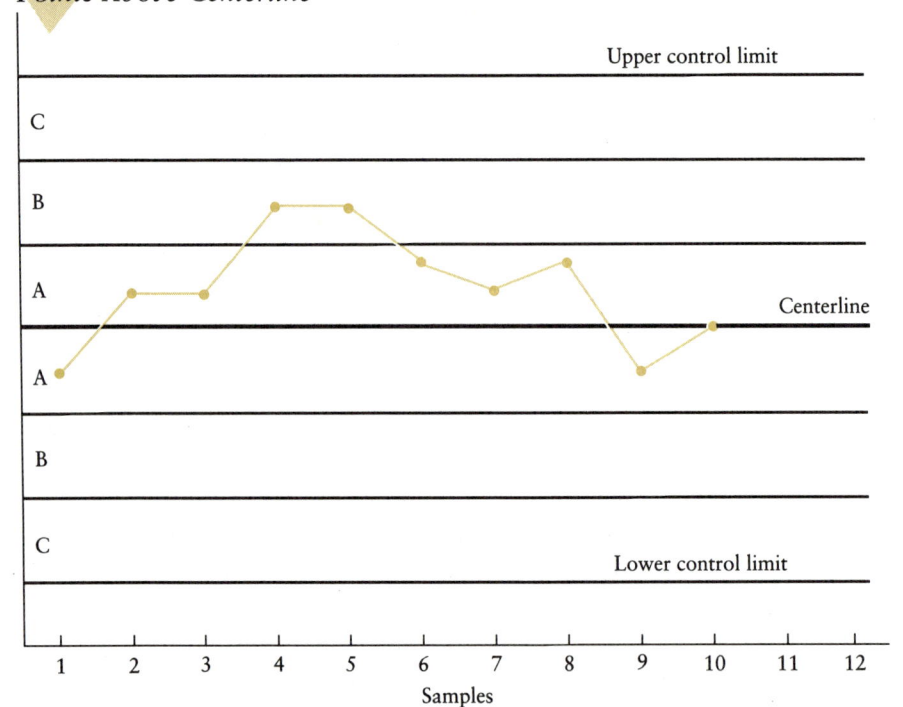

Figure 11-8

Statistical Control Chart, Decision Rule 5: Seven Consecutive Points Below Centerline

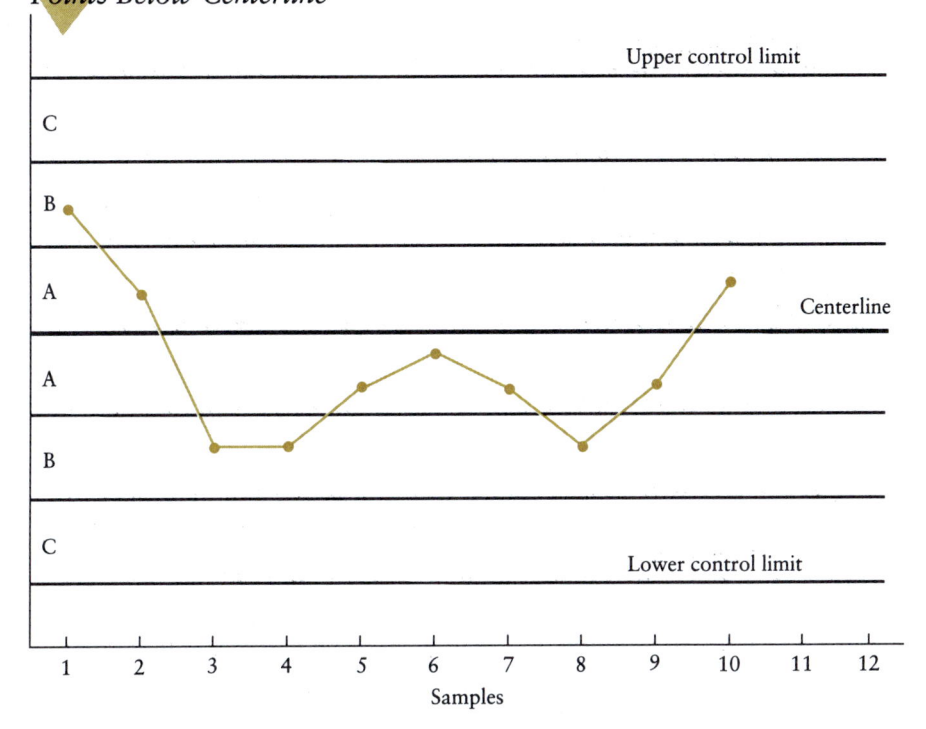

Figure 11-9

Statistical Control Chart, Decision Rule 6: Seven Consecutive Points Trending Up

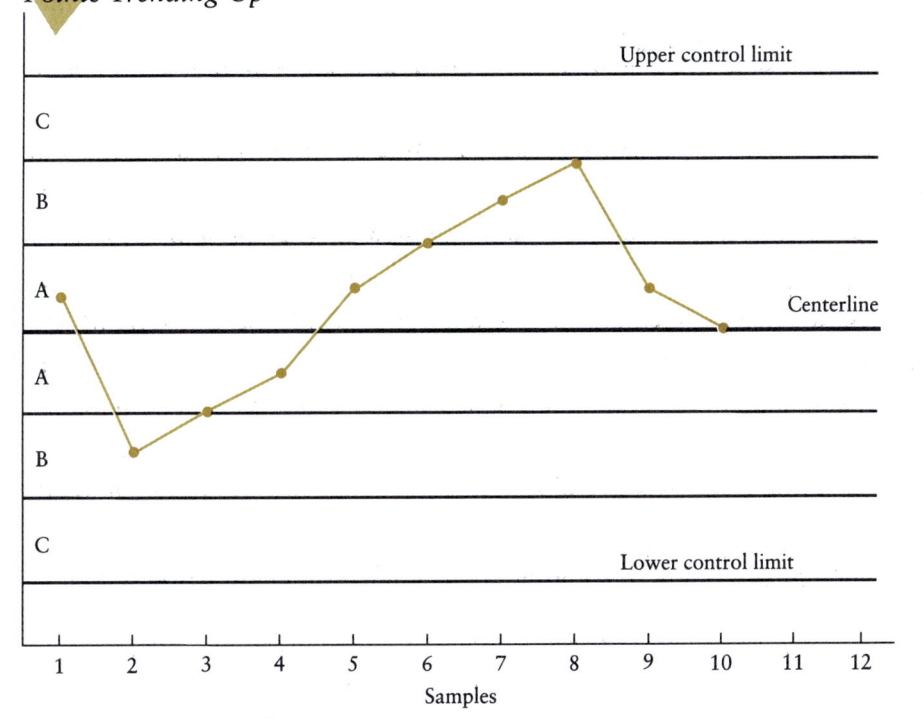

Figure 11-10

Statistical Control Chart, Decision Rule 7: Seven Consecutive Points Trending Down

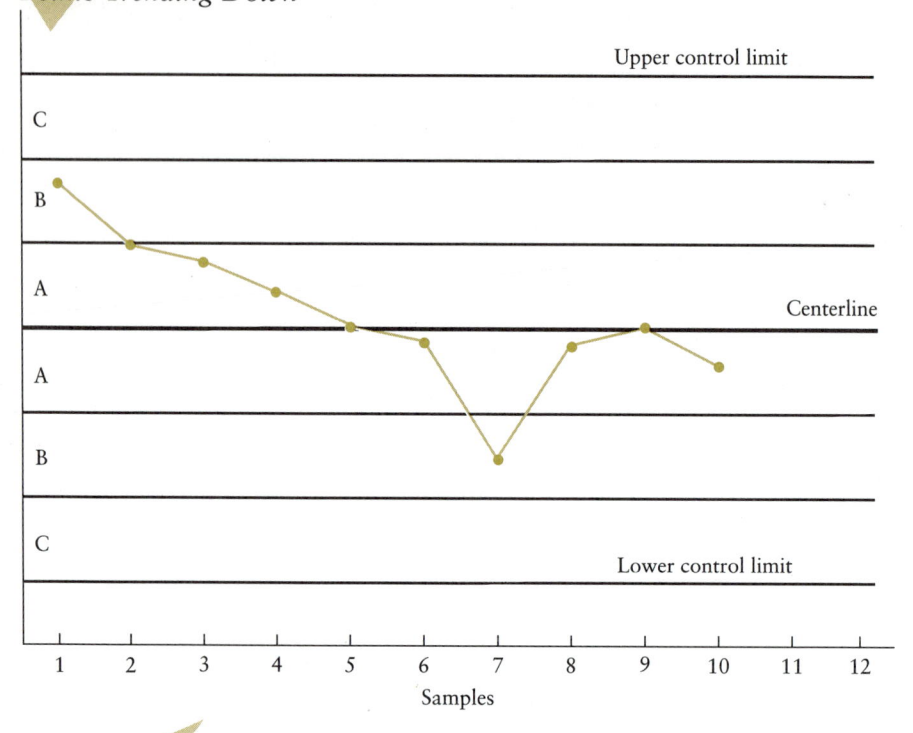

Figure 11-11

Statistical Control Chart, Decision Rule 8: Only One Out of Ten Consecutive Points Is within ±1 Sigma from Centerline

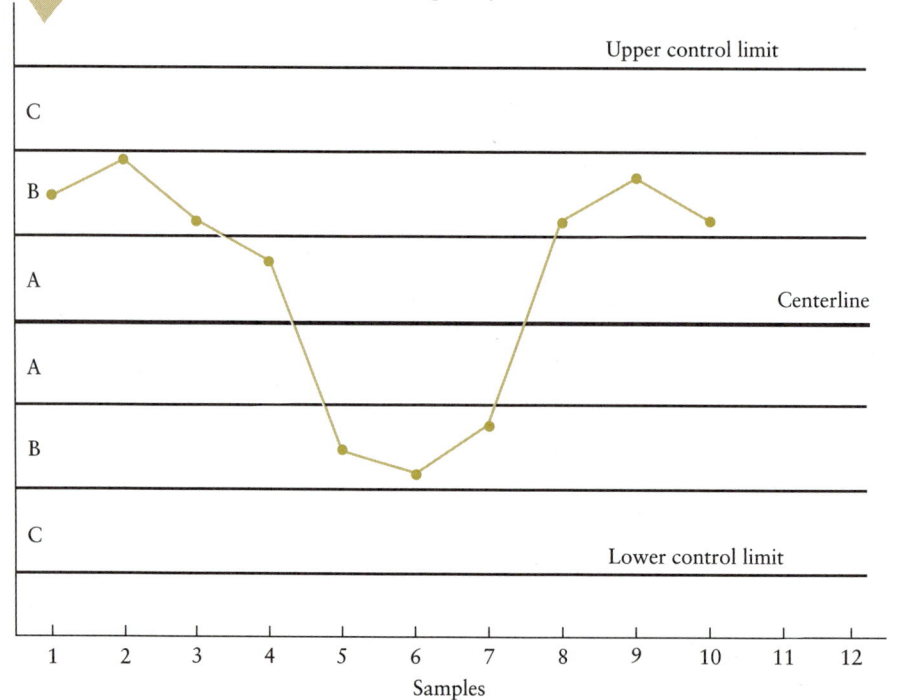

STATISTICAL CONTROL CHARTING

Figure 11-12

Statistical Control Chart, Decision Rule 9: Nine Out of Ten Consecutive Points Are Located within ±1 Sigma from Centerline

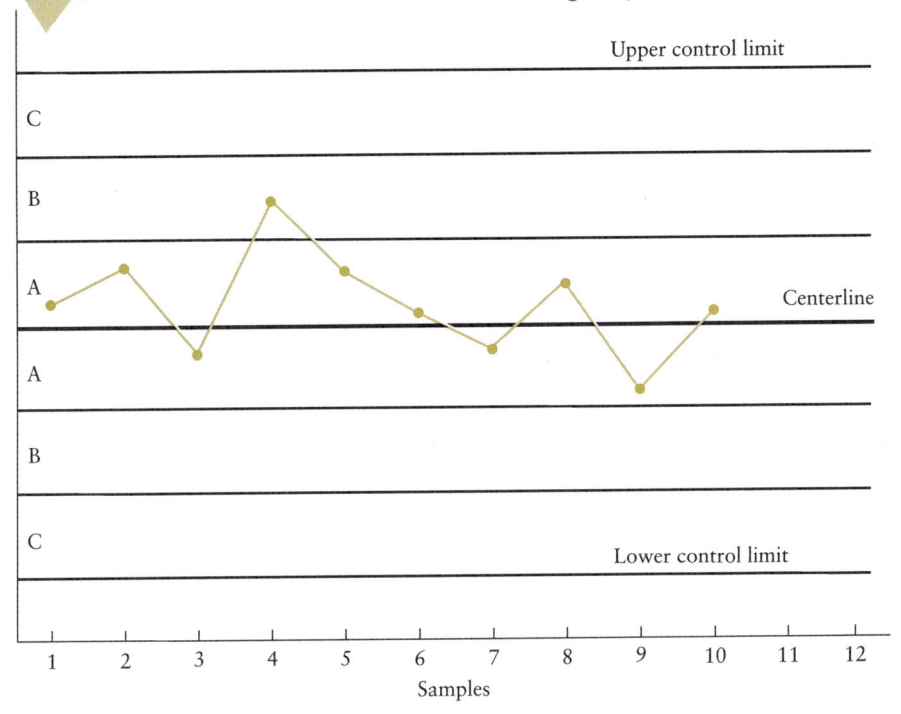

MOTOROLA'S SIX SIGMA CHALLENGE

The objective of error-free performance in products and services led Motorola to the six sigma challenge. What is the six sigma challenge? What does it mean to achieve it?

The six sigma challenge is based on the standard normal distribution. As shown in Table 11–5, the standard normal distribution is divided on the basis of the standard deviations (sigmas) that divide it in segments. For instances, the segment covering one sigma or either side of the mean (the centerline dividing it in equal halves) equals 68.27% of the total area under the curve. Plus or minus two sigmas on either side of the mean cover 95.45% of the area under the curve. Plus or minus 6 sigmas covers 99.9999998% of the area under the curve. So what does all this mean in terms of error-free performance?

The six sigma challenge's aim is to develop a production process whose range falls within plus or minus six sigma limits. This means that if the process can be maintained, only two parts per billion parts produced will fall outside the production process specification limits.

What complicates the error-free performance objectives of any firm is the fact that the quality or performance level of a product is not just determined by the production process but also by the design of the product. In other words, deviations in output can be caused by a deviation in the production process, a deviation in the design process, or both. If the production process and design process overlap exactly, a difficult-to-achieve feat, the achievement

Table 11-5
Attributes of the Standard Normal Distribution

Specification Range in Sigmas	Percent within Range	Defective Parts per Billion
± 1	68.27	317,300,000
± 2	95.45	45,400,000
± 3	99.73	2,700,000
± 4	99.9937	63,000
± 5	99.999943	57
± 6	99.9999998	2

of near error-free performance becomes easier. However, if both the production process and the design process are able to achieve output within the six sigma limits, there is room for error in the center points, the means, of the two processes.

The output of a design process is a design for a particular product, part, component, or assembly. The design specifies the dimensions, specifications, and attributes of both the product to be produced and the tools to be utilized for the production of the product. With considerable experience and expertise, the design engineers are then able to deliver a design that is able to produce a quality product within the six sigma limits.

Table 11-6
Effects of a Shift Away from the Optimal Mean by 1.5 Sigmas

Specification Range in Sigmas	Percent within Range	Defective Parts per Million
± 1	30.23	697,700
± 2	69.13	308,700
± 3	93.32	66,810
± 4	99.3790	6,210
± 5	99.97670	233
± 6	99.999660	3.4

The production process utilizes the manufactured tools and machinery designed by the design process. Then, using raw materials, which follow detailed specifications, the production process produces the product. With the proper training of personnel, the production process, after being stabilized, is able to produce the product within the six sigma limits. However, the means of the design process and the production process probably will not be identical, although they are intended to be. They generally differ, but ideally, of course, by a small amount.

Table 11-6 shows how the production process mean and the design process mean are separated by three sigmas. But because each of the two processes is able to produce within six sigma limits, the defective parts rate can still be kept to 3.4 parts per million. A defect rate of 3.4 parts per million is clearly substantially higher than the 2 parts per billion achievable if the two process means exactly coincide. But a defect rate of 3.4 parts per million is a figure most manufacturers will be quite satisfied with in the 1990s.

Conclusions

Statistical control charting is used extensively in production and service facilities where quality and productivity are constantly monitored. Statistical control charts can be used effectively for problem identification because they make deviations in a process easily visible. They are also useful for follow-up after a change in a system has been implemented. The benefits of statistical control are the time savings. Instead of having to inspect, evaluate, or measure every activity or component, random samples taken at prespecified or random intervals generate sample means. These sample means can then be charted on a statistical control chart. If the sample means fall outside of the upper and lower control limits, the process is probably in need of adjustment and appropriate action can be taken.

Control charting in order to maintain quality or other aspects of operations have become quite popular in recent years. The reason for this popularity is not just the increasing concern of organizations to improve quality, but also the relative ease with which statistical control charts can be applied.

Developing and applying control charts to a process is relatively easily learned, and maintaining the control chart can be done even by people with just a high school education. Interpretation of what control charts mean is somewhat more complex and difficult. However, the decision rule approach introduced in this chapter makes interpretation easier.

Discussion Questions

1. Why are averages ($\bar{x}$) plotted on a control chart instead of individual observations?
2. Develop an average ($\bar{x}$) control chart where the mean output of the process is 18.4 and the standard deviation of the mean is 0.16. Use three sigma control limits.

3. Why is the range ($\bar{R}$) chart preferred over the standard deviation chart?
4. Develop a range ($\bar{R}$) control chart where the mean range is 1.5. Use three sigma control limits.
5. Describe how you could use an averages chart or a proportion chart to control absences.
6. Develop a proportion control chart for $\bar{p}$ = 0.014. Use three sigma control limits.
7. For which control cases would you recommend the use of an error control chart?
8. Develop an error control chart where the mean number of errors is 4.9. Use three sigma control limits.
9. Show how you could identify change in a process even though the control chart shows that the process is under control.
10. Motorola developed seven decision rules to identify deviations in their production processes. Identify and describe three additional rules.
11. Describe in general terms Motorola's six sigma challenge.
12. How many defects per million will be produced if only five sigma limits, instead of six limits, can be achieved?

References

1. Fitzsimmons, J. A., and M. J. Fitzsimmons. *Service Management for Competitive Advantage,* pp. 210–214. McGraw-Hill, New York, 1994.
2. Goldberg, A. M., and C. C. Pegels. *Quality Circles in Health Care Facilities,* pp. 126–133. Aspen Systems Corporation, Rockville, MD, 1984.
3. Hoskins, Janice, Bob Stuart, and Jesse Taylor. *Statistical Process Control.* Motorola Inc., Semiconductor Products Sector, Phoenix, AZ, 1991.
4. Stevenson, W. J. *Production/Operations Management,* 3rd ed., pp. 838–856. Irwin, Homewood, IL, 1990.

Chapter twelve

Quality Function Deployment

Outline

Introduction
Description of Quality Function Deployment
Illustration of Quality Function Deployment
Application of Quality Function Deployment
The Taguchi Method and Quality Function Deployment
Conclusions

Introduction

Of the quality improvement tools utilized by manufacturing and service organizations, quality function deployment (QFD) is probably one of the lesser-known techniques. However, it is a powerful and valuable technique that needs to be more widely studied, evaluated, and applied. It holds high promise to improve a firm's operations, especially in terms of quality products and customer satisfaction. Clausing [2] describes QFD as a product development tool that systematically translates customer requirements into guidelines for the manufacturing or service process.

Quality function deployment rests on three important aspects: value features of products, as determined by customers; functional characteristics, as determined by the products' designers and manufacturer; and quality and value of competitors' products.

As a technique to control and promote quality, QFD is not widely known because it is not as direct and easy to understand as a control chart. It is also not easy to implement. Applying QFD takes commitment and judgment. It requires collecting a lot of information from customers of the firm's products and also from customers of the competitors' products. In addition, QFD requires detailed knowledge of the functional characteristics of the firm's products and of the competitors' products [3]. This chapter describes and illustrates the techniques of quality function deployment.

Description of Quality Function Deployment

Quality function deployment is a technique that helps firms in considering the needs and wants of customers. It is, therefore, intended to serve the function of satisfying customers. The QFD approach was developed by two Japanese scholars in the 1970s; since then, it has been widely and successfully used by the Japanese.

The interesting feature of QFD is that it not only addresses potential problems in the production process but also problems associated with the raw materials used to manufacture the products and the design of the product itself.

The QFD technique includes a customer survey to determine which features of a product customers value and like. Customers are then asked to rate the leading brands, including the products of the firm that is doing the survey.

The list of features customers value and like is then related to the product's functional characteristics. Competitors' brands, especially those that rate higher than the firm's brand, are then taken apart (reverse engineered) to determine why customers value the competitors' products. The best features in the product then become the benchmarks that are going to be used to redesign the product, to change the raw materials used in the product, or to improve the production process that is used to manufacture the product.

The QFD technique has also been fully covered by Hauser and Clausing [4] in the *Harvard Business Review*.

As reported by Scollard [6], QFD is widely used in the automobile industry, especially during the design and development stages. A specific application cited was the use of QFD in the design and development of the latest Lincoln Continental.

The QFD technique provides an important tool for management to determine how it can improve the design of a product, the raw materials used in the product, and the production process. The result is a more satisfied customer who will continue to purchase the product.

Illustration of Quality Function Deployment

We will next look at an illustration of quality function deployment in the automobile industry. The data used in the example are fictional, and the four automobile models used in the example are also fictional. We have used automobiles in order to provide more realism to the example and to provide more motivation to the student.

Table 12–1 shows the result of a questionnaire sent to about 100 randomly sampled automobile owners. The questionnaire recipients were asked to list five features in automobiles they value highly. They were then asked to rate each value feature on a scale from 1 (no importance) to 5 (high importance). Note that the five value features consist of three nonphysical features (low price, quality of ride, and interior noise level) and two physical features (interior styling and exterior styling). The importance ratings illustrate how one questionnaire respondent could select his or her ratings or how all responses can be averaged. The table represents the latter.

The next step in the quality function deployment method is to select a random sample of about 100 automobile owners who are willing to take a test drive in each of the four automobiles and then rate each automobile tested for

QUALITY FUNCTION DEPLOYMENT

Table 12–1
Value Features and Importance Ratings in Four Automobiles

Value Features	Importance Ratings
Low price	3
Quality of ride	5
Interior noise level	4
Interior styling	3
Exterior styling	2

Value features and their importance ratings were determined by asking each person surveyed the following questions: (1) What feature do you value most in an automobile? (2) What importance rating do you give each value feature? Importance ratings range from 1 (no importance) to 5 (high importance).

the five quality features listed in Table 12–1. Table 12–2 shows the kind of information that will be collected from each respondent. Note that we obtain a total of 20 automobile satisfaction ratings. Using these ratings and multiplying them by the importance rating for each value feature enables us to obtain an overall rating for each automobile. In the example, the Narima has achieved the highest satisfaction rating of 7 from the respondent whose ratings were used in the example.

Table 12–2
Customer Satisfaction Matrix

Value Features	Equus	Corda	Leo	Narima	Importance Rating
Low price	3	4	6	7	3
Quality of ride	5	4	3	6	5
Interior noise level	7	5	4	3	4
Interior styling	3	4	5	6	3
Exterior styling	6	5	3	4	2
Overall Rating of Each Automobile	83	74	70	89	

Matrix entries were obtained from one surveyed person who evaluated the satisfaction value features of each of the four automobiles on a scale of 1 (low) to 7 (high).

The importance ratings were transferred from Table 12–1.

The overall rankings were obtained by multiplying each importance rating by each satisfaction rating entry for each automobile and summing the five resultant products. The maximum attainable overall ranking is 119.

Table 12-3
Functional Characteristics and Their Ratings in Four Automobiles

Functional Characteristics	Equus	Corda	Leo	Narima
Quality of suspension system	8	6	7	9
Quality of upholstery cloth and trim	5	6	7	9
Thickness of sound insulation	9	4	6	7
Engine noise level in decibels	8	6	5	3
Road noise absorption by tires	6	5	7	5

Matrix entries were obtained from a group of automotive experts after they had evaluated the technical aspects of each automobile. The entries represent 1 (poorest) to 9 (best).

The third step in the quality function deployment process is the evaluation of a limited number (five, in this case) of functional characteristics for each of the four automobiles. The five functional characteristics for each of the four automobiles are listed in Table 12–3 and are rated by a group of automotive experts. The ratings range from 1 (poorest) to 9 (best). The ratings shown are averages derived from the individual assessments of the group of automotive experts. In order to keep the illustration as simple as possible, we use ratings instead of actual dimensions. For instance, for thickness of sound insulation we could have used the actual thickness measure. Similarly, for engine noise level in decibels we could have used the actual decibel figures.

The fourth step involves obtaining correlation coefficients for the 25 cells shown in Table 12–4. The matrix is determined by the five satisfaction value features and the five functional characteristics on each of the two respective axes.

The correlation analysis data are shown on Table 12–5. Note that each person in the survey produces four pairs of data because he or she will test drive each of the four automobiles. If we have 100 volunteers, they will collectively produce 400 pairs of observations. We have to do 25 separate correlation analyses, so the total number of pairs of observations will be 25 times 400 pairs, which equals 10,000 pairs of observations.

The fifth step involves evaluating the 25 correlation coefficients we obtain from our evaluation study, as shown in Table 12–6. Note that the highest correlation is found to exist between interior noise level (C) and thickness of sound insulation (C). This is not surprising; one would expect the level of interior noise to be at least partly and possibly greatly determined by the noise insulation thickness.

Also highly correlated are quality of ride (B) and engine noise level in decibels (D). It appears that the subjects who evaluated the vehicles' quality of ride were influenced by the engine noise level or lack thereof.

QUALITY FUNCTION DEPLOYMENT

Table 12-4
Correlation Matrix

Value Features	Functional Characteristics				
	Quality of Suspension System	Quality of Upholstery Cloth and Trim	Thickness of Sound Insulation	Engine Noise Level in Decibels	Road Noise Absorption by Tires
Low price					
Quality of ride					
Interior noise level					
Interior styling					
Exterior styling					

For each of the 25 cells in the table, a correlation analysis result must be obtained.

Table 12-5
Illustration of Data for One Correlation Analysis

Surveyed Person	Low Price	Quality of Suspension System	Automobile
1	3	8	Equus
	4	6	Corda
	6	7	Leo
	7	9	Narima
2	4	8	Equus
	5	6	Corda
	4	7	Leo
	6	9	Narima
3	3	8	Equus
	5	6	Corda
	6	7	Leo
	4	9	Narima
4	4	8	
	5	6	
	5	7	
	7	9	

Survey data are for only four persons. Sample should be for at least 25 persons, and preferable for as many as 100 persons.

Table 12-6
Correlation Matrix—Hypothetical Data

Value Features	Functional Characteristics				
	A	B	C	D	E
A	−.21	−.42	−.14	−.29	−.11
B	.46	.04	.17	.72	.41
C	.12	.04.	.77	.24	.32
D	.09	.56	.13	−.25	−.09
E	.10	.19	.13	.02	.11

The highest positive correlations are found to exist between value feature C and functional characteristic C, and between value feature B and functional characteristic D. The highest negative correlation is found between value feature A and functional characteristic B.

The highest negative correlation coefficient was found to occur between low price (A) and quality of upholstery cloth and trim (B). Subjects who value a low price and automobiles with high-quality upholstery cloth and trim are inversely correlated, a not surprising result.

The sixth step involves an analysis of the improvements required by each automobile manufacturer if it wants to attain value features that are rated at least as high as the rating received by the best of the other three competitors. Table 12–7 shows the amount by which each manufacturer must improve its ratings for each of the five value features, and also the sum of the improvements

Table 12-7
Improvements Required by Each Automobile Manufacturer

Value Features	Automobile				Best Rating	Importance Rating
	Equus	Corda	Leo	Narima		
Low price	4	3	1	0	7	3
Quality of ride	1	2	3	0	6	5
Interior noise level	0	2	3	4	7	4
Interior styling	3	2	1	0	6	3
Exterior styling	0	1	3	2	6	2
Increase in ranking required	26	35	39	20	109[a]	

[a]Maximum ranking required to be best of four.

required. The results are not surprising. The automobile that received the highest rating, of course, needs to make the least improvement, and the automobile with the lowest rating must make the most improvement in its ratings. It is important to keep in mind that the figures in the exhibit are static figures. If any one of the four automobiles is improved in any of its functional characteristics, the entire study needs to be repeated.

The seventh step is for management to determine which of the highly correlated areas (see Table 12–6) it should focus on. For instance, Narima, with its highly perceived interior noise level, might want to investigate if it should improve its already heavy thickness of sound insulation to reduce interior noise level. Similarly, Equus, with its poorly perceived interior styling, might want to investigate if it should improve its quality of upholstery and trim. The student can find other examples similar to the ones discussed above.

It must be kept in mind, however, that a quality function deployment study is done by one manufacturer in order to gain advantages over its competitors. The manufacturer who does the study in our example could be any one of the four automobile manufacturers.

Application of Quality Function Deployment

Let us now look at a very successful and complex application of quality function deployment in a firm. Keep in mind that the technique is quite complex, costly, and time-consuming, and most firms prefer not to share their findings and methods with their competitors.

At NEC in Japan, quality function deployment was used to design, develop, and build a highly complex 32-bit microprocessor chip. As many as six QFD matrices, analogous to the one in our example, were used to relate consumer demands and expectations with basic specifications, hardware and software features, and function of the microprocessor chip [5].

NEC's quality function deployment approach of breaking up the total of customers' demands and expectations into six QFD matrices was, of course, done to make the project manageable. There are also other reasons. Certain customer demands and expectations, the value features, relate to certain physical and functional characteristics, and they should be put into a single QFD matrix. For instance, one logical separation is hardware features and physical specifications on the one hand and performance features and design specifications on the other hand. NEC's microprocessor chip found it necessary to have as many as six QFD matrices.

The second reason to break up all quality features based on customer demands and expectations and the functional characteristics and hardware specifications is the enormous size of the QFD matrix that would be required if all features and characteristics were put into one QFD matrix. For instance, suppose that each of NEC's six QFD matrices consisted of five value features and five functional characteristics. Each QFD matrix would then produce 25 separate correlation coefficients, for a total of 150 correlation coefficients. This is a large but manageable number of correlations to evaluate, especially because they were separated into six categories represented by the six QFD matrices. Suppose the six QFD matrices were combined into one QFD matrix with 900 cells and 900 correlation coefficients. This clearly would become a case of information overload, and many of the correlations would be meaningless or not of importance to the design and operation of the product.

Quality function deployment's main purpose is to relate the customer's needs, wants, and demands to the functional and design characteristics of the product; not all value features directly relate to all functional or design characteristics.

THE TAGUCHI METHOD AND QUALITY FUNCTION DEPLOYMENT

The Taguchi method is related to quality function deployment or an expansion thereof. The Taguchi method pays more attention to the design and the process dimensions, dimensions that need to be addressed or perfected before the product is produced and before it reaches the customer.

The Taguchi method employs a quality loss function (QLF). The difficulty with estimating losses incurred due to poor quality hinders the use of the Taguchi method and its associated QLF. Losses due to poor quality can be caused by warranty work, rework, excessive service and installation work, and scrap losses. Hidden costs may be incurred due to long-term losses related to additional engineering costs, additional management costs, additional inventory, customer dissatisfaction, lost market share, and so on.

The basis of the Taguchi method is the underlying assumption that losses or costs are incurred whenever the product deviates from a certain target standard. The further the deviation from the standard, the higher the losses or additional costs incurred. Dr. Taguchi discovered that the quadratic cost function, as exhibited in Figure 12–1, is a good approximation of the QLF in most instances [1]. The quality loss function is loss = $k(x - T)^2$, where k is the cost coefficient, x is the value of the target dimension, and T is the target value.

If we combine the QFD method and the Taguchi method we derive the following four dimensions:

1. Value features from customers' demands, needs, and wants.
2. Functional characteristics and operating specifications of the product.

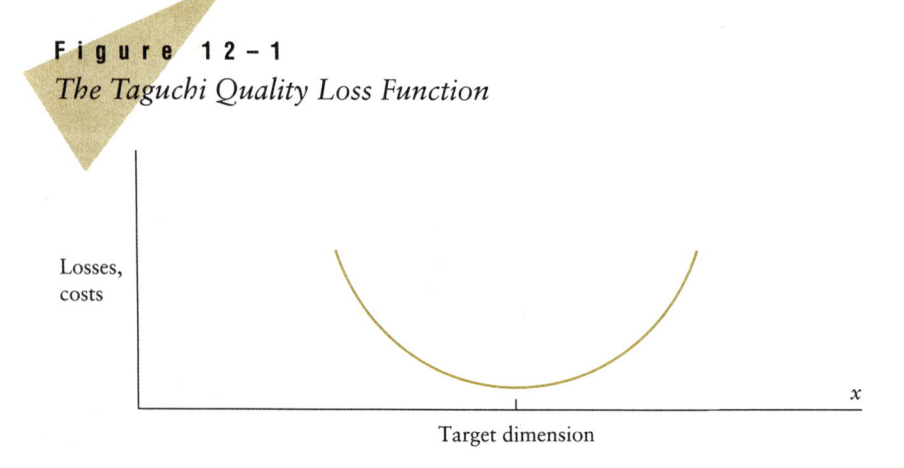

Figure 12–1
The Taguchi Quality Loss Function

3. Design considerations and characteristics, including material specifications for all aspects of the final product.
4. Processes used in the manufacture of all parts, components, subassembly, and final assembly.

The difficulty with using four dimensions is the complexity that arises. Relationships between multiple variables become more difficult to see and to relate to each other. Other techniques of statistical analysis need to be used. Simple correlation analysis (used in the quality function deployment method) no longer is applicable or suffices.

Conclusions

Quality function deployment is probably the most complex and sophisticated technique used in the total quality management field. It is not well known because of its complexity and also because of its large information needs. The latter probably most limits its use.

The information needs consist of technical product information, customer opinion of the firm's product, and customer information on competitors' products. Typically, a firm is information rich on both the technical aspects of its own products and the customer views of its products. However, the same is not necessarily true for competitors' products. The one exception is probably in the case of a product such as the automobile. External agencies commonly collect and publish large amounts of both technical and consumer information on all products available in that industry.

Relatively little information is available on the application of quality function deployment in industry. However, as more firms gain experience with the technique, and as more user-friendly software is developed, we can expect a much wider use of the technique in the future.

Discussion Questions

1. Describe QFD's definition of value features in a product.
2. Describe QFD's definition of functional characteristics of a product.
3. Who determines QFD's value features and who determines QFD's functional characteristics? Why?
4. What are the overall value feature ratings of the four automobiles in Table 12–2 if the importance ratings are changed to 2, 3, 3, 5, and 5 for, respectively, low price, quality of ride, interior noise level, interior styling, and exterior styling?
5. For your own automobile, how would you rate the five value features in Table 12–2?
6. Attach your own importance ratings to the five value features you just selected for your own automobile. Then calculate the overall value feature rating of your automobile.
7. For your own automobile, how would you rate the five functional characteristics listed in Table 12–3?

8. Plot the loss values for the Taguchi quality loss function for values of $x = 3$, 4, 5, 6, and 7, where $k = 1.5$ and $T = 5.5$.

References

1. Byrne, D. M. "Taguchi Methods," in N. E. Ryan (ed.), *Taguchi Methods and Quality Function Deployment*, pp. 11–22. ASI Press, Detroit, MI, 1988.
2. Clausing, D. "Quality Function Deployment," in N. E. Ryan (ed.), *Taguchi Methods and Quality Function Deployment*, pp. 63–76. ASI Press, Detroit, MI, 1988.
3. Fitzsimmons, J. A., and M. J. Fitzsimmons. *Service Management for Competitive Advantage*, pp. 202–207. McGraw-Hill, New York, 1994.
4. Hauser, J. R., and D. Clausing. "The House of Quality," *Harvard Business Review*, May-June 1988, 63–73.
5. Neff, Robert. "No. 1—And Trying Harder." *Business Week/Quality 1991*, 20–24.
6. Scollard, W. E. "Putting Quality Function Deployment to Work," in N. E. Ryan (ed.), *Taguchi Methods and Quality Function Deployment*, pp. 89–96. ASI Press, Detroit, MI, 1988.

Chapter thirteen

Process Quality and ISO 9000 Standards

Outline

Introduction
Components of the ISO 9000 Quality Systems Standards
ISO 9000 and Global Sourcing
ISO 9000—A New Approach to Productivity
Conclusions

Introduction

The ISO 9000 quality systems standards were introduced in 1987 as an umbrella set of quality systems standards by the International Organization for Standardization (ISO), a worldwide federation of national standards organizations, to serve as a link between the standards of various national organizations. With the globalization of world product markets and especially the globalization of parts, components, and raw material sourcing, a set of international standards became a necessity [6].

The two U.S. national organizations are the American National Standards Institute (ANSI) and the American Society for Quality Control (ASQC). Most national organizations, including the two U.S. quality standards organizations, have their own designators for the ISO 9000 quality systems standards. Specifically, the common set of ISO 9000 standards includes ISO 9000, ISO 9001, ISO 9002, ISO 9003, and ISO 9004. The U.S. equivalents are ANSI/ASQC Q90, Q91, Q92, Q93, and Q94. As of mid-1993, 55 countries had adopted the ISO 9000 series of standards. In nearly all cases they had assigned their own designators to these standards.

The benefits of having common international standards are significant. Manufacturers of raw materials, processed materials, parts, components, and subassemblies in one country can much more easily compete against suppliers in the home country of the customer, assuming, of course, that they have achieved internationally recognized ISO 9000 quality systems certification.

To become certified, a firm needs to do an enormous amount of preparation, including assignment of management responsibility; development of detailed operations descriptions; preparation of quality control procedures, documented in a quality manual; vendor relations procedures; product identification and testing; procedures for handling storage, packing, and shipping of products; training procedures; description of inspection, measuring, and test equipment; procedure for maintaining quality records; and numerous other processes and procedures.

Upon completion of the firm's preparatory activities for ISO 9000 quality systems certification, the firm's operations are evaluated by a registrar. The registrar is a third party independent of the firm seeking ISO 9000 certification. The registrar is certified by a national accreditation board. In the United States, it is the Registrar Accreditation Board.

If accredited, the firm must undergo periodic audits by independent registrars. In other words, ISO 9000 accreditation is not given permanently but is subject to suspension if the ISO 9000–certified firm does not adhere to its certified process, procedures, and quality systems and products. ■

Components of the ISO 9000 Quality Systems Standards

The ISO 9000 quality systems standards is not just one single comprehensive set of standards, but rather a series of five individual standards, identified as ISO 9000, ISO 9001, ISO 9002, ISO 9003, and ISO 9004.

The ISO 9000 series provides guidance for suppliers of products who want to implement effective quality systems or improve existing ones, and it provides generic requirements against which a customer can evaluate the adequacy of a supplier's quality system. The ISO 9000 standards consist of the following:

ISO 9000. Guidelines for selection and use of the standards—a road map of the entire series.

ISO 9001. Quality systems—a model for quality assurance in design, development, production, installation, and servicing of a company's products.

ISO 9002. Quality systems—a model for quality assurance in production and installation of company products.

ISO 9003. Quality systems—a model for quality assurance in final inspection and testing.

ISO 9004. Quality management and quality system elements—provides guidance to all organizations for internal quality management purposes [4].

Note that ISO 9000 and ISO 9004 provide guidance to the firm in its preparation for ISO 9000 certification. In other words, these two standards describe what the firm can and should do in order to implement effective quality systems or to improve on existing quality systems.

The other three standards, ISO 9001, ISO 9002, and ISO 9003, are prescriptive standards. They specify what the firm needs to do to become ISO 9000 certified. The first two standards appear to be somewhat overlapping, and they are purposely so. For instance, a firm in the chemical industry producing processed chemicals for use in a chemical production process by an industrial customer typically does not need to be concerned with design and development of a product, or with its servicing after delivery. A chemical products firm therefore would prepare for ISO 9002 certification. On the other hand, a firm supplying electromechanical subassemblies to an automobile manufacturer will be involved in design, development, and servicing of its products. That automotive supplier firm therefore must prepare for qualification under the more extensive ISO 9001 quality systems standards.

A separate standard, ISO 9003, has been prepared for quality assurance in final inspection and testing. Firms prepare for qualification of this standard separately from either ISO 9001 or ISO 9002. Not surprisingly, most customers of materials supplier firms require that ISO 9003 compliance be obtained in addition to either ISO 9001 or ISO 9002.

Exhibit 13-1 lists the elements of the ISO 9000 quality systems standards, and Exhibit 13-2 provides a simple road map that will lead a firm to ISO 9000 certification. Further details of the ISO 9000 standards have been published by the American Society for Quality Control [1–3].

Exhibit 13-1
Elements of ISO 9000 Quality Systems Standards

1. Management responsibility
2. Quality system principles
3. Material control and traceability
4. Inspection and test status
5. Product inspection and testing
6. Measuring and test equipment
7. Control of nonconforming products
8. Handling, storage, and delivery
9. Document control
10. Quality records
11. Training
12. Use of statistical methods
13. Internal audit
14. Quality in marketing
15. Purchasing
16. Process control
17. Control of production
18. Corrective action
19. Purchaser-supplied products
20. Quality in research and development
21. After-sales servicing
22. Cost considerations
23. Product safety and reliability

Exhibit 13-2
Road Map to Certification

A simple road map to certification:
- Determine which one of the ISO 9000 conformance standards best fits the general description of your business.
- Set up a coordinating council representing all functions within the organization and assign responsibility and authority to drive the project.
- Set up your documentation hierarchy in pyramid form so that it cascades from one level to the next, meeting all traceability and control requirements. For example:

  - Level one: quality manual
  - Level two: procedures
  - Level three: work instructions
  - Level four: records

The Quality Manual is a policy document and should describe the basis of your system with regard to all the elements defined by the appropriate standard. Keep it simple!

Procedures should describe the what, when, where, and who of the system.

The work instructions should be machine, task, and product specific and should be written by those who know how to perform the tasks.

The quality manual, procedures, and work instructions should be controlled documents that are numbered and kept up to date.

Source: Adapted from Dean, Terry C. Private communication.

ISO 9000 AND GLOBAL SOURCING

The quality measure has many components, such as reliability, dependability, performance, aesthetics, taste, smell, and consistency. One of the important success factors for the large fast-food chains such as McDonald's, Burger King, and Pizza Hut has been their ability to provide a consistent quality of products and services. They have been able to achieve their consistent quality by depending on standardization of processed food and materials, standardization of food preparation processes, and standardization of employee training. Proper execution of standardized processes ensures that the product or service produced by that standardized process will be of consistent quality.

The basis of the ISO 9000 quality systems standards can be found in the above-described scenario. ISO 9000 quality systems standards focus on the process, procedures, activities, operations, controls, and management of an operation, and only secondarily on the product. The process-oriented focus makes the ISO 9000 standards largely universal to most firms. There are, of course, variations; the processes in a chemical products firm, for instance, are substantially different than those in a mechanical or electrical products firm. And processes in service firms differ widely depending on the type of service being offered. But in all cases, ISO 9000 quality systems standards focus on setting standards for each activity that is performed in the firm. If these standards are properly adhered to, the output of that process will be a quality product or service with a consistent quality level.

Because of the benefits that ISO 9000 can provide, industrial firms have quickly become enamored of the ISO 9000 certification process. These firms see it not only as a way to improve and maintain their own quality products or services but as a way to control the quality of the materials they purchase from their industrial suppliers. With the trend toward decreased rearward vertical integration, manufacturers have become increasingly dependent on their supplier organizations to provide them with subassemblies and numerous other supplies and services. Imposing ISO 9000 certification requirements on their suppliers is a win-win solution for them.

Companies outside of the European Community (EC) that want to sell materials and supplies to EC firms must be ISO 9000 certified. Within the EC, firms are quickly pushing to ISO 9000 compliance by all supplier firms. As of mid-1992 the German electronics giant Siemens required ISO 9000 compliance in 50% of its supply contracts. Other suppliers are on notice to obtain ISO certification if they want to continue as suppliers [5].

The quality leaders in U.S. industry, such as Motorola, Xerox, and IBM, are forcing suppliers to prepare for ISO 9000 certification. As of mid-1992, only about 400 U.S. facilities were ISO 9000 certified. By 1996 there will be thousands. Without ISO 9000 certification it will be impossible for a supplier firm to function in a few years. Hence, firms should begin exploring how soon they can qualify. Preparation typically takes about two years, and the time is now to begin if a firm wants to be in business as a supplier after 1996.

ISO 9000—A NEW APPROACH TO PRODUCTIVITY

Because ISO 9000 certification is still very much in its infant stage, especially in the United States, it is difficult to ascertain its benefits. Costs clearly are incurred to attain certification and especially for the preparation before a firm can apply for certification. The magnitude of the costs varies considerably from firm to firm depending on how well a firm has documented its processes and operations, how well its employees are trained, and the status of its control processes.

The major benefit a firm seeks and expects to attain is an improved level of quality and consistency of quality. This is, of course, also the main reason why industrial customers want their supplier firms to become ISO 9000 certified. It provides them with a high level of assurance that the raw or processed materials they purchase from their suppliers are of high and consistent quality.

The other potential benefit is improved productivity. Are productivity improvements being attained by ISO 9000–certified firms? It is probably a little early to tell because not many U.S. firms are ISO 9000 certified, and those certified have been in certified status for a relatively brief period of time.

However, in the United Kingdom, where ISO 9000 certification began in 1980, ISO 9000 certification is showing promising examples of productivity improvements. A 1991 study commissioned by the British government found the following productivity improvements: 89% of firms reported greater operational efficiency, 47% reported increased profitability, 76% reported improvements in marketing, 26% reported increased export sales.

The British study surveyed firms in both the manufacturing and service sectors. The majority of firms surveyed stated that they had attained improved operational efficiency, and they attributed it to ISO 9000 certification [8].

In a more recent survey of company executives in the United Kingdom, all respondents reported increased productivity and savings in overtime payments, administrative costs, and unnecessary procedures following ISO 9000 certification. These same executives also reported that they had recouped the costs of registration within three years. Ten percent recouped registration costs in less than two years [8].

From a theoretical point of view, we can argue that the operational, procedural, and control changes necessary in a firm that wants to be ISO 9000 certified must produce improved productivity and improved quality. What ISO 9000 quality systems standards impose on a firm is a discipline in the management and operation of the firm. Waste is generally produced by firms because of laxness in management and in the execution of the value-added work that needs to be done. Training of employees, standardized operating procedures, quality control processes, operations control, and other management-directed activities form the foundation of the ISO 9000 standards. If these standards are implemented and adhered to, a firm is well on its way to total quality management attainment.

Therefore, we must view the implementation of ISO 9000 quality systems standards as a cog in the overall TQM process. If properly executed, there is no doubt that it will produce improved quality and productivity.

Conclusions

In this chapter, we have provided a brief overview of the ISO 9000 quality systems standards. The ISO 9000 standards focus on the execution of a high-quality, standardized, and consistent productive process with raw material and other inputs of high and consistent quality.

The underlying premise of ISO 9000 quality systems standards is the reasonable presumption that a high-quality, consistent process utilizing high-quality, consistent operations and procedures will produce a high-quality, consistent product. The procedures, of course, include quality control and inspection of the final product, thus ensuring that slip-ups in the process or in the procedures will not produce inadequate or poor-quality products.

Because of the focus on the process and procedures, there is bound to be high variability between firms in their readiness for ISO 9000 certification. Some firms may already have nearly all the procedures, processes, and controls in place to satisfy the ISO 9000 requirements. Some, however, will need to do a major revamping of their operations and retraining of their employees before they are ready to apply for ISO 9000 certification. It is, of course, the latter group of firms that is going to attain the maximum benefit of the ISO 9000 preparation process.

Discussion Questions

1. What are the two primary roles of the ISO 9000 standards?
2. List seven possible attributes of a product quality measure.
3. Why is the focus of ISO 9000 on the process and not on the product?
4. Why is there such a large difference in time required to qualify for ISO 9000 certification among firms?
5. Why do some large firms insist that their suppliers obtain ISO 9000 certification?
6. How can ISO 9000 improve productivity?

References

1. ASQC. *Quality Management and Quality Assurance Standards—Guidelines for Selection and Use.* ANSI/ASQC Q90. American Society for Quality Control, Milwaukee, WI, 1987.
2. ASQC. *Quality Systems—Model for Quality Assurance in Design/Development, Production, Installation, and Servicing.* ANSI/ASQC Q91. American Society for Quality Control, Milwaukee, WI, 1987.
3. ASQC. *Quality Management and Quality System Elements—Guidelines.* ANSI/ASQC Q94. American Society for Quality Control, Milwaukee, WI, 1987.
4. Dean, Terry C. Private communication.
5. Fouhy, Ken, Gulam Samdani, and Stephen Moore. "ISO 9000: A New Road to Quality." *Chemical Engineering*, October 1992, 43–47.
6. Krishnan, R., A. B. Shani, R. M. Grant, and R. Baer. "In Search of Quality Improvement: Problems of Design and Implementation." *Academy of Management Executive*, 7(4), November 1993, 7–16.
7. Levine, Jonathan B. "Want EC Business? You Have Two Choices." *Business Week*, October 19, 1992, 58–59.
8. O'Donnell, Chris. "Companies Report at Least 5% Savings after Registering," *Quality Systems Update*, 3(2), February 1993, 4–5.

Part four

Improvement Strategies

Productivity and Its Measurement	14
Benchmarking	15
Cycle-Time Reduction, Time-Based Competition, and Managerial Use of Time	16
Just-In-Time Operations	17
Flexibility and Adaptability of the Firm	18
Reengineering Systems	19
Concurrent Engineering and Integration of Functional Areas	20
Activity-Based Costing	21

Introduction

This section is the largest in the book, comprising eight chapters. The first chapter, "Productivity and Its Measurement," is an apt introduction to this section because all chapters have a strong productivity focus. The second chapter addresses benchmarking. Benchmarking is now viewed as an efficient way to identify flaws, inefficiencies, and ineffectiveness in a firm's operations. Most progressive firms devote considerable time to comparing their operations to their competitors'.

The third chapter is focused on cycle-time reduction. It is based on the premise, which has been proven true in numerous cases, that reducing the cycle time or turnaround time of almost any activity, task, or process will lead to improved productivity and also to improved satisfaction of the customer, external or internal.

Just-in-time operations is related to cycle-time reduction but has a longer history, and also focuses more on processes, inventories, and supplies. It continues to be an important area that can contribute to increased productivity.

Flexibility of the firm in in its ability to rapidly change over to produce other products, to change rapidly to respond to increased or decreased demands, and to rapidly develop new or modified products is a valuable capability. Truly flexible firms have an important competitive edge.

Reengineering consists of modifying and simplifying processes in the firm so that they are able to provide better-quality services and/or products to the ultimate consumer at reduced costs. Reengineering activities are often triggered by information derived from benchmarking and from ideas generated from cycle-time reduction activities.

Concurrent engineering and integration of functional areas aim to break down the barriers between functional departments in the firm. By eliminating the boundaries between functional departments, improved product designs and improved operations can be achieved.

Activity-based costing is a topic not frequently found under total quality management. It is, however, an important area because activity-based costing identifies what the true costs of a product, a service, a process, or an activity are. Because true costing is important for productivity measurement and comparison, the attention paid to activity-based costing is warranted. ■

Chapter fourteen

Productivity and Its Measurement

Outline

Introduction
What Is Productivity?
The Productivity Level of the American Economy
Productivity Improvement through Empowerment and Control
Productivity Improvement through Engineering and Design Changes
Productivity Improvement through Incremental Managerial Changes
Conclusions

Introduction

The term *productivity* is widely used to compare how effective firms and industries are in converting inputs—human resources and other inputs—into outputs consisting of the products or services they deliver to their customers. Because productivity is based on many inputs used to produce at least several, and for some firms many, outputs, it is virtually impossible to find agreement on a common and single metric to indicate the level of productivity for a firm or an industry.

Because of this, productivity is commonly reported in terms of differences or changes. Government agencies report how productivity changes from period to period—usually year to year. Similarly, studies done by think tanks or government agencies report how much lower or higher the productivity is between industries in different countries. By focusing on changes or differences, the reported productivity figures are generally quite accurate and therefore are closely watched and tracked.

Disagreements between different organizations about the magnitude of changes that are occurring can usually be traced to how the respective organizations measure productivity. In its simplest form, we can define productivity as output per man-hour. In its most complex form, we can use a weighted average of numerous productivity measures, such as output per man-hour, inventory turnover, absenteeism, employee turnover rate, warranty rates, scrap rates, obsolete products in inventory, equipment utilization, and output per dollar of capital employed. In other words, a firm must always determine the comprehensiveness of the productivity measures on which reported changes or differences in productivity are based.

When we begin to explore comprehensive measures, we must include such issues as effectiveness, quality of product or service delivered, timeliness of deliveries, customer service, flexibility, and numerous others. Richardson and Gordon [10] addressed the comprehensiveness problem in their study on manufacturing performance of Canadian firms. They concluded that distinction should be made between manufacturing performance and productivity. Their conclusion is particularly valid if productivity is measured in simple output-input terms.

An excellent survey of U.S. productivity, including about 50 examples of how U.S. firms had managed to increase productivity, was prepared by Seidman and Skancke [11]. The study shows that many firms are taking productivity seriously and are determined to survive in the current age of global competition.

Below we will explore in more detail how productivity is measured and what firms are doing to improve it.

What is Productivity?

Productivity is defined in terms of how an organization is effective in maximizing the utilization of all of its inputs (capital, energy, technology, human resources, knowledge, reputation, experience) to produce its required outputs.

Productivity is measured by the ratio of outputs over inputs in terms of measurable resources. Because all organizations usually have numerous outputs and require by necessity several types of inputs, it is difficult to obtain aggregate measures of productivity. One commonly used surrogate for productivity is, of course, profitability. However, profitability is not a completely satisfactory substitute for productivity because it can vary by industry and is notoriously variable over successive time periods for individual firms.

Productivity measures are used and frequently reported by firms. They are nearly always productivity measures in terms of a specific measurable input measure, such as output per man-hour or output per dollar of capital. Because outputs are usually heterogeneous, the dollar measure of output is frequently used. Note, however, that productivity is extremely difficult to or impossible to define in terms of technology, knowledge, reputation, experience, or knowledge level of human resources. Because these five inputs are currently considered to be overwhelmingly important factors in determining aggregate levels of productivity (and profitability), the aggregate productivity measure is essentially unknown or cannot be determined. The two quantifiable measures of aggregate labor and aggregate capital productivity are weak indicators of a firm's overall productivity.

Ideally, of course, productivity is defined in terms independent of monetary terms such as units per man-hour or its reciprocal, man-hours per unit. This approach is frequently used in the automobile industry—for instance, man-hours to assemble an automobile or man-hours to produce the entire automobile. It is reported that Ford uses 16 hours to assemble its Taurus automobile. However, Mercedes-Benz uses as many as 100 hours to assemble their luxury automobiles. This productivity measure is free of direct monetary terms, but it ignores the indirect monetary terms of retail value of the automobiles. Productivity measures that show hours to produce an entire automobile are usually deceptive because they typically ignore the differences in outsourcing rates—the amount of parts and components purchased from outside suppliers. For instance, General Motors outsources about 30% of the parts and components in its automobiles. Toyota, on the other hand, outsources about 70%. Hence, the amount of hours to produce an automobile cannot be used to compare G.M.'s productivity with Toyota's.

Federal government agencies regularly report productivity increases or decreases in aggregate terms and also by industry. The productivity measures are usually based on outputs per man-hour standardized for a given industry. For traditional industries, these measures are probably quite accurate in showing changes from period to period because products do not change dramatically over time. In newer industries, and especially in high-technology industries, measuring productivity, even from period to period, becomes much more problematic because the nature of the output changes dramatically over relatively brief periods of time. For instance, the personal computer available in 1988 is dramatically different from the one available in 1995.

In the services industry, which now makes up about 70% of our employment, productivity is even more difficult to measure. Output is more difficult to define because the nature of outputs produced changes as rapidly as in high-technology product industries. There have been criticisms about the way federal agencies measure service industry productivity [5]. These critics claim that service productivity is rising much faster, at least in the United States, than is reported by government statistical agencies.

THE PRODUCTIVITY LEVEL OF THE AMERICAN ECONOMY

Much debate has raged in recent years about the productivity of the American worker and the competitiveness of American industry. It is true that in certain industries American firms lag behind foreign (particularly Japanese) firms. But overall, the United States still leads the rest of the world in productivity.

As a matter of fact, out of five major industry areas, Japan leads the United States in only one, and Germany is behind the United States in all five. Table 14–1 shows the five sectors and the manufacturing productivity indices of the Unites States, Japan, and Germany. Only in machinery, electrical engineering, and transport equipment is Japan ahead, and substantially, of the United States and Germany. But note how low Japan's productivity is in food products, beverages, and tobacco, an industry that serves its very large population.

What the table also does not show is the very high productivity of the United States in such services as retailing, communications, entertainment, and financial services. The productivity levels of these major service sectors are substantially lower in Japan and Germany.

Table 14-1
Comparison of U.S., Japanese, and German Productivity Levels—1989

Industry Sector	United States	Japan	Germany
Machinery, electrical engineering, and transport equipment	100	117	80
Metals and metal products	100	98	85
Chemicals, petroleum, rubber, and plastics	100	92	70
Textiles, apparel, and leather	100	63	92
Food products, beverages, and tobacco	100	25	69

Source: Adapted from Stewart, Thomas A. "U.S. Productivity: First but Fading." *Fortune,*

In manufacturing, U.S. productivity has at least doubled between 1966 and 1991. Eighteen million workers manufactured twice as much in 1991 as 19.2 million workers manufactured in 1966. These figures may be slightly exaggerated because in 1991 manufacturers did a lot more outsourcing of services [3].

PRODUCTIVITY IMPROVEMENT THROUGH EMPOWERMENT AND CONTROL

The human element is critically important in improving productivity in all its dimensions. A common way of involving the employee more in the productivity improvement process is by empowering him or her. What does empowerment mean? In its simplest form, empowerment means giving the employee more decision-making power about all or nearly all aspects of his or her job, and at the same time specifying the responsibilities that accompany that decision-making power [2].

Traditional firms managed by managers with a history of top-down and autocratic management do not find it easy to turn over the decision-making power to lower-level employees. Giving up power is very threatening, especially to lower-level managers. The threat is, of course, real because if empowerment is implemented as described above, the need for the lower-level, first-line manager ceases to exist.

Empowerment of employees clearly cannot be done overnight. It takes a lot of training for employees to be able to make good decisions that are in the interest of the enterprise and ultimately, of course, of the employee.

The more successful cases of employee empowerment and also the most visible are related to empowered teams of employees. The employees are not empowered individually but collectively, as teams. The empowerment of teams can be limited or quite extensive. At Saturn, a General Motors subsidiary, teams are empowered to a very extensive degree. At Saturn, all teams are responsible for budgeting, training, scheduling, supplies, and safety. Job rotation is common, thus allowing the team to function uninterruptedly even if one or more team members are absent. Each team selects its new members, and 20% of the pay of the team member is at risk if productivity, quality, and profitability is not achieved [6, 9]. An illustration of the work team concept at Saturn follows.

The work team responsible for car doors decided that productivity and quality could be improved if equipment and machinery could be rearranged. The 14-member team implemented the change and decided that the team could be reduced to 12 members without sacrificing output and quality. The two discharged team members were absorbed by other teams in the plant [9].

One of the bonus benefits of empowered work teams is the control aspect of teams, an attribute often overlooked by the anecdotal reporting of teams in the popular press. Because the team is empowered as a team and the welfare of each individual team member is directly tied to the success of the team, the structure of the team provides considerable control on the output and quality of its work. It is less likely that a group will commit a blunder in comparison with an individual employee.

Each team is expected to set goals that need to be approved by management. Each team works toward achieving the set goals, and the performance measured in terms of goal achievement is usually the determinant of team performance [1].

Chrysler created teams in its New Castle, Indiana, components plant in 1986. Individual team members were renamed "technicians" and line supervisors either left the company, were reassigned, or became "team advisors." Time clocks were removed.

Chrysler's successful experiment resulted in 77 teams in operation in 1992. The teams assign tasks, confront sluggish performers, order repairs, talk to customers, and even have a modicum of control over work hours in conjunction with the labor-management steering committee. Applicant members to a team are interviewed and evaluated by the team. The team decides whether to accept the candidates or not.

The Chrysler experiment at New Castle, Indiana, was quite successful. Absenteeism dropped from 7% to 2.9%. Union grievances tumbled to 33 in 1991; before 1986, they exceeded 1000 per year. On the quality front, the number of defects per million parts made fell to 20 from 300 in 1988. Overall, productivity has increased dramatically [4].

Productivity Improvement through Engineering and Design Changes

One of the more powerful ways of improving productivity is by changing product design and process design. Virtually all products are developed for a functional purpose and wrapped in a targeted package. Within the constraints of being able to perform its function according to specifications and within an acceptable artistic design, a product can be designed in numerous ways. The product design can be complex and costly to manufacture or it can be simple and easy to manufacture. The ultimate level of productivity can be achieved through simple product designs that can be manufactured at low cost, yet provide high quality and consumer satisfaction. This is becoming an increasingly popular way to lower cost.

One particular illustration of the above approach is the Ford Taurus. The Taurus bumper has only 10 parts, whereas the Pontiac Grand Prix, a competitive G.M. model, has over 100 bumper parts [8].

The automobile industry is focusing on how how to use product redesign to lower manufacturing costs. As the Taurus example shows, it is clear that many more simplifications will be made in the future.

The U.S. electrical appliance industry was actually one of the forerunners of improving productivity through product redesign. The General Electric appliance division made major design changes to its line of electrical appliances in order to lower cost. One particular example was the G.E. dishwasher, which was redesigned in such a way that the number of parts in the redesigned dishwasher was less than half the number of parts in the old design.

Productivity Improvement Through Incremental Managerial Changes

The power of making incremental improvements in operations is often overlooked by management as a powerful way to improve productivity. Incremental improvements can emanate from management, manufacturing engineering, or employees.

Ford attributes most of its productivity improvements over the past 10 years to increased cooperation among its workforce. However, it is clear that this increased cooperation is the direct result of managerial approaches and ways of managing the workforce. Over the past 10 years, Ford's management has been successful at co-opting its workforce in its striving to higher productivity.

One illustration of Ford's success is its Walton Hills metal-stamping plant outside Cleveland. Since 1985, with the cooperation of the workforce, labor and overhead costs have declined by an average of 3.2% per year [8]. A metal-press operator suggested a way to save metal on one of the parts made in his press. His suggestion produced savings for Ford of $70,000 per year. The suggestion won the press operator an award of $14,000.

Ford has a similar metal-stamping plant in Woodlawn, New York, a suburb of Buffalo. According to management of this plant, over the past 10 years the workforce in the plant has been halved, but output has remained unchanged.

Based on Ford's incremental improvements over the past 10 years, Ford uses one-third fewer man-hours to build its cars than General Motors. This difference gives Ford a cost advantage over G.M. of about $800 per vehicle [8].

Under competitive pressure, American management has shown innovation to alter work practices and employee relations in order to improve productivity. The realization that the employee can make considerable contributions to productivity improvement has also helped firms to lower costs while maintaining output and quality levels.

Conclusions

Productivity is a concept that is widely used and reported in the popular business press, but is generally poorly understood. It would be desirable if standards of productivity measurement could be developed, at least by industry. If these standards were widely disseminated, comparison of industries between countries could be facilitated, and productivity measurement standards by firms within an industry would be significantly facilitated.

With the need for firms to be competitive in the global marketplace, it is increasingly important that firms be constantly aware of where they stand and where they have to go in order to become or remain globally competitive.

With service industries making up about 70% of the U.S. economy, it is becoming increasingly imperative that productivity measurement standards be developed by industry sectors, especially those industry sectors that compete in global markets. Examples of established global industry service sectors are information technology services, communications, transportation, banking, entertainment, financial services, and consulting. Emerging global industry sectors include retailing, education, franchising, and entertainment parks.

Because productivity is the ultimate driver of competitiveness in open world markets, we can expect the development of comprehensive productivity indexes in the future. These future productivity indexes will be analogous to the financial security market indexes currently in use for the major financial markets. There will be productivity indexes that measure aggregate productivity for an entire country, productivity indexes for individual industries, and productivity indexes for individual firms in an industry.

Discussion Questions

1. Identify six productivity measures for an industrial firm.
2. Productivity is usually measured in outputs-to-inputs ratios. Which five inputs are virtually impossible to use in productivity ratios?
3. Profitability is a potential but problematic measure of productivity. Which measure of profits would be a better measure of productivity than net profits after taxes?
4. The figures in Table 14–1 show that the United States has higher productivity than Japan and Germany. How, then, is Japan able to maintain a large trade surplus with the United States?
5. Extensive use of teams is made to improve quality and productivity. What mechanisms and controls must be in place to prevent laggards and freeloaders from remaining team members?
6. Based on the topics discussed in this chapter, identify several ways in which productivity can be improved through design changes in a product.

References

1. Bell, R. R., and J. M. Burnham. *Managing Productivity and Change,* pp. 228–249. Southwestern, Cincinnati, OH, 1991.
2. Kiernan, M. J. "The New Strategic Architecture: Learning to Compete in the Twenty First Century." *Academy of Management Executive,* 7(1), February 1993, 7–21.

3. Levinson, Marc. "America's Edge." *Newsweek,* June 8, 1992, 40–43.
4. Lublin, Joann S. "Trying to Increase Worker Productivity, More Employers Alter Management Style." *Wall Street Journal,* February 13, 1992, B1.
5. Magnet, Myron. "Good News for the Service Economy." *Fortune,* May 3, 1993, 46–52.
6. O'Hara, Don. "Teamwork Is Saturn's Secret to Job Satisfaction." *The Buffalo News,* June 18, 1993, A9.
7. Stewart, Thomas A. "U.S. Productivity: First but Fading." *Fortune,* October 19, 1992, 54–57.
8. Templin, Neal. "A Decisive Response to Crisis Brought Ford Enhanced Productivity." *Wall Street Journal,* December 15, 1992, A1.
9. Woodruff, David, James B. Freece, Sunita Wadekar Bhargava, and Karen Lowry Miller. "Saturn." *Newsweek,* August 17, 1992, 85–91.
10. Richardson, P. R. and J. R. M. Gordon. "Measuring Total Manufacturing Performance." *Sloan Management Review,* Winter 1980, 47–58.
11. Seidman, L. W., and S. L. Skancke. *Productivity—The Proven Path to Excellence.* Simon and Schuster, New York, 1990.

Chapter fifteen

Benchmarking

Outline

Introduction
Achievements of Benchmarking
Benchmarking the Product
The Process of Benchmarking
Benchmarking the Process
Benchmarking in the Administrative Sector
A Benchmarking Pitfall
Benchmarking Networks
Conclusions

Introduction

Benchmarking by its simplest definition is the search for a better way of doing something by observing how others do it better. The most difficult part is to identify the best-in-class performers, and when they are identified to determine how and why those best-in-class firms are both more efficient and more effective than you are. Last but not least comes the difficult task of convincing your employees and managers to change what they have been doing, that is, to implement an improved method that was identified through benchmarking.

Benchmarking is not entirely new. In the product design sector, firms have practiced reverse engineering for a long time. Reverse engineering involves taking a competitor's product apart to find out all of its technical and design details. You can then evaluate whether your product design is as effective and as efficient as the competitor's.

The present benchmarking activities are largely process oriented. Who has the most effective and efficient process for a given activity, and how can we obtain detailed information on it so that we can determine if it fits our needs and if we can adopt and implement it? In essence, it is thus "process reverse engineering." The difficulty is that you cannot take your competitor's process apart in the quiet of your laboratory. The best you can expect to achieve is to observe your competitor's process, learn from it, and hope that your competitor will share with you why his or her process is as efficient as it is.

Robert Camp [1] defines benchmarking as the process of continually searching for new ideas, methods, practices, and procedures. If any of them are benchmarks—that is, if they are superior to the ones you are using now—adopt them or adapt them to your needs, and implement them.

Benchmarking is a continual process. Even after you implement an improved process, how do you know it is the best, the most efficient, and the most effective? You don't. You need to keep searching for improvements.

Camp identified four distinct types of benchmarking:

1. *Internal Benchmarking.* Compare your operations against other similar or identical operations in your own organization, but probably at a different division, location, plant, or other facility.
2. *Competitive Benchmarking.* Compare your operations with those of your direct competitors. This information may not always be easy to obtain, but it is frequently available through professional organizations, vendors, trade organizations, and other types of networking.
3. *Functional Benchmarking.* Functional areas do not differ much among organizations. Hence, there is an abundance of benchmarking potential. The difficulty here is to identify which organization is the benchmark. Trade publications are potential sources of information, and professional organizations provide excellent networking opportunities.
4. *Generic Benchmarking.* This is probably the most difficult approach to benchmarking. The underlying assumption is that you may discover a benchmark for any one of your processes almost anywhere in another organization or in your own organization. The process for this type of benchmark search is complex and vast. It is difficult to do this type of benchmarking systematically. Hence, the best approach for generic benchmarking is probably training your employees to always keep alert in the search for that elusive benchmark.

Regardless of the difficulties associated with effective benchmarking, numerous companies have implemented benchmarking with a vengeance. This frantic activity is probably the result of the enormous success achieved by some well-known benchmarking studies. Many major and well-known companies are actively involved in benchmarking. Examples of companies engaged in benchmarking include Xerox, NCR, Motorola, Digital Equipment Corporation, Kodak, Hewlett-Packard, General Motors, and Ford Motor Company.

This chapter reviews benchmarking in some detail and reports a number of success stories. However, the potential utilizer of benchmarking should realize that not every benchmark study provides huge improvements. But if benchmarking is correctly utilized by a firm on an ongoing basis, management can be assured that positive results will flow from it. ■

Achievements of Benchmarking

The widest and most comprehensive information on benchmarking available for one company is the information released by and for Xerox. Ross [6] reports the following quantitative results of benchmarking by Xerox:

1. Suppliers were reduced from 5000 to 300.
2. Commonality of parts increased from 20% to about 65%.
3. Quality problems were reduced by two-thirds.
4. Manufacturing costs were reduced by one-half.
5. Development time was reduced by 65%.
6. Direct labor was reduced by 50%.
7. Corporate staff was reduced by 35% while output volume increased.

Xerox also introduced concurrent engineering, and its hierarchical management structure was flattened significantly.

Motorola is one company that can be considered best in its class. It was able to achieve this by closely observing (benchmarking) what the Japanese were doing in those product lines where Motorola was active. As a result, Motorola has been able to reduce its defect rate in manufacturing by 99%. It also has been able to generate cost savings of about $900 million in 1992, and over $3 billion by the end of 1992 in cumulative terms [4].

These achievements in benchmarking by two highly visible multinational companies clearly indicate that benchmarking can produce substantial savings and improve overall competitiveness.

Benchmarking the Product

Benchmarking a product has been around for many years, since well before the term "benchmarking" became popular. It is usually referred to as "reverse engineering." Automobile firms are known to use it extensively to identify features in competitors' products that are or may be more desirable than the firm's own products. Automobiles are taken apart piece by piece and each component is analyzed to determine how it compares with similar components in the firm's own products. Needless to say, this kind of process has a tendency to standardize products and many components in automobiles are interchangeable among competitor products. This reverse engineering process, now known as benchmarking, has served the industry well by helping its members to improve product quality.

A specific example of product benchmarking is the Taurus automobile produced and marketed by the Ford Motor Company. Ford determined through a customer survey what the important features in an automobile are and then interviewed customers in order to determine what they disliked and liked about each feature. Ford then determined for each of the features what the competition had done to each feature. It then selected the best implementation of each feature for the design of the Taurus automobile. Ford's extensive and serious attempt at product benchmarking has produced one of the more successful automobiles ever produced. In 1992, Taurus was the top-selling automobile in the United States [5, 6].

The Process of Benchmarking

Benchmarking is an opportunistic activity that firms should be involved in all of the time, so it is probably somewhat pedantic to describe it as a process. On the other hand, in most organizations it is difficult to be systematic in pursuing potential benchmarks unless there is a written process, a procedure, in place. The benchmarking process can be described as follows [3]:

1. Rank the functions, activities, and processes that are in need of improvement. Then focus on those that rank high in importance and develop a plan to search for benchmarks either internal or external to the organization.
2. Identify the key cost, time, and quality performance indicators. These indicators should be related to customer needs and customer satisfaction.
3. Identify the organizations that have good reputations, especially in the area where the activity you are benchmarking is located. This step is probably the most difficult because the information you are seeking is difficult to locate and when located is not always easy to acquire.
4. Measure the performance of the indicators identified in step 2 for the potential benchmark sources. Compare the performance indicators of the benchmark firms with your own.
5. If substantially better performance is indicated at one of the benchmark companies, change your own process, activity, or function to at least exceed the best benchmark. Investigate how you can improve over and above the benchmark firm so that you can become the benchmark firm for the particular activity, process, or function.

Benchmarking the Process

A survey of 580 firms worldwide from four industries, consisting of computers, automobiles, hospitals, and banks, found that 31% of U.S. enterprises regularly benchmarked their products and services and only 7% never did any benchmarking [5]. These figures indicate that U.S. firms are more heavily engaged in benchmarking than either German or Japanese firms.

Most of the anecdotal information on benchmarking clearly indicates that the benchmarking that is done is on the production or operations process. There are few stories on product benchmarking.

Companies involved in benchmarking are well known to those engaged in observing or studying American industry: Xerox, Motorola, General Motors, Ford, Chrysler, AT&T. The practice of benchmarking has become pervasive.

If we review the benchmarking process, two alternative methods of benchmarking emerge. The first is a detailed, comprehensive, time-consuming approach intended to make a major cost-reducing change to the current process. The other is a more modest and brief approach intended to make incremental improvements in an operations process.

Xerox became involved in a lengthy process when it discovered that its midsize copiers were no longer competitive on the basis of price with similar Japanese copiers. The Japanese were selling midsize copiers at a price equal to what it costs Xerox to produce its midsize copier. This proved to be the "wake-up call" to Xerox to benchmark its manufacturing process against that of the Japanese. Xerox did a comprehensive study, including site visits by its manufacturing managers at all levels, to convince them how much change Xerox needed to make in order to achieve those cost reductions required to compete with the Japanese in the midsize copier market [5, 7, 8].

Another study by Xerox, also a comprehensive benchmarking study, was of its order-processing operations. Xerox's order processing costs amounted to $80 to $95 per order. After benchmarking the order-processing activity at 14 other companies, Xerox found that other companies only spent a fraction of what it costs Xerox to process orders. One particularly effective order-processing system was discovered at L.L. Bean. After this became known, numerous other companies visited L.L. Bean's order processing complex to study its order-processing operations. After a comprehensive study, Xerox achieved substantial savings in its order-processing operations [5].

Not all benchmarking studies are elaborate or excessively time-consuming. Westinghouse Corporation prefers to focus on small incremental improvements. These improvements can usually be achieved after brief and low-cost benchmarking projects. Whether the use of benchmarking to achieve incremental improvements is more effective than comprehensive benchmarking is difficult to say. Future research studies will probably reveal what the most effective approach to benchmarking is.

Benchmarking in the Administrative Sector

Mellon Bank of Pittsburgh became involved in benchmarking in 1991. For its first project it picked credit card billing disputes. Customer disputes are a major area of concern for banks, and any way to speed up their resolution is an important goal for any bank.

Mellon used a team made up of eight staff members from different departments to find ways to resolve the problem. The team benchmarked seven companies, including a bank, an airline, and credit card companies. Only three actual site visits were required. Information about the others was collected by phone conversations. The approach that eventually reduced the customer dispute problem for Mellon consisted of a computerized database that enabled the customer service clerk to communicate with the customer about all aspects of the dispute. The number of complaints was cut by more than half, and dispute resolution was shortened from 45 to 25 days [5].

Another classic case of benchmarking in the administrative area was Ford Motor Company's discovery that its accounts payable staff was several times larger than the accounts payable staff at its partner, the Mazda corporation. A thorough benchmarking study revealed that Mazda paid their supplier accounts in response to actual receipt of shipments or after completion of services. Ford used the traditional system of paying suppliers in response to invoices. Invoices needed verification, frequent modification, and numerous adjustments. By adopting a major process change, enormous savings were achieved.

A Benchmarking Pitfall

Hammer and Champy [3] identify one specific pitfall of benchmarking: benchmarking based only on what is being done in one's own industry. They point out that this limits the improvements that can be attained; benchmarking is then only a tool for catching up to the best performer in the industry. The moral of this example is to benchmark outside of your own industry.

If a firm is going to benchmark, it should benchmark from the best in the world, not just the best in its own industry. Ideas in entirely different industries may hold more promise than those emanating from your own industry.

The classic case is Xerox's adoption of L.L. Bean's order-fulfillment process. Xerox and L.L. Bean are in entirely different industries, but the two functions were similar and L.L. Bean had the best benchmark [5].

Benchmarking Networks

Benchmarking is of mutual benefit to all firms. Hence, it makes sense for companies to cooperate with other companies in studying each other's operations. Most companies do cooperate with each other. But, of course, there are holdouts. For companies that have achieved substantial internal competitive advantages, it is, of course, not surprising that they are reluctant to cooperate.

One organization that promotes exchange of information between companies is the American Productivity and Quality Center. It has established the nonprofit International Benchmarking Clearinghouse and has achieved a large number of company members who pay an annual fee to support its activities.

Another organization is the Strategic Planning Institute Council on Benchmarking. It is smaller than the American Productivity and Quality Center, but it has similar aims. The benefits of these organizations include their ability to provide communications, statistics, and data banks of benchmarking information to their memberships.

Still another way firms can learn from each other is through informed networking. Major consulting firms such as Towers Perrin and A. T. Kearney provide conduits for information on benchmarking to flow between competing firms. Collaboration between competing firms is frowned on for a variety of reasons. Through the use of consultants, collaboration is avoided while the necessary benchmarking can still be done through intermediaries [5, 7]. However, many processes in a firm do not necessarily have to be benchmarked on a competitor's process. Most administrative processes, for instance, are common to most firms, but may be performed differently. Benchmarking identifies the firm that does a particular process most efficiently.

Conclusions

Benchmarking is one of the many activities that firms engage in to either become more competitive or remain competitive. Benchmarking has become popular in recent years because of the globalization of not only product markets but also product sources. Products purchased in stores in Asia, Europe, or North America may have been manufactured in a wide variety of countries. Even before international trade agreements such as the North American Free Trade Agreement are fully implemented, trade in finished products and components of finished products is widely practiced. One can even argue that many international trade agreements result from extensive trade movements between the involved countries. The common wisdom is that international trade agreements produce increased trade. But are they the real motivators? Or are they just a "rubber stamp" of approval on existing activities?

Benchmarking will evolve over time and may even be called by a new name in the future. What will not change, however, is the need, born out of competitive necessity, to have a process in place that is as good or nearly as good as the best-in-class process. Firms that are not best-in-class, especially firms that compete in world markets, will not be able to remain in business much longer.

Discussion Questions

1. Contrast the major and minor benchmarking approaches.
2. Contrast benchmarking with reengineering.
3. Describe reverse engineering and discuss its similarities with benchmarking.
4. How does process benchmarking information typically become available?
5. What does Ford's accounts payable benchmarking study suggest about administrative operations?
6. Describe the seven benchmarking improvements achieved by Xerox.
7. Rank the seven improvements achieved by Xerox in terms of cost savings achieved.
8. Does benchmarking hold more promise for productivity improvements in the manufacturing or service sectors? Justify your rationale.
9. Why are U.S. firms more actively involved in benchmarking than either German or Japanese firms?
10. Discuss how membership in local chapters of professional and trade organizations by employees can be beneficial to benchmarking for the firm.

References

1. Camp, R. C. *Benchmarking.* ASQC Quality Press, Milwaukee, WI, 1989.
2. Dean, J. W., Jr., and J. R. Evans. *Total Quality Management, Organization and Strategy,* p. 93. West Publishing, Minneapolis, MN, 1994.
3. Hammer, M., and J. Champy. *Re-engineering the Corporation,* pp. 132–133. HarperCollins, New York, 1993.
4. Hill, Christian, and Ken Yamada. "Motorola Illustrates How an Aged Giant Can Remain Vibrant." *Wall Street Journal,* October 14, 1992, A1.
5. Main, Jeremy. "How to Steal the Best Ideas Around." *Fortune,* October 19, 1992, 102–106.
6. Ross, A. M. *Total Quality Management,* pp. 206–209. St. Lucie, Delray Beach, FL, 1992.
7. Whiting, Rick. "Benchmarking: Lessons from the Best-in-Class." *Electronic Business,* October 7, 1991, 25.
8. Xerox Corporation. *Profiles of Malcolm Baldrige Award Winners,* pp. 51–57. Allyn and Bacon, Boston, MA, 1992.

Chapter sixteen

Cycle-Time Reduction, Time-Based Competition, and Managerial Use of Time

Outline

Introduction
Cycle-Time-Based Competition in Day-to-Day Operations
Cycle-Time-Based Competition in New Product Designs
Cycle-Time-Based Competitions and the U.S. Armed Forces
Managing Time for the Manager/Leader
Conclusions

Introduction

Reducing the cycle time of every task, activity, or project in an organization is now considered by many firms to be the means for lowering cost, improving quality, reducing excess inventory, becoming more flexible, motivating employees, and improving customer satisfaction. The question that a cynic may pose is that if cycle-time reduction is able to achieve all of these improvements, why was it not thought of and implemented before?

There is no question that consumer satisfaction and cycle-time reduction are closely related. The success achieved by many businesses that focus on quick or instant service is clear. Instant banking, 24-hour restaurants and supermarkets, frequent flight schedules, and airline shuttle service with on-board ticketing are all examples of time-based competition allowing the customer quick turnaround times or reduced cycle times [1, 8, 11].

A wide variety of tools and techniques are available to management to develop and implement time-based tactics and approaches. Examples are concurrent engineering, electronic data interchange, process simplification, efficiency improvement, project management techniques, and numerous others.

In this chapter we will explore in detail how time-based competition, cycle-time reduction methods, and managerial use of time are useful in manufacturing, retailing, wholesaling, transportation, and other service industries, including the U.S. military.

CYCLE-TIME-BASED COMPETITION IN DAY-TO-DAY OPERATIONS

There are many benefits to be derived from reducing cycle time in day-to-day operations. What is meant by cycle time is broadly defined. We do not just mean the cycle time of a manufacturing operation, but the turnaround time for almost any activity an individual is engaged in as part of his or her daily work activities. For instance, responding to a customer inquiry, request, or complaint can be done right away, tomorrow, or next week. Clearly, the customer likes a response right away, but in most cases must wait. Another example is performing a project that requires many people and involves many activities, interactions, or consultations. How can this project be completed in the shortest possible time through effective coordination, rapid responses, swift communication, and continual interaction among all participants in the project [3]?

One specific example of cycle-time reduction was conveyed to me by a department manager of a supplier plant. He stated that much of their incoming communication was by mail. The mail usually was delivered by the local post office around noon, and was then sorted and delivered to the addressees within the organization late that same afternoon. The addressees generally did not open their mail until the next morning and then responded to it as necessary. To decrease the cycle time (i.e., speed up the mail-handling process), they arranged with the local post office to have their mail ready by 8:00 A.M. so it could be picked up by one of the supplier's employees on his way to work. The employee who picked up the mail arrived at the plant at 8:30 A.M.; the mail was then sorted and delivered to the addressees before 10:00 A.M. The addressees were thus able to respond to the mail that same day. As a result, the change in the process speeded up the mail cycle response time by 24 hours.

This example mainly involves personally controlled activities. There are, however, many other cases where cycle-time reduction provides considerable benefits to the organization and especially to the customer served by that organization. For instance, reducing sizes of orders and shipping orders out more frequently lowers finished goods inventory levels and improves customer satisfaction. Similarly, ordering smaller batches of products from suppliers lowers supply inventory levels and reduces inventory holding costs, pilferage costs, and obsolescence costs. To be able to achieve all of these benefits requires better organization, improved planning and scheduling, and especially more rapid response times from suppliers [4].

Modifications in operations to achieve cycle-time reduction require not only the internal cooperation of employees, including extensive retraining, but also cooperation and training of suppliers and, probably, customers. To be successful as a time-based competitor requires cooperation from all parties that interface in day-to-day operations.

Considerable assistance in achieving time-based competition is derived from electronic and computer-based technology. Electronic data interchange systems now connect many suppliers with the central or hub firm, and many customers are similarly connected with the central or hub firm. This new communications technology provides considerable potential improvement through its ability to compress activities such as ordering supplies, receiving orders from customers, and sending modifications of orders or specifications to suppliers. Customers, similarly, can revise their orders instantaneously and modify specifications, lodge complaints, and otherwise communicate with the hub or central firm instantaneously. Electronic data interchange thus provides rapid communications between customers and suppliers. However, cycle-time reduction can only be fully achieved if the receivers of the information react immediately or at least promptly to the information transmitted by electronic data interchange messages.

Cycle-time reduction or time-based competition is beginning to be actively practiced by many firms. It has proven to be a focused way to improve operations, reduce waste, and improve quality and customer satisfaction. Waste not only consists of material waste but especially of valuable time wasted by employees. Quality is improved because changes are incorporated in products quickly, customers' complaints are responded to quickly, and obsolescence is reduced. Customers become more satisfied because their requests, orders, and specification changes are responded to quickly. The comprehensive improvements thus improve operations for the firm in general.

CYCLE-TIME-BASED COMPETITION IN NEW PRODUCT DESIGNS

The success of the Japanese in world markets for manufactured goods, and especially for traditional goods, is often traced to their ability to produce a higher quality and more dependable product for the same or for a lower price than the traditional competition.

As Romm [6] reports, Honda's Acura division and General Motors' Saturn division were announced at about the same time, but Honda's Acura division had already completed three major Acura model changes before Saturn automobiles appeared in showrooms. The Acura–Saturn comparison is only one of many comparisons where the ability to respond quickly to changing markets is a major competitive weapon.

Another cycle-time example is the Mitsubishi heat pump [9]. Every year between 1979 and 1988 Mitsubishi introduced either a major design change or a new feature to its three-horsepower heat pump, including the introduction of integrated circuits to control the heat pump cycle in 1980. The American firms that were competing against Mitsubishi were unable to respond to the rapid technological changes introduced by Mitsubishi and began sourcing their critical components from Mitsubishi. Mitsubishi, as a result, substantially increased its market share of the value added to heat pumps sold.

A third cycle-time example relates to the two major Japanese motorcycle manufacturers, Honda and Yamaha [9]. Honda was able to defeat Yamaha by introducing new product features or new product models at a faster pace than Yamaha, its major competitor. This rapid response to customer tastes and preferred customer features is also referred to as getting inside a competitor's time/cycle loop. Both Honda and Yamaha started with about 60 models of motorcycles. Within a period of 18 months, Honda introduced new models or replaced its existing models at such a rapid pace that it turned its product line over twice. Yamaha, on the other hand, managed to turn over only about half of its product line in the same time period. In addition, Honda introduced new features, such as four-cycle engines and components made from composite materials that strengthened and lightened the motorcycles. The negative impact on Yamaha was significant. It had difficulty selling its inventory of motorcycles, which at one point had increased to a 12-month supply in its dealers' showrooms.

The Honda–Yamaha example of time-based product design competition shows how one firm, by being able to change product designs quickly, was able to gain a significant competitive advantage on its major competitor. It did not destroy the competition, but it weakened its major competitor significantly.

Another area where time-based product design methods were utilized effectively was in the Ford Taurus automobile model development. Ford abandoned its rigidly hierarchical, top-down pyramid organization and replaced it with a hub-rim approach. The hub-rim approach had the overall design and development program management in the center (the hub) and all other design and development activities on the rim, connected by the spokes of the wheel. Design and development activities consisted of automobile styling, product engineering, manufacturing engineering, manufacturing, purchasing, logistics, suppliers, and so on [7, 10].

The approach used by Ford for its Taurus design and development process also included quality function deployment. QFD is discussed in detail in Chapter 12.

CYCLE-TIME-BASED COMPETITION AND THE U.S. ARMED FORCES

The U.S.-led coalition of United Nations forces had an easy time beating the Iraqi armed forces in the Gulf War. What was one of the key strategies that led to the United Nations success?

You could argue that the U.N. forces were successful because they had overwhelming air power and had technologically superior equipment. Both strengths were successful in keeping the Iraqi army contained, but they contributed only marginally to the success of the final attack and routing of the Iraqi forces. What contributed to the U.S.-led final attack and routing was surprise and rapid deployment of strategies. Similar strategies were employed by the Germans in their blitzkrieg attack on western Europe in 1940 and earlier in their attack on Poland in 1939.

The German World War II general Gunther von Blumentritt described the blitzkrieg as rapid, concise assessment of situations followed by quick decisions and quick execution based on the premise that each minute ahead of the enemy is an advantage. The Gulf War was fought in a similar way. To be prepared for a worst-case scenario, sufficient reserve units were held back to be utilized if the blitzkrieg approach did not reach its planned success. The planning and preparation for the final phase of the Gulf War took a long time because of the enormous logistical problems involved. But when the final attack took place, it was rapid, unpredictable to the enemy, filled with surprises, and a true time-based effort.

Another example of cycle-time-based competition was the ability of the American F-86 Sabre Jet to consistently beat the Soviet-built MIG-15 in aerial dogfights even though the MIG-15 was a "superior" airplane by many performance standards. The MIG-15 had faster acceleration, could climb faster, and could generally make tighter turns than the F-86. But the F-86 had several crucial advantages [6]: it could change from one maneuver to another much more quickly, it could decelerate and turn, and it could dive and switch directions more quickly than the more powerful MIG-15. The F-86 also had a glass-domed bubble canopy that enabled the pilot to observe the opposition more easily than the MIG-15 pilot could.

The F-86 was thus able to defeat the MIG-15 consistently because the F-86 pilot had more information earlier and was also able to react more rapidly because of the F-86's superior maneuverability. The F-86 versus MIG-15 example is a clear illustration of the F-86 being able to get inside the MIG-15's time/cycle loop.

In the next section, we will explore how a manager's use of time during the day is an important factor in his or her effective utilization of the available time, a very scarce resource.

MANAGING TIME FOR THE MANAGER/LEADER

The conventional wisdom about how managers, especially managers serving in senior leadership positions, should manage their time is rather straightforward. It is generally recommended that the managers structure their day and use assistants or secretaries to shield them from "unnecessary" interruptions. The conventional wisdom is based on the premise that a general manager's time is scarce and valuable and therefore should be rationed out only to important activities.

The problem with the conventional wisdom is that it is difficult to decide what is important. And how do we know what the really important activities are for a general manager? Two empirically based studies, one recent and one done in the early 1980s, have challenged the conventional wisdom.

The first study was done by John Kotter, a Harvard Business School professor. It is reported in his book, *The General Managers* [5]. Kotter studied 15 executives who were judged to be good performers. He found that these successful executives did not plan most of their time while at work. They used their time to communicate with many people, many of whom were not managers reporting to them but staff members at lower levels. The communications were interactive, were not necessarily all related to work or the task at hand, included humor and banter, and did not consist of giving orders. In these communication activities, the general managers used such tactics as nudging, convincing, and cajoling instead of giving direct orders. During their typical workday, the general managers interacted at many levels and with many people, establishing over time hundreds and in some cases thousands of contacts. These numerous contacts served as motivators and established networks of communications.

By utilizing most of their time on the job talking and communicating with colleagues, subordinates, clients, customers, and others who call or drop by or are encountered in hallways, general managers stay tuned in to what is going on in their environment. They have up-to-date information and are able to make decisions based on that up-to-date information. They thus achieve control of the organization and are able to positively affect the output of the organization.

The second empirically based study was done by Stephanie Winston [2]. Winston's study is based on interviews with 48 senior executives. She found that an executive's workday consists almost entirely of interruptions. Executives try not to have their days organized with appointments and meetings. They largely work in response to what comes next. The successful executives use a communications style that allows for a wide range of interactive communications, including questions, comments, updates, and requests. All types of communication means are used, such as face-to-face, telephone, fax, notes, and brief memos. Through their management approaches, these executives were able to maintain a thorough and solid contact with what was going on in their organizations. They were also able to influence what was going on, motivate their subordinates, identify weak links in the organization in a timely fashion, maintain customer contact, maintain external contact, and serve in a true leadership position.

How do these managers take care of their paperwork, how do they respond to memos, how and when do they conduct meetings, how and when do they respond to external contacts, how and when do they respond to customer complaints, and when do they do their readings? The answer is that the general managers work long hours and must utilize blocks of time outside of their day at the office to get these things done. Paperwork can be done at home, during travel, or early in the morning. The important thing is that the successful managers see their main responsibility, their workday, to consist of interacting on an ad hoc and open basis with the people in and outside their organization. They view it to be very important that they are able to maintain open communication with as many people as possible in the organization. They probably are distrustful of the wall that could be built around them; it would deprive them of knowledge of what is going on in the organization.

Conclusions

In this chapter, time formed the focus of attention. Time-based competition is an idea that management cannot ignore. It must pay close attention to it. Time-based competition arises when attempts are made to reduce cycle time, but it is also critical when top management decides what to do with its own time.

The notion that time is a very important ingredient in the management of a firm is not surprising. The familiar phrase "time is money" rings clear. And the practice of having employees punch a time clock, now becoming less popular, was done as much for stressing the importance of time as for ensuring that employees spent the required time on the job.

What was not so clear in the past was the notion that time is also valuable to the customer; time forms an important component of the value of a product or service. In addition, mismanagement of time has important repercussions in other aspects of the organization. Mismanagement in purchasing and supplier relations can increase inventories, a costly component of being in business. Similarly, mismanagement of design and development can delay product introduction and put the firm at a competitive disadvantage.

The importance of time-based competition is a fact of the 1990s and will remain so into the next century. After the turn of the century it will probably be referred to by a new name, but the importance of time will not lessen.

Discussion Questions

1. How does cycle-time reduction improve customer service?
2. How has technology assisted in production process cycle-time reduction?
3. How has technology helped reduce product design cycle time?
4. Give examples of how reduced cycle time is important to counter competitors' tactics or strategies.
5. How does cycle-time reduction lower inventories for a firm?
6. Why is communication with subordinates important for upper-level management?
7. Describe a time/cycle loop.
8. Give an illustration of a time/cycle loop.

References

1. Bower, J. L., and T. H. Hout. "Fast Cycle Capability for Competitive Power." *Harvard Business Review,* November-December 1988, 110–118.
2. Deutschman, Alan. "The CEO's Secret of Managing Time." *Fortune,* June 1, 1992, 135–146.
3. Hill, G. C., and K. Yamada. "Motorola Illustrates How an Aged Giant Can Remain Vibrant." *Wall Street Journal,* October 14, 1992, 91.
4. Kotler, P., and P. J. Stonich. "Turbo Marketing through Time Compression." *The Journal of Business Strategy,* September-October 1991, 24–29.
5. Kotter, John P. *The General Managers.* The Free Press, New York, 1982.
6. Romm, Joseph J. "The Gospel According to Sun Tzu." *Forbes,* December 9, 1991, 154–162.
7. Ross, A. M. *Total Quality Management,* pp. 204–205, 1992.
8. Sengstock Jr., C. A. "Pursuing the Not-So Elusive Goal of Perfection," *Public Relations Journal,* August 1991, 22–23.
9. Stalk, George, Jr. "Time: The Next Source of Competitive Advantage." *Harvard Business Review,* July-August 1988, 41–51.
10. Stalk, G., Jr., and T. M. Hout. *Competing against Time.* The Free Press, New York, 1990.
11. Vesey, J. T. "The New Competitors: They Think in Terms of Speed-to-Market." *Academy of Management Executive,* 5(2), May 1991, 23–33.

Chapter **seventeen**

Just-in-Time Operations

Outline

Introduction
Just-in-Time Philosophy
Just-in-Time Purchasing
Just-in-Time at a Corning Plant
Just-in-Time in the Retail Chain Store
Conclusions

Introduction

The concept of just-in-time (JIT) operations is important in the logistics, manufacturing, wholesale, and retail trade fields. The concept of JIT forces management to focus on the management of internal operations. Without focus, inventories, especially work-in-process inventories, tend to build up. A focus on JIT provides a policing function to maintain operations as efficiently as possible.

This chapter discusses the history and current practice of just-in-time operations. Just-in-time in the management of operations is a concept that emerged in Japan and is now practiced in various forms by all progressive manufacturers and other organizations in the developed world. The benefits of just-in-time include reducing work-in-process inventories and the imposition of a discipline and operations improvement on the system.

Just-in-time purchasing and its accompanying format of just-in-time delivery are discussed and explored. Next, a review of Corning's approach to JIT is explored and analyzed. Finally, JIT applied to retail chain store operations is reviewed and discussed.

JUST-IN-TIME PHILOSOPHY

Just-in-time originally referred to a method of controlling and managing production and especially work-in-process inventory in order to keep it to a minimum. The original Japanese approach to JIT utilized an inventory control

171

procedure that went by the term *kanban*. Kanbans are cards or tags that are attached to each container or batch of work-in-process or supplier inventory. By controlling the number of kanbans in circulation, manufacturing management could control the amount of work-in-process or supplier inventory in circulation.

Since then the concept of JIT has encompassed all of a firm's operations because almost any activity can be improved if it is done just-in-time. JIT can be applied to manufacturing, inventory management, maintenance, purchasing, logistics, distribution, retailing, wholesaling, and so on.

The term JIT has become a generic term for the above concept. However, many firms use their own descriptions, as reported by Gaither [1]. IBM uses the term "continuous flow manufacturing," Hewlett-Packard identifies JIT as "stockless production and repetitive manufacturing systems," General Electric calls it "management by sight," and in Japan it is called "the Toyota production system." In the United States it also goes by the name of "lean manufacturing."

The movement of JIT from a work-in-process inventory reduction tool to a companywide practice is largely the result of the not surprising discovery that high levels of work-in-process inventory are frequently used to cover up production problems. If a machine, in a chain of machines, breaks down, large buffers of inventory allow the other machines to continue their production throughput. The benefit of these high buffer inventories is the continued operation of the facility, thus reducing both machine and worker downtime. Unfortunately, the benefits of reduced machine and worker downtime seldom exceed the cost of maintaining the high work-in-process inventories [7].

JIT imposes a severe discipline on any operating system. All components of the system must be in good operating condition, and the production output must always be of high or at least acceptable quality. JIT has been called a system of enforced problem solving. Nothing can be left to chance. There should be no weak links in the production or operations chain. However, every link is as weak as the next, and breakdown can occur anywhere. Therefore, all links must have backups or substitute equipment that can be utilized in case of a breakdown of the regular equipment. In fact, one of the important components of a JIT system is a system of backups that can be used to avoid shutdowns of the production system.

To implement JIT therefore requires considerable changes, additions, corrections, modifications, and, generally, a strengthening of the manufacturing process to ensure that the system can function uninterruptedly. When this is achieved, the organization has achieved JIT manufacturing. The benefits of an implemented JIT system are manifold. The production operations typically are more focused, production and supplier lot sizes are substantially smaller, setup times are substantially reduced, the work environment is less cluttered and more spacious, waste is all but eliminated, production schedules are more stable, and work satisfaction among employees is generally higher. The quality of output will be stable and at a much higher level than prior to JIT implementation.

Gaither [1] identified five specific benefits of JIT implementation:

1. Inventory levels, and specifically work-in-process inventories, are drastically reduced.

JUST-IN-TIME OPERATIONS

2. The throughput time for a product—that is, the time it takes to produce a product from start to finish—is substantially reduced, thus enabling manufacturing management to respond much more quickly to specifications or design changes.
3. Quality is increased and waste due to poor-quality or unsatisfactory products is reduced substantially.
4. More open space is available between pieces of machinery and equipment, allowing a reorganization of the production facilities to a smaller floor area.
5. Fewer problems arise, so management time is freed up for more productive work.

To achieve these benefits, major efforts must be made by the organization. Reduction of work-in-process inventory levels requires substantial reductions in setup times, improved scheduling of production, and rescheduling of operations to a more product-oriented layout as opposed to a process-oriented layout of machinery and equipment.

Improving throughput time for a product also requires focus on setup times, production schedules, and a process orientation. For both inventory reduction and improvement of throughput times, the kanban operations scheduling method may be used. Kanban is a method whereby each batch of work-in-process inventory and raw material is tagged with a kanban (card). By limiting the number of kanbans in use, the inventory can be controlled.

Quality improvement is achieved by increased focus on the design and manufacturability of the product, and by employee training to ensure that each operation is performed as specified. Availability of a satisfactory production capability, including up-to-date machinery, tools, and equipment, is, of course, also mandatory to achieve high-quality. With higher quality output, less waste will be generated.

If management is able to achieve lower work-in-process inventory, higher-quality products, and faster throughput times, it usually follows that the workplace will be cleaner and less cluttered. Clean and uncluttered workplaces have been found to be motivators for employees to produce at a higher level, resulting in higher productivity and quality.

These improvements generally produce lower operating costs even if the work-in-process inventory reductions are tabulated separately. A more organized and trouble-free production process, although costly and time-consuming to install and implement, will in the long run produce substantial operating cost reductions [5].

JUST-IN-TIME PURCHASING

Just-in-time purchasing is not a new idea thought up by Japanese manufacturers. Before the arrival of the refrigerator and the supermarket, people in urban areas used to shop daily for their food. The objective of their daily just-in-time shopping was not to keep their food supplies at a low level because of a shortage of storage space; their objective was to obtain fresh food and avoid spoilage. By substituting "quality" for "freshness" we can apply this example to JIT: today's adopters of just-in-time purchasing do so to avoid obsolescence, spoilage, and pilferage, in addition to reducing inventory holding costs.

To achieve just-in-time purchasing requires a number of cooperative activities with suppliers, subcontractors, and other parties in the supplier chain. Development of suppliers and improving supplier relationships are the first steps required. Just imposing just-in-time deliveries on a vendor is not sufficient to achieve it. What can vendors do to modify their operations in order to minimize or eliminate cost increases? If necessary, the buyer firm may want to work closely with the supplier to help the supplier reduce costs and to find mutually beneficial ways to achieve just-in-time delivery of the ordered materials.

Another way to achieve just-in-time delivery is to establish long-term contracts with suppliers. With long-term contracts, suppliers can afford to invest in training of employees, in acquiring cost-reducing equipment, and in other ways to reduce costs and improve on-time and just-in-time delivery of materials and supplies [2, 8].

Just-in-time delivery cannot necessarily be attained at zero additional costs. Even the Japanese are now finding out that just-in-time purchasing and the associated frequent deliveries are choking the already congested Japanese roads, are aggravating pollution, and are generating other social and labor problems. With Japan's labor shortage, the transportation industry is facing some major labor problems because of the difficulty to acquire transportation workers [4].

Price is not the only consideration in just-in-time purchasing. Other performance factors, such as delivery schedules, product quality, timely communication, and mutual trust and dependence, are important considerations in selecting a long-term supplier.

One very important recent development between the buying firm and the supplying firm is electronic communication, which is now able to link buyer's and supplier's computer systems electronically. This electronic data interchange (EDI) system facilitates communication for placing orders, modifying orders, revising specifications, making payments, communicating regarding quality problems, and any other communications that are necessary.

Establishing just-in-time purchasing that provides as nearly as possible just-in-time delivery of products, supplies, components, and parts is an important factor in keeping costs and quality under control. Just-in-time purchasing has become an important competitive tool and firms can no longer afford to ignore it.

JUST-IN-TIME AT A CORNING PLANT

The visible benefits of just-in-time operations are reductions in inventory and specifically work-in-process inventory. To achieve these visible benefits, however, requires that many operating and administrative activities be changed to achieve just-in-time operations. For instance, the purchasing department must ensure that orders to suppliers are filled by small batches at exact and specified times. To achieve this requires that suppliers have the discipline and ability to do so. It also probably means reducing the number of suppliers. Manufacturing management must schedule their operations such that small batches are processed in a timely manner without requiring accumulations of work-in-process inventory. Shipping must ensure that finished products are shipped to the customer or warehouse immediately upon completion at the plant. In other words, a coordinated and collaborative approach among suppliers, purchasing department, manufacturing, shipping, and the customer is needed to achieve just-in-time operations.

The result of a well-executed just-in-time operations plan provides not only substantially lower inventories but also more effective and efficient operations, a satisfied customer, and a higher-quality product or service.

An illustration of the above approach is Corning's Erwin, New York, plant, which manufactures kiln-baked ceramic parts for automotive catalytic converters. Before converting to just-in-time operations, the Erwin plant warehoused large supplies of raw materials, components, and shipping boxes. A study of their in-plant inventory revealed that only 6% of its inventory was active at any moment. The remainder was inactive, serving as a backup or buffer, or waiting to be used at some future time. Space required to house all of this excessive inventory took over a large amount of space in the plant, and additional storage space had to be leased in locations nearby. Total space devoted to storage amounted to 185,000 square feet.

Following implementation of just-in-time operations, the leased warehouses are no longer necessary, and about two-thirds of the factory inventory was also eliminated. Annual inventory holding costs amount to about 25% of the inventory value, so the adoption of just-in-time operations has saved the Erwin plant about $8 million [6].

Under the new system, customers are supplied with finished goods only as needed, and they are supplied directly from production, not from finished goods inventories. Another benefit of the new system is the closer contact with the customer and the speedier service to the customer.

This illustration has sketched the benefits that can be achieved from just-in-time operations. Achieving these benefits requires a major restructuring of operations; training managers and employees to alter their work methods; training suppliers to deliver specific quantities at specified times, and be highly dependable and punctual; and staying in close contact with customers to know and anticipate their orders.

For a system such as the Corning operation to be effective also requires installation and implementation of electronic data interchange, a technological communication link between Corning and its customers and suppliers. This was done in Corning's Erwin operation.

JUST-IN-TIME IN THE RETAIL CHAIN STORE

Just-in-time systems are commonly thought to be related only to manufacturing systems. It is in the manufacturing area where just-in-time is most widely practiced. But the idea for just-in-time operations as originally developed by Toyota was based on the American supermarket system, with its system of continually refilling the supermarket shelves as they are depleted.

It is not surprising, therefore, that just-in-time is of interest to other retailers, or at least suppliers of retailers. One such corporation is the VF Corporation. VF Corporation is the $3.8 billion per year manufacturer and distributor of such well-known clothing brands as Lee and Wrangler jeans, Jantzen sportswear, and Vanity Fair lingerie.

VF Corporation uses what it calls a flow replenishment inventory management system. The system is driven by a market response system (MRS), which is a computerized network that links its manufacturing and distribution plants directly to more than 36,000 retail store customers.

The market response system is able to identify on a daily basis how well its current products in the 36,000 retail centers are selling. This information not only identifies the popularity of certain kinds of clothing but also the preferred styles, fabrics, colors, and sizes. This collected information is then sent by satellite to VF's computer communication center, which relays it to product managers, designers, buyers, and others who track consumer preferences. The collected information is then analyzed to determine trends in customer tastes and buying patterns. This information is then used to design new styles and place orders for popular and well-selling styles, fabrics, colors, and sizes of clothing.

The market response system has enabled VF Corporation to respond quickly by restocking retailers with the proper mix of products. In stores where Lee products are sold, for instance, VF Corporation has been able to maintain a 97% in-stock rate of Lee products. The industry average is only 70%. Excess inventory of Wrangler stretch jeans has been reduced by 85% and sales have increased by 40%. For products such as those VF Corporation produces, a sale occurs only if the desired product is on the shelf. Being able to achieve nearly 100% in-stock rates is therefore a tremendous advantage. And customers who can find exactly what they are looking for are customers who will return.

The market response system developed by VF Corporation is therefore an indirect just-in-time system. It helps reduce excess inventories and ensures that VF's products will be on the shelves of its retailers at the right time. That feature is a true customer response system.

One other benefit of the system is the service it provides to the retailers. Retailers want products that sell, and they abhor stockouts of products. The market response system therefore serves the dual purpose of satisfying the end customer, the purchaser of the garment, as well as the retailer, the seller of the garment [3].

Conclusions

Just-in-time operations are now widely practiced by all progressive firms, but the concept is still widely misunderstood. Toyota of Japan is generally viewed as the originator of the JIT idea because of space limitations in Japanese factories and in Japan generally. The close proximity of most of Toyota's suppliers to its automobile assembly plants made JIT particularly attractive and also easier to utilize.

The idea for JIT came from the American supermarket, with its routine shelf-filling replacement system. We may also give some credit to the parsimonious shoppers of the world who like fresh products and who do not like to see their purchases spoiled. Both of these examples are strongly analogous to the JIT systems utilized in many organizations [9].

The important benefit of JIT systems is not just the reduced inventory levels but the necessary importance of disciplined control and management, and the elimination of all possible breakdowns and actual or potential bottlenecks.

A JIT system needs to be nearly foolproof and failproof. The successful JIT system must be in operating status nearly all the time. To achieve this requires a highly functioning operating system that is well managed and has extensive backup systems and procedures in case a link has a temporary failure. Not all JIT systems are as dependable as this, of course, but the truly successful ones are.

Discussion Questions

1. Just-in-time is intended to make improvements in several activities in the operations of a firm. Describe and discuss four important improvements.
2. Some firms use their own terms for just-in-time. Identify four of them and describe in your own words why the respective firms chose those terms.
3. Describe Gaither's first benefit of JIT: reduction in work-in-process inventories. How is it achieved?
4. Describe Gaither's third benefit of JIT: increase in quality and reduction of waste. How is it achieved?
5. Will JIT require more or less machinery and equipment in a factory? Explain your rationale.
6. Discuss just-in-time purchasing and delivery. Describe the benefits that are accrued by the firm using these tactics.
7. What are the limitations of a retail store for just-in-time purchasing? Could you refer to it as stockless operations?
8. Discuss how electronic communications and information technology can benefit just-in-time approaches for multi-store retail operations.

References

1. Gaither, Norman. *Production and Operations Management,* 4th ed., pp. 520–534, 598–600. Dryden Press, 1990.
2. Hay, E. J. "Implementing JIT Purchasing." *Production and Inventory Management Review,* 10(1), 1990, 30–32.
3. Hessan, Diane, and Jerry Bowles. "The Customer-Driven Company: Listening and Responding at VF Corporation." Advertising Insert in *Fortune,* January 1993.
4. Kameyama, Naoyuki. "Recent Debate Over Just-In-Time Systems." *Japan Labor Bulletin,* November 1, 1991, 4–6.
5. Nayak, R. P. "Planning Speeds Technological Development." *Planning Review,* November-December 1990, 94–98.
6. O'Boyle, Thomas F. "Firm's Newfound Skill in Managing Inventory May Soften Downturn." *Wall Street Journal,* November 19, 1990, A1.
7. Schniederjans, M. J. *Topics in Just-in-Time Management.* Allyn and Bacon, Boston, 1993.
8. Willis, T. H. and C. R. Huston. "Vendor Requirements and Evaluation in a Just-in-Time Environment." *International Journal of Operations and Production Management,* 10(4), 1990, 41–50.
9. Zipkin, P. H. "Does Manufacturing Need a JIT Revolution?" *Harvard Business Review,* January-February 1991, 40–50.

Chapter eighteen

Flexibility and Adaptability of the Firm

Outline

Introduction
Operations Flexibility in Japan
General Motors: Flexibility through Increased Plant Utilization
Flexibility in Managing the Computer Hardware Industry
Flexibility through Product Modularization
Agile Manufacturing and Operations Systems
Adaptability in Strategic Alliances
The Adaptive and Flexible Corporation
Conclusions

Introduction

In its narrowest definition, flexibility consists of operations flexibility and product development flexibility. Operations flexibility is a measure of a firm's ability to respond to market demands by changing over from one product to another through rapid production line changeovers. Product development flexibility is a measure of a firm's ability to bring out new or redesigned products quickly to respond to changes in customer tastes and demand. The U.S. automotive industry's ability to shorten vehicle design and development times is an example of improving one's product development flexibility.

However, flexibility and adaptability need to be more broadly defined. The flexible and adaptive corporation of the future will be strongly customer responsive, and must be highly flexible and adaptive to respond to the customer's current and future needs and wants. In other words, being responsive to current needs and wants is necessary but not sufficient. The ability and creativity to develop products and create future needs for the customer is an important aspect of the new flexible and adaptive corporation [5].

This will require a change in the traditional corporate organization from a functional area orientation to a more activity or project orientation. Major activities and projects will be managed and executed by multifunctional teams. These teams will change in membership over time as requirements change. The team approach needs to be flexible and adaptive at all times.

This chapter will review how the Japanese are changing their organizations to be more flexible and responsive. Next, it will review how firms in several U.S. industries are changing their organizational structures to become more responsive to customer needs while simultaneously strengthening their competitiveness through increased flexibility and adaptiveness [6]. The chapter closes with a look at developments in the future, including agile operating systems and adaptability through strategic alliances, and a view of the adaptive and flexible corporation of the future.

Operations Flexibility in Japan

Japan in the past has provided the leadership in improving product quality and low-inventory production and operations. Japan's industry is now focusing on operations flexibility and product variety. The latter is a direct result of the former. By developing operations that are flexible in terms of their ability to provide a wide variety of product models at a low cost, the Japanese are strategically positioning themselves to be formidable competitors not only in high-volume but also in low-volume product markets.

Product flexibility is achieved by two important flexibility factors. The first flexibility factor allows a company to produce many different models of a product with the same machinery and usually on the same assembly line at low cost and with little disruption in the production process when models are changed. That is, small production runs can be made of any component or any final assembly, and the production process can be switched quickly, with little or no disruption, to another model or product.

The second flexibility factor is the ability to require only minimum disruption in production operations when introducing an entirely new model to the production process. This is extremely important because in the past this second flexibility factor created considerable lost production.

The Japanese have been focusing their attention on both flexibility factors and have achieved considerable progress. They have achieved this progress at a price: massive capital investment in advanced technology had to be added to production operations to achieve these abilities in flexible production.

Japan's flexibility drive was fueled by capital spending as reported by Steward [10]. Between 1986 and 1991, Japan's industry spent $3 trillion in domestic plants and equipment. Japan's industry on a per capita basis spent an equivalent of two and a half times as much on new plants and equipment than U.S. industry in 1991. Not all of this investment was targeted for flexibility, of course, but much of it was.

An example of the first flexibility factor is Toshiba's ability to assemble nine different word processors on one assembly line and 20 different laptop computers on an adjacent assembly line. Batch sizes of each model number about 20. Assembly workers receive instructions for each different model from a computer screen in front of them [10].

An example of the second flexibility factor, the ability to add new models to the production process at low cost, is Nissan's ability to prepare an automobile plant for a new model while the assembly line keeps assembling automobiles. This process now takes 3 months; it used to take 12 months. Toyota is able to do its model changeover as quickly. After several months of preparation, only one shift of downtime is needed to add a new model to the assembly line. Toyota has been able to increase its capacity utilization of its assembly lines from 75% in 1982 to 95% in 1992, through the one-shift model change. Before 1982, model changes took lengthy shutdowns of the entire automobile assembly line [7, 10].

The two flexibility factors described above are clearly strong competitive advantages that enable Japanese manufacturers to take advantage of changes in customer taste and to be competitive not only in terms of cost but also in terms of model variety to meet customers' changing tastes and preferences.

General Motors: Flexibility Through Increased Plant Utilization

An airline would never consider idling an airliner because pilots and cabin crews prefer to not work on weekends. The immense investment in capital equipment by the airlines as well as the expectations of the traveling public make seven days per week and around-the-clock operations mandatory.

In U.S. and European manufacturing operations, the idea of working on weekends is strongly resisted by labor unions and by the majority of nonunion employees. The idea of having the weekend off for recreation is a strongly embedded custom. If weekend work is done at all, it usually requires time-and-a-half or double-time pay. Yet manufacturers have enormous investments in plants and equipment that sit idle on weekends unless overtime is worked.

In a global competitive environment, the underutilization of plants and equipment puts Western manufacturers at a distinct disadvantage. The practice of seven days per week plant operation is common in Japan and other Asian countries.

In order to close the gap in plant and equipment productivity, General Motors instituted a third shift at its Lordstown, Ohio, plant in 1991. This change in work practices took place after extensive labor-management negotiations and after concessions made by both sides. To entice the workers to the less popular shifts, monetary incentives were provided. Workers had to select their preferred shifts, and shift assignments were then made on the basis of seniority. The most popular shift was the Monday through Thursday day shift (no premium pay) and the Friday through Monday swing shift ($100 per week premium pay). The least popular shift was the Tuesday through Friday night shift ($50 per week premium pay). The labor-management agreement stipulated that workers could not change shifts for the first six months to ensure continuity of worker teams and to get workers accustomed to their designated shift. Each weekly shift consisted of four days of 10 hours per day for a total of 40 hours per week [11]. Table 18–1 shows a mapping of the three shifts on a

Table 18-1
Diagram of Three Shifts at Lordstown

Tuesday	Wednesday	Thursday	Friday	Saturday	Sunday	Monday
Night shift 5:30 P.M.–4:00 A.M.					Swing shift 7:00P.M.–5:30P.M.	
Day shift 6:00 A.M.–5:00 P.M.			Swing shift 6:00 A.M.–5:00 P.M.			Day Shift 6:00 A.M.–5:00 P.M.

Source: Adapted for Treece, James B., and Patrick Oster. "General Motors Open All Night." *Business Week,* June 1, 1992, 82–83.

normal workweek. The benefit to General Motors was that the third shift added 50% more production time to the plant. In addition, less overtime wages had to be paid. However, on average there was a $50 per week per worker wage premium associated with the change.

With three shifts per week, the plant turned out automobiles for 120 hours out of a total of 168 hours. The 48 idle hours per week were utilized for plant and equipment maintenance, replenishment of supplies, and general get-ready activities for each work shift. Being able to attain 120 hours of output out of 168 available hours is quite an achievement for an automobile assembly operation.

FLEXIBILITY IN MANAGING THE COMPUTER HARDWARE INDUSTRY

Flexibility is not required only in product design, design modification, and manufacturing product variety; it is also required in organizational systems. This is known as organizational flexibility.

One of the main organizational problems of large organizations is organizational, operations, and management flexibility. Organizations, especially large organizations, tend to prefer the status quo. Large organizations tend to discourage change through their bureaucratic systems and procedures, their hierarchical or established management style, and their quest for stability.

Unfortunately, many large organizations have run into serious trouble because of the organizational inflexibility. In industries that are undergoing rapid product, technological, structural, and other changes, large organizations are notoriously vulnerable. Large organizations, and especially very large organizations, are similar to large oil tankers. To turn or stop them takes an enormous amount of time. The larger the organization, the more difficult it is to change the organizational structure, operations, and overall direction of the organization.

There are a number of recent examples of large organizations not responding quickly enough to rapid technological, structural, and competitive changes in their respective industries. In the computer hardware industry, both IBM and Digital Equipment Corporation (DEC) stumbled badly and were forced to make major changes, including changes in their leadership, their organizational size, their workforce, and the strategic direction in which they had been moving. In the retailing field, the erstwhile symbol of retailing and mail-order sales, Sears Inc., had to make major structural and organizational changes, including the closing of its mail order business. Numerous smaller, less well-known firms had to restructure, reorganize, or go out of business entirely.

These examples illustrate how important it is for large and small organizations to remain flexible. Alert management, continuous environmental scanning, and benchmarking not only of new products or processes but also of the entire organization on a continuing basis are just a few of the important attributes of a flexible management organization.

One organization that tried to remain flexible but got caught in organizational inertia is Hewlett-Packard (HP). HP followed a highly participatory management style, utilizing the committee structure widely and extensively. The idea behind this structure was originally sound when it was instituted because it engendered wide participation by many engineers and middle-level managers in the management process. However, as HP grew larger, the committee structure snowballed into an unmanageable format and caused serious delays in product development, operational decisions, and marketing projects. In the spring of 1991, HP had to radically change its management structure in order to speed up the decision-making process and simultaneously bring new products to the market quicker. The change was a major organizational one. It allowed engineers and middle managers to spend more time on technical work and problems and it produced a much more rapid decision-making style. It also, of course, reduced the committee structure but did not entirely eliminate it [1].

The HP experience received much of its impetus from HP's independently functioning and highly successful laser printer subsidiary located in Boise, Idaho. Not only the geographic location, away from Palo Alto headquarters, but also its unique mission allowed this business unit to function nearly independently from HP's other units. The Boise operation's mission was the design, development, production and marketing of a laser printer for stand-alone desktop computers. The unit was able to bring a reasonably priced laser printer to market in record time, well ahead of the competition, and sell it at a highly competitive price. The HP Boise unit was so successful that it quickly captured a large part of the laser printer market, and even after other competitors entered the laser printer market HP was able to maintain a 60% market share [1].

The HP example illustrates the importance of organizational, structural, and operations flexibility. It is a concept that organizations, large or small, ignore at their peril.

FLEXIBILITY THROUGH PRODUCT MODULARIZATION

A classic case of product modularization to provide flexibility in switching from one product model to another is the automobile engine. Automobile engines were traditionally built in engine plants designed for one engine model only and with high-volume output. Producing 400,000 to 500,000 engines in one engine plant, all basically of the same design, was not all that unusual in the past. The traditional manufacturing process of building automobile engines of only one design in one plant was quite economical and efficient, provided the demand for that particular engine remained unchanged. However, customer tastes for automobiles change constantly, and technological developments obsolete engines much more quickly now than in the past.

In response automobile manufacturers are in the process of building new engine plants that will enable them to produce a variety of different engine types and sizes in one engine plant. As demand for a given engine type changes, they can quickly vary the production mix of engines [7].

Woodruff [12] reports that Ford is developing a type of engine plant that will allow Ford to build V8 and V6 engines around a basic building block, the combustion chamber, designed for maximum fuel economy. Ford's new engine plants, utilizing flexible manufacturing equipment, will be able to produce more than a dozen engine sizes and configurations on one engine production and assembly line. The key to achieving this product flexibility on one engine production and assembly line lies in the sharing of about 350 common parts for each engine size or configuration. This approach to manufacturing is called modularization because several modules or subassemblies are identical for each engine model or configuration.

Ford is by no means the first to utilize modularization to produce automobile engines. Caterpillar utilized modular design to produce V12, V10, and V8 engines on the same engine production and assembly line. Toyota Motor Corporation utilizes the same flexible manufacturing approach to produce several basic engines on the same engine production and assembly line.

One basic benefit of modular automobile engines is the ability to switch to new engine designs more quickly. Toyota has switched to the four valves per cylinder engine, a much improved version of the two valves per cylinder engine used in virtually all U.S. automobiles. The main reason U.S. manufacturers are lagging behind the adoption of the 30% more efficient four valves per cylinder engine is the enormous investment they have in engine plants that specialize in only one type of engine.

Modularization to attain flexibility is used in many other products also. It is extensively used in automobile components other than engines. It is also used in the household appliance industry, in electronic and computer products, in farm equipment, and in numerous other products.

The concept of modularization is not new. What is new and also extremely difficult and challenging for manufacturers is to force themselves to utilize the concept and implement it for their products. The degree to which they are able to implement modularization will determine the degree of manufacturing flexibility they are able to attain. And manufacturing flexibility will determine how well manufacturers will be able to compete in the future.

AGILE MANUFACTURING AND OPERATIONS SYSTEMS

The term *agile manufacturing systems* was coined by Lehigh University's Iacocca Institute for a conceptual system of designing, manufacturing, and marketing products that would leapfrog Japan's current system of flexible, high-quality, lean, low-cost manufacturing.

Agile manufacturing has developed into a movement called the Agile Manufacturing Forum (AMEF). AMEF is a collaborative movement supported by over 100 of the largest U.S. companies plus such national organizations as the National Center for Manufacturing Sciences (NCMS), the Microelectronics and Computer Technology Corporation (MCC), Sandia National Laboratories (SNL), Massachusetts Institute of Technology (MIT), the U.S. Department of Defense, the U.S. Department of Commerce, and numerous other organizations [8].

The focus of AMEF is a 25-year plan for erecting a high-technology infrastructure that can develop, design, manufacture and market high-quality, innovative, low-cost products quicker than competing industries in other areas such as Japan and Europe.

The foundations of accomplishing AMEF's objectives are advanced information technologies and communication, and the collaboration between corporations and support organizations through strategic alliances. The means of accomplishing AMEF's objectives are such techniques or approaches as concurrent engineering, electronic data interchange, benchmarking, design and product flexibility, cycle-time compression and time-based competing, and modular manufacturing.

The concept of concurrent engineering would be extended beyond the individual firm to alliance members. Two or more companies would collaborate on design and development of new products, thus pooling resources and avoiding unnecessary duplication. Electronic data interchange and computer-aided design (CAD) and computer-aided manufacturing (CAM) will be able to provide rapid communication between members of the concurrent engineering teams. Utilizing this approach will, it is hoped, enable the alliances to compress time significantly and bring new products to market faster than the competition.

Modular manufacturing is not a new concept, but it is expected to become a more widely practiced approach in the future. Modular manufacturing provides more potential for customization of products in response to customer demand. With the alliances there is also more potential for sharing modular systems in each alliance member's products. For instance, there is the potential in the automobile industry for more sharing of such major components as engines, drivetrains, braking systems, pollution control systems, and electronic systems.

The objective of all of AMEF's approaches is to lower cost, provide more variety, provide rapid response to new demands, raise quality and reliability to the highest level, and improve overall competitiveness to the alliance members.

There is, however, a potential problem to the AMEF approach. What about antitrust violations because of the close cooperation between competing firms? How will the competing firms maintain competitiveness for these products? Will there be sufficient competition to maintain each firm in a lean and active condition? These are important questions that need to be addressed by AMEF as it proceeds along its way of implementing agile manufacturing systems.

Adaptability in Strategic Alliances

Joint ventures or strategic alliances are an important vehicle for a company to enter a market in a foreign country, especially if the economic activity in the foreign country is tightly controlled by the government (as in mainland China) or if the economic structure of the country is difficult to penetrate (as in Japan). However, in recent years strategic alliances have become more and more common between corporations within a developed country or economy (within the United States or Europe) and also between corporations from different developed countries with the purpose of serving multiple countries.

The purpose of strategic alliances is seldom strictly economic (for economies of scale); more likely, it is to benefit from each others' technological, engineering, financial, or marketing strengths. The purpose is also frequently to get access to a new market, beat others to a new market, or attain flexibility.

An example of a strategic alliance that over the years has proven to be very successful is between Ford and Mazda. In the engineering area, Mazda designs the small cars and Ford designs the four-wheel drive vehicles. Both types of vehicles are then marketed and sold under Ford and Mazda brand names. In the manufacturing area, the two firms also share resources and produce vehicles that are sold under both the Ford and Mazda brand names. By sharing engineering and manufacturing, both firms can offer a broader array of vehicles than either one could alone. Both firms also benefit from each other's expertise in the design, development, manufacturing, and marketing areas. Violation of antitrust laws is a constant concern in the Ford-Mazda strategic alliance. But because Mazda is a Japanese firm and Ford is a U.S. firm, and joint marketing does not occur, the antitrust laws are not violated.

The Ford-Mazda strategic alliance can be viewed as a strategic alliance that has as its main purpose economies of scope through each firm's ability to offer a wider array of vehicles. However, there are also considerable technological benefits associated with the Ford-Mazda strategic alliance. Both firms share each other's engineering and manufacturing expertise [7, 9].

The success of any joint venture is highly dependent on the way it is structured. The most successful ventures are those in which the two partners bring equal strengths to the venture. Management of the joint venture usually works best when one of the partners takes control and responsibility, a condition to be agreed to prior to the formation of the venture. If both sides share in the management of a joint venture, it is almost certainly doomed to failure. In large joint ventures, the two partners may even set up a separate corporation with its own board of directors. For example, Dow Corning Inc. is a joint venture between Dow Chemical and Corning. Dow Corning has grown into a large corporation and is a member of the *Fortune* 500. Other joint venture partners include Merck and Johnson and Johnson; Merck and DuPont; Merck and A. B. Astra of Sweden; IBM, Siemens of Germany, and Toshiba of Japan; Corning and Siemens of Germany; Corning and Vitro of Mexico; Corning and Dow Chemical; Ford and Mazda of Japan; Microsoft and Apple; and General Motors and Toyota [9].

The most important aspect of strategic alliances is the flexibility inherent in them, in established ones as well as in those yet to be formed. These alliances provide management with the means to take advantage of opportunities, share risks, and remain viable, profitable, and competitive.

The Adaptive and Flexible Corporation

The successful corporation of the future will be adaptive and flexible, with a focus on the customer and the customer's needs and wants. For many decades, the successful corporation was one with a hierarchical management organization, focused on efficiency and economies of scale and with a vast marketing division to promote and sell its products. The organization was organized along functional lines, with each functional area operating somewhat independently and focused on its own interests. Control was exercised through strong financial controls but relatively weak controls in the critical areas that add value, such as quality, manufacturing, inventory, engineering, and product development.

The new adaptive and flexible corporation must be flexible to respond to changes in its industry, its industry structure, its customer base, its technology, and other critical areas that will determine its success or failure. Its focus will be on the customer and how to satisfy his or her actual needs and potential needs. In other words, the new corporation must anticipate the needs of the customer and respond to them by developing products and/or services to meet those new needs and wants.

The organization of the adaptive and flexible corporation will utilize teamwork and forge close cooperation between members of functional areas in cases where those functional areas still exist in their traditional formats. Teams will be flexible and changeable. They will be organized around tasks, activities, and projects. Activity or project management will in many cases replace the traditional functional area framework. Functional areas, where they still exist, will become service activities providing support and services to the activities and projects.

In the product development area, the focus will be on customers in global markets. Borders will gradually disappear, at least in terms of product development. This does not imply that products will be standardized for all global markets. Diversity is and will increasingly become a key requirement to remain competitive. Different cultures, different countries, different languages, and different tastes will require a wide variety of different modes of products for each market. But central focus on product development, design, and manufacture through project teams will ensure that response to market changes will be quick and thorough. The adaptive and flexible corporation will need to compress time, be agile, and respond to the changing needs and wants of its customers.

The new adaptive and flexible corporation will have to develop and maintain efficiencies of scope: the ability to deliver a wide variety of products or services to a constantly changing marketplace. Economies of scale will still be important in many high-volume markets, but economies of scale alone will not be sufficient to be competitive in the global marketplace of the future [3, 7].

An example of time-based competing with economies of scope instead of economies of scale is Wausau Paper Mills Company. Wausau found that to compete against larger competitors it needed to invest $600 million in new high-volume equipment. Instead, it decided to differentiate itself with its customers on the basis of speed of delivery of orders. Instead of several days or several weeks of lead time, it was able to focus on rapid response to customers' orders. Wausau quickly attained 24-hour delivery on 95% of its orders, thus becoming a competitor on time-based delivery. These rapid response times enabled Wausau's customers to reduce their inventories substantially, thus saving themselves substantial inventory holding costs. Through time-based competing, Wausau offset some of its cost disadvantages [2].

In the traditional hierarchical command and control structure inherent in many companies, managers become responsible to each other instead of to their customers. In the customer-driven company, the focus on the customer affects how management and employees think about their work, their responsibilities, and how they fit into the organization. The customer focus has provided a new focus, a focus that provides motivation to the employees and incentives to serve the customer and satisfy his or her needs.

To accomplish all of the above requires teamwork, focus on major activities and projects, continual focus on time compression, and focus on quality and durability of products and services.

Conclusions

This chapter has tried to paint a broad picture of the flexible and adaptive corporation of the future. Tomorrow's corporations must be flexible and adaptive to respond to changes in its environment, and they must be proactive by creating uncertainties that competitors find difficult to deal with or to which competitors cannot respond immediately [4].

What has not been adequately addressed is the fact that flexibility has costs associated with it. These costs must of course be borne by the corporation in order to be competitive. However, excessive flexibility may be unnecessarily costly and should be reduced or at least controlled. It is important to be aware that competitiveness in the future will not be solely based on flexibility, adaptiveness, and customer focus. Always of importance will be cost and the ability to be cost-competitive.

It is fairly clear that economies of scope are going to be increasingly important in the future. The ability to be flexible and adaptive will greatly assist the firm in attaining economies of scope. Above all, however, the firm must remain focused on the customer's needs and wants.

Discussion Questions

1. Describe and discuss operations flexibility.
2. Describe and discuss product design flexibility.
3. Develop an improved three-shift work schedule in comparison with the one shown in Table 18–1.
4. Describe the concept of an agile manufacturing system.
5. Why have Western manufacturing firms been slow in increasing their manufacturing plant utilization?
6. Explain why Japan's industry is a leader in operations flexibility.
7. Why is it so much more difficult for large organizations to be flexible and adaptable?
8. Explain why Japan's industry is a leader in design flexibility.
9. What are the roadblocks to AMEF's success?
10. Describe the adaptive and flexible corporation.
11. What are the flexibility benefits of Ford's strategic alliance with Mazda?
12. What are the flexibility benefits of General Motors' strategic alliance with Toyota?

References

1. Buell, Barbara, Robert D. Hof, and Gary McWilliams. "Hewlett-Packard Rethinks Itself." *Business Week,* April 1, 1991, 76–79.
2. Byrne, John A. "Paradigms for Postmodern Managers." *Business Week/Reinventing America,* 1992, 62–63.
3. Garvin, D. A. "Building a Learning Organization." *Harvard Business Review,* July-August 1993, 78–91.
4. Gerwin, Donald. "Manufacturing Flexibility: A Strategic Perspective." *Management Science,* 39(4), April 1993, 395–410.
5. Hamel, D., and C. Prahalad. "Strategic Intent." *Harvard Business Review,* May-June 1989, 69.
6. Hamel, D., and C. Prahalad. "Strategy as Stretch and Leverage." *Harvard Business Review,* March-April 1993, 75–84.
7. McGrath, M. E., and R. W. Hoole. "Manufacturing's New Economies of Scale." *Harvard Business Review,* May-June 1992, 94–102.
8. Port, Otis. "Moving Past the Assembly Line." *Business Week/Reinventing America,* 1992, 177–180.
9. Sherman, Stratford, "Are Strategic Alliances Working?" *Fortune,* September 21, 1992, 77–78.
10. Steward, Thomas A. "Brace for Japan's Hot New Strategy." *Fortune,* September 21, 1992, 61–74.
11. Treece, James B., and Patrick Oster. "General Motors Open All Night." *Business Week,* June 1, 1992, 82–83.
12. Woodruff, David. "A Dozen Motor Factories—Under One Roof." *Business Week,* November 10, 1989, 90–94.

Chapter nineteen

Reengineering Systems

Outline

Introduction
Pitfalls of Reengineering
Reengineering Management Information Systems
Reengineering in the Packaged Goods Transportation Industry
Reengineering at Ford Motor Company
Reengineering at IBM Credit Corporation
Reengineering at Boeing
Conclusions

Introduction

Reengineering by its simplest definition is radical redesign of work. This statement, of course, begs the question of how work can be or should be redesigned if it is to become more efficient and more effective. In this chapter, we will describe and illustrate how reengineering, applied to numerous tasks, operations, and projects, has provided significant if not radical benefits [1, 8].

In its simplest form, reengineering is based on the simple tenet that there is always a better way. Although the expression "a better way" or, even more strongly, "an optimum way" is often used, attaining the actual optimum approach is rather elusive and difficult to achieve. If you think you have found the optimum approach, someone else may come along and find a better way to do it. The best that can be attained is to find the best possible approach that can be attained at that time.

The illustrations in this chapter use two different approaches to accomplish reengineering. The most prominent approach is information technology. If you are going to invest in information technology, be sure that it is applied to a reengineered operations system or to entirely new operations that did not, and without information technology could not, exist.

The other approach is to do away with a functional organization and focus on the process, activity, or project. It has been found that in many reengineering projects, much wasted effort resides in the functional organization of work.

Finally, reengineering should also speed up the work to be accomplished. Time is valuable and important. A reengineered system should not only do the work more efficiently but also much more speedily [3, 4]. In other words, reengineering should be able to reduce the cycle time of a task, activity, operation, or project, and also make the task, activity, operation, or project more efficient and productive. ∎

PITFALLS OF REENGINEERING

The success stories of reengineering applications usually report large reductions in cost. Because of these success stories, managers contemplating a reengineering study and implementation frequently have unrealistic expectations.

A recent study of 20 reengineering projects found that 11 of the 20 projects provided less than 5% in performance improvement. But 6 of the remaining 9 achieved an average reduction in business-unit costs of 18% [5].

Relatively modest improvements result from reengineering studies because the reengineering is commonly applied only to small segments of the business unit. For instance, suppose an operating segment achieves a 50% cost reduction because of a major reengineering effort. The operating segment makes up only 10% of the overall business unit in terms of operating cost. Thus, the overall cost reduction to the business unit will amount to only 5% (50% of 10%). This scenario is by no means a story of a failed reengineering study. But management, if it had expectations that were too high, may have been disappointed with the overall results.

To counteract the potential disappointment, it may be advisable to do reengineering studies with more breadth. Alternatively, several segments of a business unit may need to be reengineered sequentially over a period of time. The latter approach may also be preferred because any reengineering study and implementation requires considerable effort and commitment of all staff members, especially top management.

REENGINEERING MANAGEMENT INFORMATION SYSTEMS

Massive amounts have been invested by organizations in computer and information systems over the last few decades. Yet many organizations have not seen significant productivity benefits from these massive investments. To be sure, one should not judge the newly installed information systems strictly on the basis of productivity improvements. Many other benefits are also derived from computer-based management information systems, such as higher-quality products or services, improved control over costs, better control over inventories, improved quality, and other improvements to the organization's operations. However, large investments in information technology are usually made with the expectation that efficiency and productivity improvements will be achieved.

One of the main reasons why information systems do not always produce significant cost reductions is that the information systems are installed to computerize existing operating systems. If the existing operating systems are inefficient to begin with, no amount of computerization will improve them. What is needed is a complete revamping of the traditional way of doing things before computerization is attempted. This approach is called reengineering.

An example of reengineering is Banc One's mortgage application review. The traditional mortgage application review involved a large amount of paper flow among many different departments. The reengineered approach for the mortgage application process involves a series of work cells analogous to cellular manufacturing, where machines are grouped together to form a manufacturing cell. Each of Banc One's work cells consists of 17 people who, using computers, convene electronically to work together on all aspects of a mortgage application. The mortgage applications are processed much more rapidly than before, and mortgages can be granted, or applications rejected, within days instead of weeks under the old system. What Banc One did was reengineer the mortgage application processing system prior to computerizing it. The combined application of reengineering and computer technology produced not only significant savings and improved productivity but also a significant improvement in performance measured on the basis of timeliness and customer satisfaction [10].

Another application of reengineering combined with information technology is Hallmark Cards' product design operations. The traditional way to design new products at Hallmark takes up to two years. Hallmark decided to reengineer its product design operations with a goal of completing a design in less than 12 months using small teams of employees from the art, design, and sales departments who were utilizing computerized databases for common electronic access by all team participants. Hallmark's reengineering approach is analogous to concurrent engineering at such companies as Boeing and Ford Motor Company. To obtain rapid feedback from customers, Hallmark is also equipping its 1700 major retailers with computer-based point-of-sale terminals to obtain feedback on which of Hallmark's products are selling well and which products are not selling well [10].

The two examples described above point out how important it is for firms to reengineer their operations before installing information technology. Just computerizing the traditional, inefficient way things were done in the past is no longer appropriate. If work can be computerized, it probably needs to be reengineered first.

REENGINEERING IN THE PACKAGED GOODS TRANSPORTATION INDUSTRY

With the rapid proliferation of just-in-time operations systems, it has become increasingly important to speed delivery of packaged goods from manufacturer to warehouse, from warehouse to wholesaler or retailer, from wholesaler to retailer, and from mail-order warehouse to customer. Speed of delivery is of the essence. Delays are unacceptable.

The pioneer in overnight small package delivery is Federal Express. It pioneered the airline hub small package delivery system, guaranteeing overnight delivery virtually everywhere in the United States. Federal Express was also the pioneer in using information technology for package tracking. Pickup and delivery drivers using handheld computers collect all data on the sender and addressee and then transfer that data to a central computer system. With this central computer system, the location of the package can be tracked and its location determined at any time while the package is in the Federal Express system.

A potential competitor for Federal Express was United Parcel Service (UPS), the world's largest medium-size package delivery organization, generating annual revenues in excess of $15 billion. The UPS operations were very efficient, but until the mid-1980s UPS had not considered information technology to be a necessary component of their operations. With Federal Express beginning to encroach on UPS's small package delivery and with Federal Express's ability to provide much better delivery times and package tracking, UPS decided it had to reengineer its operations to remain competitive in the last decade of this century. UPS decided to adopt a modified form of the Federal Express package tracking system, and it also decided to enter the airfreight business so it could compete with Federal Express and the Federal Express service imitators. The UPS investment in information technology to compete with Federal Express and other competitors was well over $1 billion, and the investment in a fleet of airfreight airliners amounted to several billion dollars [2].

Another large organization that viewed information technology as a competitive weapon was Wal-Mart, now the largest retailer in the world. While it was still smaller than its major competitor, Kmart, Wal-Mart decided to invest heavily in information technology to track its flow of products from suppliers to its warehouses and from its warehouses to its retail stores. Wal-mart also developed a point-of-sale tracking system that allowed it to keep track of how well each one of its products sold in all of its stores. This critical information allowed the purchasing department to increase or decrease orders quickly in response to demand changes. It also allowed Wal-Mart to provide demand information to 3800 vendors on a daily basis. With this information, both Wal-Mart and its 3800 vendors can keep inventories to a minimum and thus reduce manufacturing and distribution costs [2].

These examples show how large organizations such as Federal Express, United Parcel Service, and Wal-Mart reengineer their operations not just by using information technology to computerize existing operations but also by using information technology to speed up delivery and to provide information and services to suppliers and customers. The benefits of these examples of reengineering applications consist of improved information flow, more timely availability of products, availability of demand information on a timely basis, and improved productivity and efficiency.

REENGINEERING AT FORD MOTOR COMPANY

A classic case of reengineering involves Ford Motor Company's accounts payable department (see also Chapter 15). Before reengineering took place, the accounts payable department, before authorizing payments to vendors, would ensure that the invoices sent by Ford's vendors to its accounts payable department were for valid orders and the goods had actually been received by Ford. The process to validate each invoice was laborious, time-consuming, and complex. The validation process required the input of receiving departments, purchasing departments, and quality control departments. It involved orders, order modifications, order cancellations, rejects, returns, receipts, and just plain errors. To sort out all this information was time-consuming, costly, and frequently created conflicts between Ford and its vendors because of discrepancies and payment delays [6].

Ford's accounts payable department employed 500 people to perform this process. In its quest for cost reduction, Ford discovered that at its Japanese partner, Mazda, the entire accounts payable operation was handled by only 5 people. Mazda was much smaller than Ford, but not 100 times as small.

Ford studied the Mazda accounts payable operation and decided to adopt much of its structure. Under the new reengineered system, Ford authorizes payment to vendors in response to shipments received at receiving departments of Ford plants or other operations. The receiving department verifies that an order is outstanding for a shipment prior to acceptance of the shipment. If an order is outstanding, the receiving department authorizes payment to the vendor. If there is no order outstanding for the shipment, the shipment is refused.

Ford was able to reduce its accounts payable department staff from 500 people to 125 people. The same reengineering procedure was applied to other Ford divisions. At Ford's engine manufacturing division, accounts payable staff was reduced by 95% [6].

The Ford example is a dramatic one. It illustrates that we should never accept anything we do as absolutely necessary, or that it is the proper way to do it. There probably is a more efficient way of doing almost anything. The challenging task is to find out where reengineering can be applied and where it will produce dramatic or at least significant results.

Reengineering at IBM Credit Corporation

The basic thrust of reengineering is to break down the overall operations to be reengineered into separate processes or projects that can stand on their own and that can be identified as processes producing end products or services.

One such process was identified at IBM Credit Corporation. It consisted of a process that evaluated the credit of potential customers for IBM's products. A field salesperson who had made a sale for an IBM system or product would forward the information to IBM Credit for approval of the financing.

The traditional method used for checking the potential IBM customer's credit was handled by a number of different departments each doing its own check in sequential order. The checking process involved a credit check, determination of what interest rate to charge, and other checks. The overall process took anywhere from 6 days to 2 weeks as the credit application bounced from department to department. The lengthy process not only frustrated the ultimate customer but also the IBM field salesperson, because during the credit application process the customer could change his or her mind about the deal.

A detailed reengineering study revealed that the work done on the credit application by each department was rather routine and with proper computer support could be handled by one person in less than two hours. IBM Credit Corporation restructured (reengineered) its credit application process from a multifunctioning activity to a single process or project. Each credit application now goes directly to a deal structurer, who completes the entire credit application and the approval process, including the pricing (interest rate) process, in less than four hours. The IBM sales representative, at the time of the sale, can inform the client that the deal will be approved or rejected within four hours.

The IBM Credit Corporation example is one where reengineering is able to produce massive improvements. Turnaround time was reduced from an average of six days to four hours. Credit applications increased a hundredfold and were handled without the necessity of having to add additional employees.

REENGINEERING AT BOEING

Boeing has the reputation of being a highly efficient, high-technology, high-quality, progressive manufacturing firm. This reputation is largely based on its past performance and on its ability to build world-class airliners with quality and technology levels well ahead of its competitors.

What has been somewhat ignored is the fact that Boeing's competition is rather weak. The only American competitor Boeing faces is McDonnell-Douglas, and it competes only with two airplane models. On the international level, Boeing competes with Air Bus, a multinational European consortium. Air Bus is less efficient and has higher costs than Boeing but is able to compete with Boeing because it receives substantial subsidies from the governments in the countries in which Air Bus is located.

Another "phantom" competitor has entered the competitive arena. It is the fleet of aging, lower-technology airplanes being operated by the world's airlines. These aging airplanes are less efficient and more costly to operate, but cost much less on the used airliner market than the new, efficient, high-technology airplanes Boeing produces. Because airplanes have very long lives, the threat of aging airplanes competing with Boeing's new airliners will not soon disappear; in fact, as more airplanes are built and become part of the world's stock of airplanes, the threat of these aging airplanes will become even more prominent.

To overcome the threat of these aging airplanes, Boeing must reduce its new airplane cost by 25 to 30%. If the cost of new airliners can be reduced, airlines will find it advantageous to replace their older, inefficient airplanes with the new, high-technology airplanes. If Boeing can achieve its cost reduction target, it will, of course, also become a much stronger competitor in the world market for passenger and freight airplanes [9].

The question is, How can Boeing achieve such a massive reduction in its costs? The answer is that Boeing must utilize such techniques as reengineering, just-in-time operations, concurrent engineering, and cycle-time compression methods to achieve its targeted cost reductions by 1998.

The first areas Boeing is focusing its attention on are concurrent engineering and just-in-time inventory management. Boeing turns over its inventory about twice per year. It has over $8 billion in inventory in its commercial aircraft operations. In other industries, inventory turnovers of ten times per year are not unusual. Inventory holding costs are conservatively estimated at 25% per year, so a reduction of Boeing's inventory from $8 billion to $4 billion will produce a savings of $1 billion.

Boeing justifies its high inventory levels by the fact that no two airliners it builds are alike. Each airplane order has its unique requirements of interiors, cockpit configuration, and engines. Although this argument is used for holding large volumes of inventory, it can also be used for lowering inventories by using just-in-time inventory management approaches for all special-order airplanes manufactured. With a more organized and more coordinated vendor communication and training system, Boeing should be able to achieve the needed inventory reductions by 1998 or earlier.

Boeing's second reengineering target is the design engineering area. Boeing's traditional approach to designing an aircraft consists of three phases. The first step involves the design of the plane's shape and its components. The second step involves manufacturing engineering, which designs the manufacturing processes to build the airplane. The third step involves the tooling experts who design the tooling, machinery, and equipment needed. Each of the three steps essentially follows a process that is independent and sequential. Because the three groups involved in each process have little contact with each other, the overall engineering processes are inefficient and create cost-producing design problems at the second and third steps. The engineers at the first step essentially dictate to the engineers at the second step what they must do, whether feasible or not. In turn, engineers at the second step dictate to the engineers at the third step what they should do, again whether feasible or not. This traditional process is not rational, tends to produce unnecessary additional design costs, and also has the tendency to make it more difficult to produce quality products [9].

The new approach, called concurrent engineering, allows the three steps to be combined in one concurrent design process. Each engineering group is constantly aware of what the others are doing through computer-aided design databases accessible to all engineers at any one of the three engineering steps. Hence, if engineers at step 2 or 3 note that the design engineers at step 1 have decided on designs that will be difficult to build or for which tooling is difficult to design, they can let them know immediately. They can then offer advice on alternative design configurations. Similarly, engineers at the step 3 process can evaluate what engineers at step 2 propose.

This new concurrent engineering process, facilitated by modern computer-driven design and communication technology, is not only avoiding costly design mistakes and poor designs but is also speeding up the overall design process considerably. Boeing applied the new concurrent engineering design technology to the design of a cargo version of the Boeing 767. Boeing was able to reduce design cost by 25% and design time from 47 months to 33 months, a 30% reduction.

Computer-aided design methods have also been able to provide substantial savings through the elimination of costly mock-ups of new aircraft models and supporting systems. Under the new approach, three-dimensional configurations on computer screens are able to evaluate the designs as well as the mock-ups did under the traditional design methods.

The reengineering applied to inventory management and design engineering clearly will not produce enough savings by themselves to reduce Boeing's overall airplane manufacturing cost. Considerable additional process changes in the actual manufacture of the aircraft will have to generate the balance of the necessary savings [9].

Boeing's 1992 revenues amounted to about $30 billion. A 20% savings means that Boeing must slash about $6 billion of its 1992 cost. About $1 billion of that is attainable from just-in-time inventory management. Will Boeing be able to achieve the additional $5 billion of savings through other reengineering options? Time will tell.

Conclusions

The term *reengineering* evokes thoughts of machinery, equipment, and technology. To be sure, many applications of reengineering appear in the manufacturing and technology industries. But just as many, if not more, applications of reengineering appear in clerical-related or in white-collar operations.

The purpose of reengineering is improvement in efficiency, productivity, and quality of product or service. Other reengineering objectives are reduction of resources needed, compression of time to get things done, improved operations scheduling, and other performance factors [7].

The motivation for reengineering is usually the realization that there is a need to speed up the process, lower cost, improve productivity, and improve competitiveness. Ignoring the need for reengineering can be dangerous because it may result in poor cost and quality competitiveness and, if not corrected, may ultimately force the organization into bankruptcy.

Ideas for reengineering require creative thinking. One useful technique for setting a goal for reengineering is to do benchmarking. However, benchmarking an operation only allows you to keep up with the competition, not to leap ahead of it. Creative ideas provide the sources of reengineering applications that may put you ahead, and possibly way ahead, of the competition.

Reengineering is not a fad. It will be around, possibly in modified form, for a long time.

Discussion Questions

1. Define reengineering in your own words. Your definition should be about 50 words long.
2. Why should production or service operations be reengineered before major changes are made in their information systems?
3. Reengineer the mail delivery process of the U.S. Postal Service.
4. Reengineer the process of monthly bill paying by households for utilities, mortgage payments, lease payments, and so on.
5. How have package handling and delivery systems gone through major reengineering changes in recent years?
6. How has information technology enabled major changes in the package delivery industry?
7. Boeing has been able to cut its operating costs by about $1 billion per year by reducing its inventory by 50%. What other actions can it take to achieve other additional and substantial cost reductions?
8. Why did Boeing not implement its major reengineering years ago? Give several reasons and explanations.
9. Ford Motor Company plans a major restructuring (reengineering) of their vehicle design operations with a projected savings of several billion dollars

per year. Why was this change not made years ago? Give several reasons and explanations.
10. Reengineer the process of higher education. Focus on the undergraduate division of a college or university.

References

1. Byrne, John A. "Management's New Gurus." *Business Week,* August 31, 1992, 44–52.
2. Coy, Peter. "The New Realism in Office Systems." *Business Week,* June 15, 1992, 128–133.
3. Ehrbar, Al. "Reengineering Gives Firms New Efficiency, Workers the Pink Slips." *Wall Street Journal,* March 16, 1993, A1.
4. Fuller, J. B., J. O'Conor, and R. Rawhinson. "Tailored Logistics: The Next Advantage." *Harvard Business Review,* May-June 1993, 87–98.
5. Hall, G., J. Rosenthal, and J. Wade. "How to Make Reengineering Really Work." *Harvard Business Review,* November-December 1993, 119–131.
6. Hammer, M., and J. Champy. *Reengineering the Corporation.* HarperCollins, New York, 1993.
7. Hayes, R., and G. P. Pisano. "Beyond World-Class: The New Manufacturing Strategy," *Harvard Business Review,* January-February 1994, 77–86.
8. Stewart, T. A. "Reengineering—The New Hot Management Tool." *Fortune,* August 23, 1993, 41–48.
9. Tully, Shawn. "Can Boeing Reinvent Itself?" *Fortune,* March 8, 1993, 66–70.
10. Verity, John W., and Gary McWilliams. "Is It Time to Junk the Way You Use Your Computer?" *Business Week,* July 22, 1991, 66–69.

Chapter twenty

Concurrent Engineering and Integration of Functional Areas

Outline

Introduction
Alternative Means of Achieving Integration
The Traditional versus the Integrated Approach
Proposed Product Development Routing Integrated Approach
Proposed Frameworks for Integrating Functional Areas
The Three-Managerial-Level Approach to Functional Area Integration
Technical Aids—Flowchart and Cost Graph
Comparison of Organizational Alternatives and Alternative Tools and Processes
Implementation
Conclusions

Introduction

The typical organization chart in Western industries shows a functional format that creates considerable barriers to communications between the various functional areas. Although this has always been recognized as undesirable, it was not until about 10 years ago that it was realized that it affected a firm's competitiveness. In other words, the firm whose functional areas were not communicating with each other—that is, the firm whose functional areas were not integrated—was at a competitive disadvantage as compared with its integrated competitor. The term "integrated functional areas" as used here has been termed the "overlapping approach" by other authors [7]. It is in contrast to the traditional Western approach (the sequential approach).

Shapiro [11] was one of the early authors to question if marketing and manufacturing could coexist. He cited situations where lack of cooperation between the two functions could lead to open warfare. Especially dangerous is the situation where either one or the other becomes dominant. If marketing dominates, the firm could become so sales minded that manufacturing cannot operate effectively. Alternatively, the firm can become so manufacturing oriented that the needs of the customer are forgotten in the name of smooth operations. Top management must be alert to prevent conflict from developing.

In more recent years, the problem of conflict or separation between the product design and engineering function on the one hand and manufacturing and manufacturing process engineering on the other has become an issue of serious concern. To resolve the conflict, a process called concurrent engineering has been proposed. Tuttle [14] refers to this conflict as the "wall" between product design engineering and manufacturing engineering. The article reported on a conference in which five participants from Pitney Bowes, Dresser Industries, divisions of United Technologies, Perkin Elmer, and Avco Corporation reported on the degree of success they had attained in breaking down the wall. If the wall can be eliminated, concurrent engineering has been achieved. None of the five participants was totally satisfied that his or her company had eliminated all the barriers between product design engineers and the manufacturing process engineers. Each of the organizations was aware of the problem and was working on eliminating the barriers. Each also had bad experiences arising from inadequate attention being paid by product design engineers to the manufacturability of the product.

International Management [15] reported on the experience at Whirlpool Corporation, which in 1979 established procedures aimed at boosting productivity and quality by forcing product design engineers and manufacturing process engineers to work closely together. The results were significant. For a new generation of automatic washers and dryers, Whirlpool achieved a 33% reduction in the number of parts used in each model. More than 50% of the parts used were common across model lines, thus reducing both manufacturing cost and inventories. Significant savings were also achieved in reducing rejects and warranty costs.

The major impact of cooperation and communication between product design and engineering and manufacturing process engineering was reported by Mitchell [8] for Ford Motor Company's successful development and introduction of its Ford Taurus and Mercury Sable product lines, a triumph in the application of concurrent engineering. The approach Ford took was a "program management" approach, in which representatives from product planning, product design, product engineering, manufacturing process engineering, and manufacturing worked together as a group. The Ford Taurus and Mercury Sable automobiles achieved high sales and popularity among consumers.

Putnam [10] identified the lack of cooperation between critical functional areas as an organizational problem. Traditional concepts of departmental and functional organization are becoming obsolete. Current technology, launch lead time, and quality problems require teamwork not only between manufacturing and engineering but among other functions as well. Hence, the structural barriers that prevent team spirit from crossing departmental lines must be eliminated. Approaches such as Ford's must be experimented with to improve interdepartmental cooperation.

Hayes and Wheelwright [6], in their detailed review of what ails U.S. manufacturing, also refer to the need to integrate product design and process design, that is, implement concurrent engineering approaches.

Abita [1] has proposed the imposition of a development-production transition. He compared the transition phase to a prototype or pilot phase, and stated that he intended it to mean the transition phase from advanced product development to production.

Management must seriously consider how it can improve cooperation and communication among various functional areas. We will explore how this can be achieved. ■

Alternative Means of Achieving Integration

The objective that needs to be achieved is improved communication and cooperation among the various functional areas involved in developing a product, from the point of concept to delivery of the product to the customer. That is, concurrent engineering needs to be implemented [2, 5].

The following list presents five organizational alternatives. Each has the potential of promoting communication and cooperation among functional units.

1. *Joint Program Meetings.* Institute frequent joint program meetings with representatives from each affected functional area. The General Motors experience in this field was reported in an article in *Production* [13].
2. *Matrix organization.* Institute a matrix organization that allows a program manager's authority to cut across functional areas. Epperley [4] reported how this approach worked in the chemical industry.
3. *Sign-off stages.* Institute a system that requires each affected functional area to sign off all plans at various stages in the product design. Disagreements must be resolved by joint meetings.
4. *CAD/CAM.* Utilize a computer-aided design system and develop a database that can be checked constantly by the affected functional areas. Disagreements need to be communicated via the database and resolved by the affected functional areas. An article in *Production* [3] reported on the experience of one firm with CAD/CAM for functional integration.
5. *Program management.* Develop a unique system in which each design and development program is a separate organizational unit that is wholly responsible to a design and development manager. This group would consist of product design engineers, manufacturing process engineers, and manufacturing people. Mitchell [8] reports on Ford's program management approach to the Taurus automobile.

Below we will identify and explore a number of alternative tools or processes to improve communication and integrated action on the part of all participants. Following that, we will review how these alternative tools and processes relate to the alternative organizational means of achieving functional integration.

THE TRADITIONAL VERSUS THE INTEGRATED APPROACH

We will contrast the traditional or sequential approach, known as sequential engineering, with the proposed integrated or overlapping approach, known as concurrent engineering. To illustrate the contrast between the two approaches, we will identify the following functional areas, based on a product-oriented organization:

1. Product planning
2. Market research
3. Product styling
4. Product design
5. Product engineering
6. Prototype engineering
7. Manufacturing engineering
8. Manufacturing
9. Sourcing and suppliers
10. Marketing and promotion
11. Sales and distribution
12. Service engineering
13. Budgeting and finance

Figure 20–1 shows the functional areas organized in a traditional or sequential organization form. The product is moved from one functional area to the next when the first completes its work or has at least made considerable progress.

As shown, the product concept is developed by product planning, probably with input from marketing research. The product concept is then handed over to product styling, which develops the external appearance.

After styling, product design does the architectural work and the macro design. The product is then turned over to product engineering, which does the detailed design and engineering work on all parts, components, subassemblies, and final assembly of the product. Blueprints for the engineered product are then sent to prototype engineering, which builds the prototype and tests it to ensure that it is able to perform its intended function. Only then does manufacturing process engineering receive the detailed product design information so that it can begin the design and engineering for the manufacturing process. As the manufacturing process is being designed, manufacturing becomes involved in the acquisition and installation process of the machinery and equipment. When the machinery and the equipment are installed, the first production test run can begin, followed by full-scale manufacturing, albeit at a slow pace because of the learning curve effects.

The sourcing department and the suppliers become involved at the same time as manufacturing. The suppliers essentially function as a simultaneous

Figure 20–1
Traditional Product Development Routing

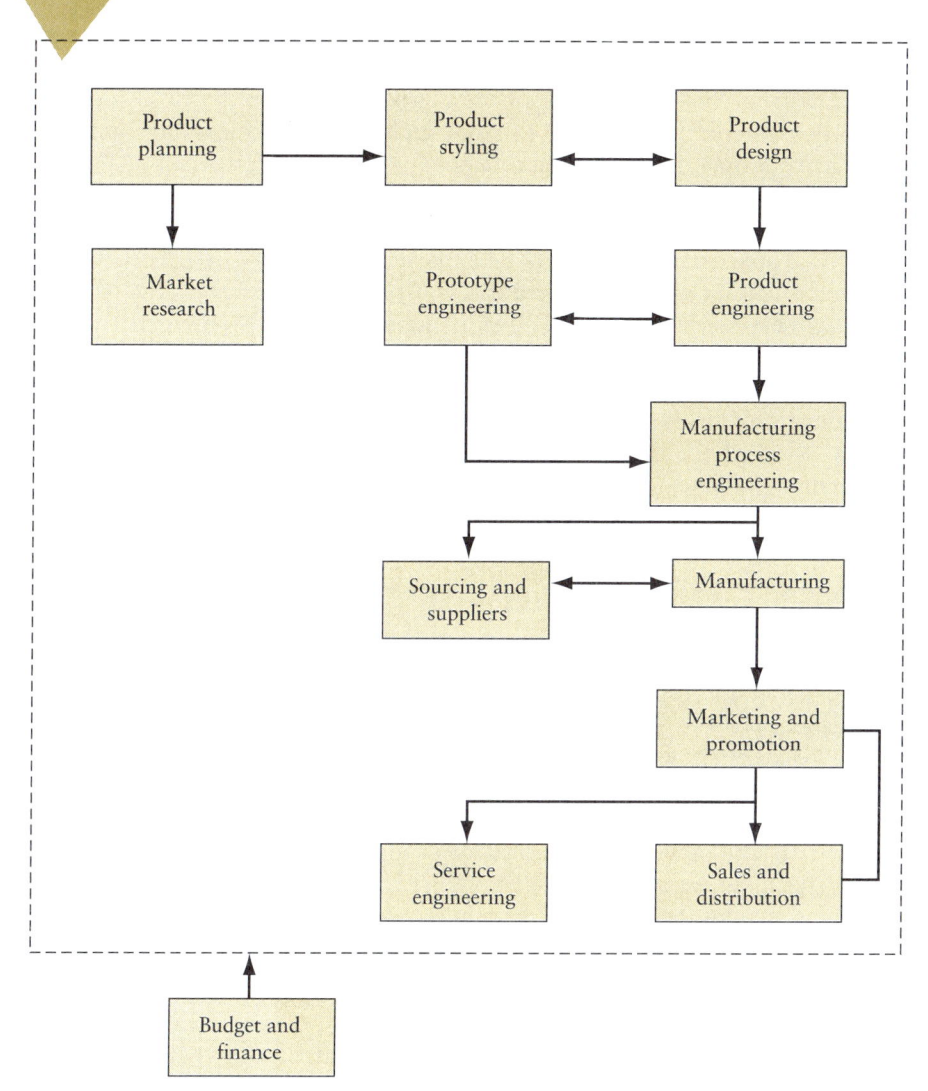

activity with manufacturing. As the product enters manufacturing, marketing and promotion will become involved to promote and begin advertising preparation. As the product is ready to hit the market, sales and distribution will become involved in the process. Finally, as the product is ready to enter into the customer's hand, the service engineering function will prepare for the product's servicing needs. Throughout this process, the budgeting and finance function will work with the affected functional areas.

This depiction of the product development process is, of course, oversimplified. In reality, there is considerable overlap between certain functional areas as the product development process moves through its cycle. However, the traditional process is undergoing considerable questioning and is in dire need of improvement.

Proposed Product Development Routing Integrated Approach

Concurrent engineering routing can take several forms, one of which is shown in Figure 20–2. In this approach there are still four multifunction groups of functional areas, but within each of these groups there will be close cooperation and communication. Among the four multifunction groups there will also be extensive cooperation, coordination, and integration. However, this form of integrated approach is not necessarily the recommended one. Each organization must assess its capabilities and needs, and on this basis it must develop an appropriate approach to functional area integration.

The proposed degree of cooperation, coordination, and integration between the departments is listed in Figure 20–3 in interaction matrix format. The degree of cooperation is measured in terms of high, medium, low, and insignificant.

So far, we have reviewed the traditional or sequential approach and a proposed integrated or overlapping approach to the product development routing process. Next we will look at how we can develop several frameworks along which functional integration can take place.

Proposed Frameworks for Integrating Functional Areas

Below we will look at several ways to integrate functional areas in order to increase communication and improve the product that will emerge from the development process.

Figure 20–4 shows a highly review-oriented product development procedure. It is based on two highly integrated multifunction groups. One group consists of product planning, product styling, marketing research, and budget and finance. The other group consists of product design, product engineering, manufacturing process engineering, manufacturing, sourcing, and suppliers and marketing. In addition, there will be numerous program reviews to ensure that

Figure 20–2
Proposed Integrated Product Development Routing (Concurrent Engineering)

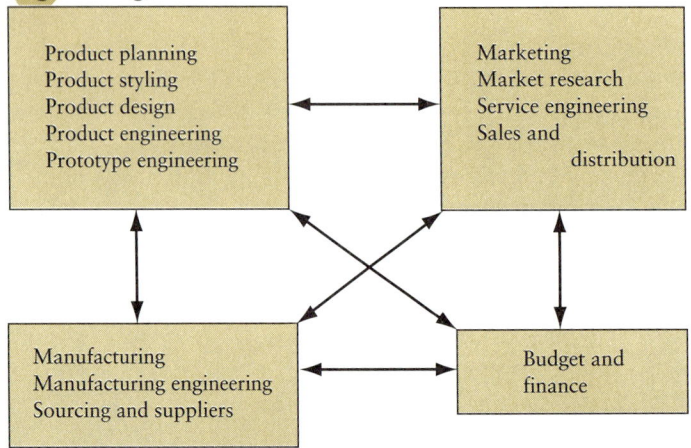

CONCURRENT ENGINEERING AND INTEGRATION OF FUNCTIONAL AREAS

Figure 20-3
Proposed Interaction Matrix for Product Development Routing

	PP	PS	BF	MK	MR	PD	ME	MF	SS	SE
PP		H	M	H	H	M	M	L	M	L
PS			L	H	H	H	M	L	L	I
BF				M	L	M	M	M	M	M
MK					H	M	M	H	L	H
MR						M	I	I	I	L
PD							H	H	H	H
ME								H	H	H
MF									H	H
SS										M
SE										

Cell identifiers—level of interaction

H =
M =
L =
I =

Legend:
- PP = product planning
- PS = product styling
- BF = budget and finance
- MK = marketing
- MR = market research
- PD = product design and product engineering (including prc
- ME = manufacturing engineering
- MF = manufacturing
- SS = sourcing and suppliers
- SE = service engineering

timely progress is made and that the product satisfies the needs of all functional area participants while simultaneously satisfying the initial product objectives. Program reviews occur after the new product concept approval, after product concept and product styling, after product design and initial manufacturing process design, after the prototype is built, after final product approval, and at the start of manufacturing.

This process depends heavily on program review. However, to function well it needs a high degree of cooperation, coordination, and integration within each multifunctional group, and especially in the second. To show the degree of cooperation, coordination, and integration we have prepared a typical milestone chart to show the times at which each functional area needs to be involved in the project. As you can see from Figure 20-5, there is a need for communication during nearly the entire product development period.

Figure 20–4
Proposed Product Development Flowchart

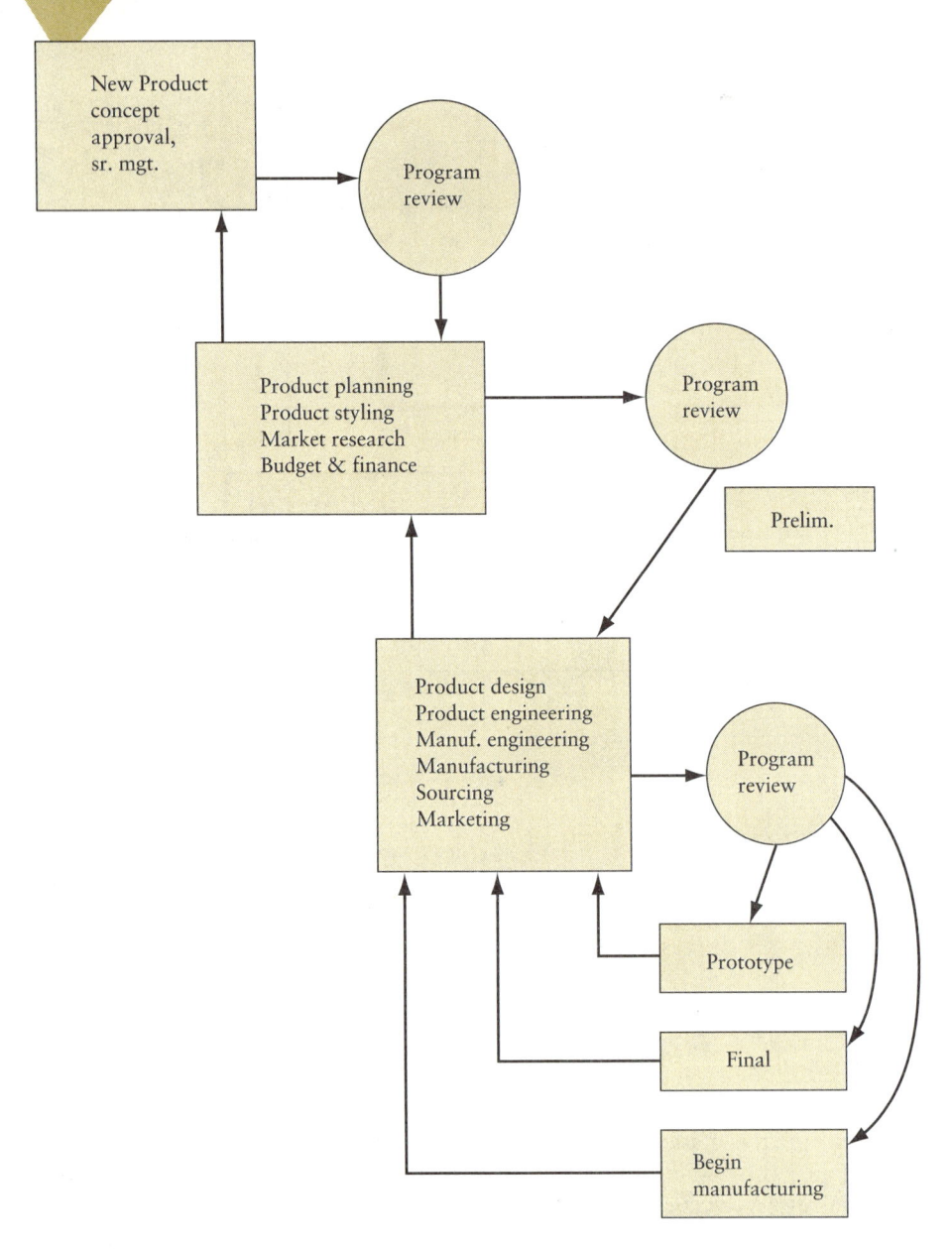

```
┌──────────────┐
│ New Product  │
│ concept      │         ╭──────────╮
│ approval,    │────────▶│ Program  │
│ sr. mgt.     │         │ review   │
└──────────────┘         ╰──────────╯
       ▲                      │
       │                      ▼
┌──────────────────┐        ╭──────────╮
│ Product planning │        │ Program  │
│ Product styling  │───────▶│ review   │
│ Market research  │        ╰──────────╯
│ Budget & finance │             │      ┌────────┐
└──────────────────┘             │      │ Prelim.│
       ▲                         │      └────────┘
       │                         ▼
┌───────────────────┐
│ Product design    │
│ Product engineering│       ╭──────────╮
│ Manuf. engineering│──────▶│ Program  │
│ Manufacturing     │        │ review   │
│ Sourcing          │        ╰──────────╯
│ Marketing         │             │
└───────────────────┘             ▼
   ▲    ▲    ▲              ┌──────────┐
   │    │    │              │Prototype │
   │    │    └──────────────└──────────┘
   │    │                   ┌──────────┐
   │    └───────────────────│  Final   │
   │                        └──────────┘
   │                        ┌──────────┐
   └────────────────────────│  Begin   │
                            │manufact. │
                            └──────────┘
```

The Three-Managerial-Level Approach to Functional Area Integration

A three-managerial-level approach to functional area integration is explored in Figure 20–6. The three managerial levels are within each functional area. The intent is to have strong communication and coordination links at the upper level, the vice president or equivalent level; the middle level, here identified as the manager level; and the lower level, here identified as the engineer level.

In addition to the three-managerial-level coordination and cooperation, there must be strong cooperation and coordination within each of the three

CONCURRENT ENGINEERING AND INTEGRATION OF FUNCTIONAL AREAS

Figure 20-5
Milestone Chart for Product Development Activities

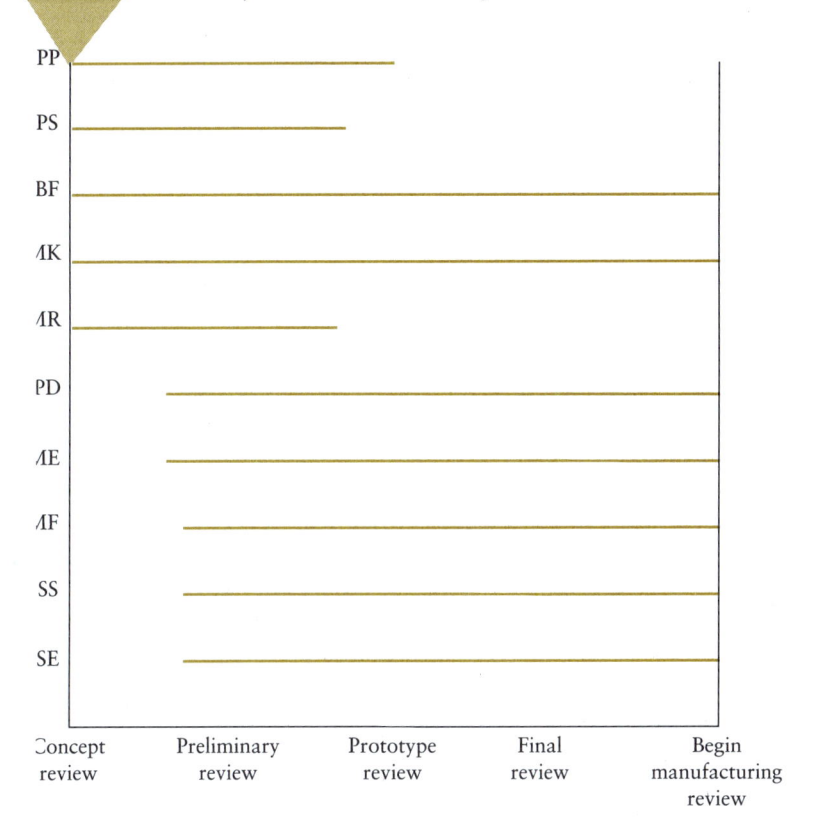

```
PP |─────────────────────────|
PS |───────────────|
BF |─────────────────────────────────────────|
MK |─────────────────────────────────────────|
MR |───────────────|
PD       |───────────────────────────────────|
ME       |───────────────────────────────────|
MF       |───────────────────────────────────|
SS       |───────────────────────────────────|
SE       |───────────────────────────────────|

   Concept   Preliminary   Prototype   Final     Begin
   review     review        review     review   manufacturing
                                                 review
```

multifunctional groups. The first multifunctional group consists of product planning, product styling, product design, and product engineering. The second group consists of manufacturing, manufacturing process engineering, and sourcing and suppliers. The third group consists of marketing, market research, and service engineering.

The three-managerial-level approach may be combined with the review-oriented approach to improve the degree of cooperation and communication in the product development process.

Technical Aids—Flowchart and Cost Graph

We now present two technical aids that may assist in the functional area integration process, that is, in concurrent engineering. The first aid is a network similar to that used in project planning (also called CPM/PERT project planning) as described by Stevenson [12]. The approach that suits the proposed functional integration processes we have discussed is illustrated in Figure 20-7.

The technical aid is essentially a flowchart. The arrows represent activities to be performed by the respective functional areas. The nodes represent connecting links between each of the activities. No activity can be started until the preceding activities have been completed. Hence, activity 1-2 must be com-

Figure 20-6
Multimanagerial Level Integration

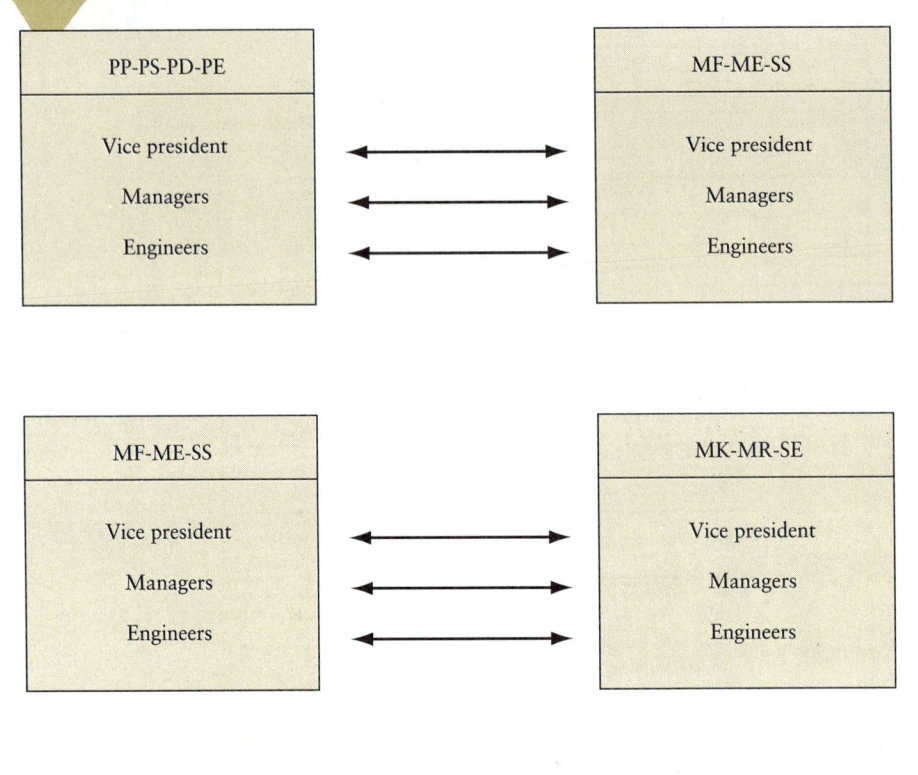

```
┌─────────────────────┐           ┌─────────────────────┐
│   PP-PS-PD-PE       │           │     MF-ME-SS        │
│                     │           │                     │
│   Vice president    │  ◄─────►  │   Vice president    │
│                     │           │                     │
│   Managers          │  ◄─────►  │   Managers          │
│                     │           │                     │
│   Engineers         │  ◄─────►  │   Engineers         │
└─────────────────────┘           └─────────────────────┘


┌─────────────────────┐           ┌─────────────────────┐
│     MF-ME-SS        │           │     MK-MR-SE        │
│                     │           │                     │
│   Vice president    │  ◄─────►  │   Vice president    │
│                     │           │                     │
│   Managers          │  ◄─────►  │   Managers          │
│                     │           │                     │
│   Engineers         │  ◄─────►  │   Engineers         │
└─────────────────────┘           └─────────────────────┘
```

Legend:
PP = product planning SE = service engineering
PS = product styling   PD = product design
PE = product engineering MF = manufacturing
ME = mfg. engineering SS = sourcing & suppliers
MK = marketing   MR = market research

pleted before activities 2-3, 2-5, and 2-4 can be started. Similarly, activities 2-3, 2-4, and 2-5 must be completed before activity 5-6 can be started. Activities 3-5 and 4-5, shown by dotted lines, are not really activities but only allow nodes 3, 4, and 5 to be connected.

Another technical aid is shown on Figure 20–8. It consists of a hypothetical situation in which costs, not necessarily monetary costs, behave as a function of the number of functional areas that are integrated. As the number of functional areas to be coordinated increases, costs of coordination also increase. However, there are considerable benefits of coordination. As the number of functional areas coordinated increases, the benefits, in terms of savings achieved, increase. Or, as shown on the exhibit, negative savings, or costs of not coordinating, decreases. Because the two costs move in opposite directions and are most likely nonlinear, there is a point at which a minimum total cost point is achieved. That minimum cost point is reached just slightly in excess of eight functional areas. The minimum total cost consists of the sum of the two costs. We must stress that the minimum cost point is hypothetical and is not based on empirical results; it is shown only for illustrative purposes.

CONCURRENT ENGINEERING AND INTEGRATION OF FUNCTIONAL AREAS

Figure 20-7
Product Development Process

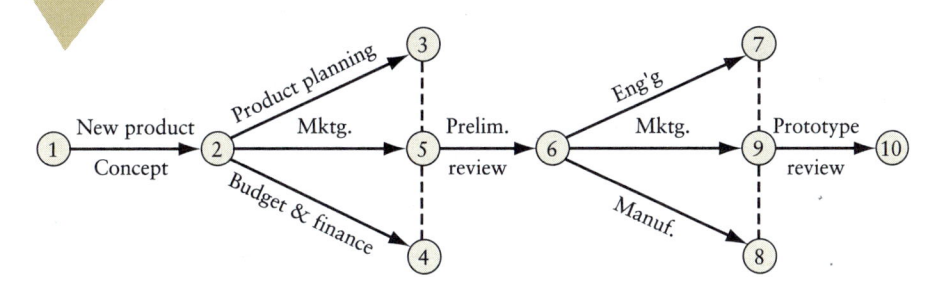

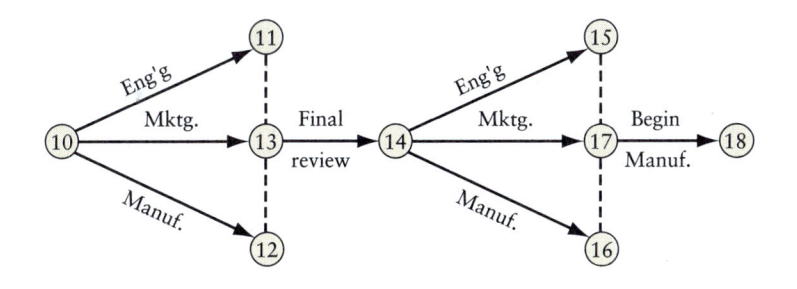

Figure 20-8
Cost Graph Approach for Product Development Process

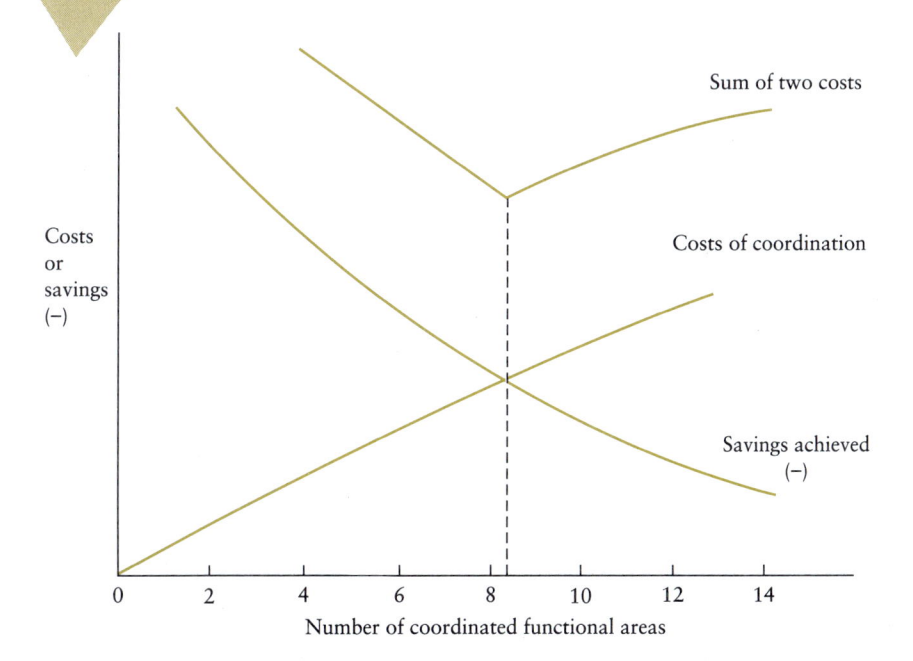

Table 20–1
Interaction Matrix for Achieving Integration

Organizational Alternatives	Alternative Tools and Processes				
	Integrated Approach	Review-Oriented Approach	Three-Managerial-Level Approach	Flow chart Approach	Cost Graph
1. Joint program meetings	H	M	H	M	L
2. Matrix organization	H	M	H	M	L
3. Sign-off stages	M	H	M	H	L
4. CAD/CAM	M	M	M	H	L
5. Program management	H	H	H	H	L

Likelihood of achieving integration: H = high level, M = medium level, L = low level.

COMPARISON OF ORGANIZATIONAL ALTERNATIVES AND ALTERNATIVE TOOLS AND PROCESSES

A comparison of the five organizational alternatives and the five alternative tools and processes is shown in Table 20–1. The comparison is made through the medium of an interaction matrix with the organizational alternatives shown on one axis and the five alternative tools and processes shown on the other.

To illustrate the comparison, we have identified that there is a high level of interaction between joint program meetings and the integrative approach. Another example shows that there is a medium level of interaction between sign-off stages and the three-managerial-level approach.

The assessments of the level of interaction between the organizational alternatives and the alternative tools and processes are estimated by the author. Other experts may very well have alternate views.

IMPLEMENTATION

Implementing functional area integration is not easy. It means changing practices and customs that have been in use for many years. However, competitive stress is an amazing motivator. We will present a number of case studies that illustrate how some firms have implemented the integration of product design and manufacturing process design.

It is important to point out that scale of operations is an important determinant of how easily integration of functional areas can be accomplished. In small-scale operations, functional integration is much easier to accomplish than in large-scale operations. As a result, you will find more anecdotes on successful functional integration from small-scale operations than from large-scale operations.

The classic older case of functional integration of engineering functions dates back about a decade and was "engineered" by General Electric's large appliance division. Through close cooperation of several engineering functions, standardization of components, and extensive use of plastic components, the cost to manufacture such appliances as dishwashers, washing machines, and refrigerators was reduced dramatically. Another classic and more recent case of functional integration of engineering functions is the National Cash Register case of designing a new checkout counter terminal. The lead time from start of design to product roll-out was only 22 months, and the new terminal had 85% fewer parts than its predecessor. The terminal could be assembled in one-quarter of the time it took to assemble its predecessor. Other successful applications of engineering integration were reported by American Telephone and Telegraph. The time required to redesign its main phone-switching computer was cut in half, from 3 years to 18 months. Deere and Company has been able to reduce its lead time for design and development of construction and forestry machinery by 60%, saving 30% of the previous development cost along the way [9].

These illustrations show the degree to which companies have been able to benefit from functional integration of their engineering departments, but they do not show in detail how this was done. For small-scale projects such as the National Cash Register case, it is feasible and desirable to merge the product design and manufacturing process design departments—in other words, use total integration. In large-scale operations such as Ford Motor Company, the program planning and control concept was used. Program planning and control requires a separate department with considerable authority to schedule, plan, and control all design and development activities across all functional areas of a particular project. This approach enables a firm to maintain separate product design and manufacturing process design departments, but the program planning and program control department is able to ensure maximum communication at all levels of the design and development phase. The program planning and control concept also allows participation by other directly affected functional areas, such as marketing, manufacturing, and financial control. In other words, the program planning and control approach enables large-scale operations to attain most of the benefits of total functional integration.

These examples show that functional area integration and especially engineering functions integration can be accomplished once firms decide to do so. The strongest motivating factor to implement functional integration is clearly the necessity to remain competitive in the national and international marketplace.

Conclusions

The point we may now want to raise is how the above proposed alternative tools or processes impact on the five organizational alternatives we proposed earlier in this chapter. The answer is that both the alternative tools and processes presented as well as the organizational alternatives provide management with a set of options to deal with the problem of functional area integration, known as concurrent engineering. There is little doubt that functional integration is necessary in order to stay competitive. How to functionally integrate, however, is a problem. We also stress the need for functional area integration for product development. There are numerous other processes in which functional areas are involved that require little or no functional integration, at least not in as many areas as in product development.

Finally, there are a number of additional requirements that must be met if functional area integration is to succeed. The requirements are top management support, proper organizational structure, appropriate management control system, effective incentive and merit system, encouragement by all management levels, and leadership by all management levels.

In other words, functional area integration needs strong top management support. The natural tendency for most functional areas is to concentrate on their own areas of concern. Having to cooperate and communicate with others is usually an additional burden. Hence, the organizational culture must be modified such that it stresses cooperation and communication in those areas, such as product development, where it is absolutely necessary.

Discussion Questions

1. In your own words, define concurrent engineering. Make your definition about 40 words long.
2. Five organizational alternatives are proposed to achieve functional integration. Discuss each one.
3. Group the 13 functional areas shown in Figure 20–1 into six groups consisting of design and product engineering, manufacturing engineering and manufacturing, purchasing and supplier relations, marketing and promotion, sales and service, and budgeting and finance. Explain your rationale for your grouping.
4. What changes in the levels of interaction would you make for the interaction matrix shown in Figure 20–3? Describe in detail.
5. Why are milestone charts such as the one proposed in Figure 20–5 important in major projects? Explain.
6. How would you describe the duties of a program manager on a major project? Identify at least six duties.

References

1. Abita, J. L. "Technology: Development to Production, Transactions on Engineering Management." *Institute of Electrical and Electronic Engineers*, EM-32(3), August 1985, 129–131.
2. Brown, W. B. "Leading the Way to Faster New Product Development." *Academy of Management Executive*, 7(1), February 1993, 36–47.
3. "CAD/CAM Stimulates Design/Production Teamwork." *Production*, May 1983, 68–70.
4. Epperley, W. Robert. "Matrix Management Can Work." *Chemtech*, November 1981, 664–667.

5. Garrett, R. W. "Eight Steps to Simultaneous Engineering." *Manufacturing Engineering,* 107(5), November 1990, 41.
6. Hayes, Robert H., and Steven C. Wheelwright. *Restoring Our Competitive Edge—Competing through Manufacturing,* pp. 197–228. Wiley, New York, 1984.
7. Imai, Kenichi, Jchijiro Monaka, and Hirotaka Jakeuchi. "Managing the New Product Development Process—How Japanese Companies Learn and Unlearn," in Kim B. Clark et al. (eds.), *The Uneasy Alliance.* Harvard Business School, Cambridge, MA, 1985.
8. Mitchell, Russell. "How Ford Hits the Bull's Eye with Taurus." *Business Week,* June 30, 1986, 69–70.
9. Port, Otis, Zachary Schiller, and Resa W. King. "A Smarter Way to Manufacture." *Business Week,* April 30, 1990, 110–117.
10. Putnam, Arnold O. "A Redesign for Engineering." *Harvard Business Review,* May-June 1985, 139–144.
11. Shapiro, Benson P. "Can Marketing and Manufacturing Coexist?" *Harvard Business Review,* September-October 1977, 104–114.
12. Stevenson, William J. *Production/Operations Management,* 2nd ed., pp. 630–648. Irwin, Homewood, IL, 1986.
13. "The General Motors Experience—Integrating New Products and Processes." *Production,* March 1986, 63–64.
14. Tuttle, Howard C. "Breaking the 'Wall' between Design and Manufacturing." *Production,* May 1983, 63–66.
15. "When Engineers Talk to Each Other—The Slow but Sure Payoff." *International Management,* July 1984, 26–27.

Source

Chapter 20 is a slightly modified version of Pegels, C. Carl, "Integrating Functional Areas for Improved Prodcutivity and Quality," *International Journal of Operations and Production Management,* Vol. 11, No. 3, 1991. Reprinted with permission.

Chapter twenty-one

Activity-Based Costing

Outline

Introduction
Activity-Based Costing
Activity-Based Costing in Different Industries
Allocating Costs in Flexible Manufacturing Systems
Conclusions

Introduction

Activity-based costing (ABC) is viewed by many as a magical way to solve many of the cost and managerial accounting problems in all types of operations, especially in manufacturing operations [1, 3]. Activity-based costing is not entirely new. It is essentially as much a philosophy as a technique to allocate all types of organizational overhead costs to the products being produced or the services being delivered. The philosophy of correct cost allocation is universally subscribed to by all cost or management accountants. The practice of correct cost allocation is, however, a different story.

Ever since the industrial revolution, direct labor has been by far the largest cost in producing products. As a result, a product costing method evolved that assigned all overhead costs to the various products of a firm on the basis of direct labor cost. In today's automated and machine-intensive manufacturing plants, direct labor is no longer the largest cost component for product manufacturing or service delivery. In some cases, direct labor is as low as 5%, and on average it is only 15% to 20%. Hence, the traditional cost allocation method, in which cost is allocated on the basis of direct labor, is no longer valid.

Allocating costs on the basis of other than direct labor is not as easy as it sounds. For instance, applying costs on the basis of other cost items, such as machine-hours used, electricity consumed, or space utilized, poses similar problems as the use of direct labor for cost allocation. What really needs to be done is a study of all overhead costs to determine how much of each overhead cost category is used or is necessary for each product or product category. For a company with many products, this is a difficult approach. Similar products can usually be grouped in product categories, but not always. Overhead costs can frequently be grouped in overhead cost categories, but again there are exceptions. And the exceptions frequently are important for correct cost allocation.

What is difficult to explain is how much additional work is required to break down overhead costs by products or product categories. Accountants must do detailed studies through interviews and other means of information and data collection methods to find out how overhead costs should be allocated in order to reflect true and accurate product costs. These detailed cost studies can be enormously time-consuming and must continue on an ongoing basis. Doing these internal and field studies are not activities that accountants typically do. They are usually more involved in using formulas for cost allocation.

With the advent and popularization of activity-based costing, there also has been a proliferation of computer-based software to assist in the ABC process. There is danger in depending too heavily on the software tools, however. They may be viewed as substitutes for doing detailed field and internal studies, but no software tool can, by itself, solve the activity-based costing problems of the firm. ■

ACTIVITY-BASED COSTING

There are numerous examples of how traditional cost allocation procedures such as those based on direct labor cost misallocate costs to products and activities.

Tektronix decided to use profit center performance from its manufacturing plants and from product lines within its plants. It found that in one of its plants all end products were unprofitable except for one that was used for internal use at one of its final assembly facilities [4]. Management threatened to shut down the plant unless better performance could be achieved for the unprofitable end products. A detailed cost study using activity-based costing revealed that the end products were profitable and the products produced for internal consumption were not profitable.

Tektronix then discovered that the unprofitable internal products were caused by internal operating conditions that were correctable. Up until that time, no attention had been paid to the bad internal operating conditions because the internal product line had shown that it was profitable, based on traditional accounting methods.

Traditional accounting methods have a tendency to overlook unnecessary and hidden costs. If profitability of a product line is achieved, the general behavioral pattern is to leave it alone. Attention is generally focused on unprofitable lines. This behavioral pattern is fine if true costs are attached to each product line. Activity-based costing assigns the costs of overhead functions to the products and services that use them. Although this seems to be an obvious and rational approach, it is commonly much easier to use traditional accounting methods, in which overhead costs are assigned on the basis of direct labor

ACTIVITY-BASED COSTING

Table 21–1
Manufacturing Costs for Three Products

	Products A	B	C	Total
Direct labor costs	$ 50	$200	$250	$ 500
Indirect labor costs	180	170	150	500
Materials and part	220	80	50	350
Total manufacturing cost	$450	$450	$450	$1350

hours. This approach works well if the product's cost is largely the result of direct labor. But in today's industries direct labor makes up only about 15% of product cost. Allocating 85% of other costs on the basis of 15% of total costs is bound to create potentially enormous misallocations of cost.

Table 21–1 provides a simplified illustration of the various options that exist for allocating cost. The three costs that are easy to allocate to a product consist of direct labor cost, indirect labor cost, and materials and parts cost. The illustration covers three different products [2].

Table 21–2 presents overhead allocation on the basis of direct labor cost. Total overhead costs for the three products combined amounts to $450. By allocating overhead costs on the basis of direct labor cost, we find for product A that the overhead cost allocation is ($50/$500) × $450 = $45. We then repeat the same calculation for products B and C. Based on the indicated revenue for each product, we find that product A provides a profit of $155, product B produces a loss of $30, and product C produces a profit of $25.

Table 21–3 presents overhead cost allocation on the basis of indirect labor cost. Overhead cost allocation on the basis of indirect labor provides for product

Table 21–2
Overhead Cost Allocation on the Basis of Direct Labor Cost

	Products A	B	C	Aggregate
Total manufacturing cost	$450	$450	$450	$1350
Overhead cost	45	180	225	450
Total cost	$495	$630	$675	$1800
Revenue	650	600	700	1950
Profit/(loss)	$155	($ 30)	$ 25	$ 150

All costs are unit costs.

Overhead cost is allocated for product A by taking the ratio of direct labor cost ($50) and aggregate direct labor cost ($500) and multiplying by the aggregate overhead cost of $450.

Table 21-3
Overhead Cost Allocation on the Basis of Indirect Labor Cost

	Products A	B	C	Aggregate
Total manufacturing cost	$450	$450	$450	$1350
Overhead cost	162	153	135	450
Total cost	$612	$603	$585	$1800
Revenue	650	600	700	1950
Profit/(loss)	$ 38	($3)	$115	$ 150

All costs are unit costs.

Overhead cost is allocated for product A by taking the ratio of indirect labor cost ($180) and aggregate indirect labor cost ($500) and multiplying by the aggregate overhead cost of $450.

A the overhead cost allocation ($180/$500) × $450 = $162. We then repeat the same calculation for products B and C. Based on the indicated revenues, we find that product A ($38) and product C ($115) are again profitable. Product C now has a $3 loss.

Table 21–4 presents overhead cost allocation on the basis of total manufacturing cost. Overhead allocation on the basis of total manufacturing cost provides for product A the overhead cost allocation ($450/$1350) × $450 = $150. We then repeat the same calculation for products B and C. Based on the indicated revenues, we again find that product A ($50) and product C ($100) are profitable. Product C is breakeven.

Table 21–5 presents overhead cost allocation on the basis of a detailed cost study. This detailed cost study reveals that overhead cost is largely attributed to

Table 21-4
Overhead Cost Allocation on the Basis of Total Manufacturing Cost

	Products A	B	C	Aggregate
Total manufacturing cost	$450	$450	$450	$1350
Overhead cost	150	150	150	450
Total cost	$600	$600	$600	$1800
Revenue	650	600	700	1950
Profit/(loss)	$ 50	$ 0	$100	$ 150

All costs are unit costs.

Overhead cost is allocated for product A by taking the ratio of total manufacturing cost ($450) and aggregate total manufacturing cost ($1350) and multiplying by the aggregate overhead cost of $450.

Table 21-5
Overhead Cost Allocation on the Basis of Actual Determined Cost

	Products A	B	C	Aggregate
Total manufacturing cost	$450	$450	$450	$1350
Overhead cost	300	100	50	450
Total cost	$750	$550	$500	$1800
Revenue	650	600	700	1950
Profit/(loss)	($100)	$ 50	$200	$ 150

All costs are unit costs.

Overhead cost is determined by a detailed study of actual overhead costs, and allocation is made accordingly.

product A ($350) and only to a minor extent to product B ($50) and product C ($50). Based on the indicated revenues, we now find that product A is generating a $100 loss, product B is profitable at $50, and product C is extremely profitable at $200.

This illustration clearly points out the necessity of allocating actual overhead costs instead of allocating overhead costs on the basis of some formula. Determining the actual overhead cost allocation for each product will require considerable additional work, but it is necessary, and the benefits justify the additional work.

ACTIVITY-BASED COSTING IN DIFFERENT INDUSTRIES

Both traditional and activity-based costing produce the same costs in the aggregate for a firm. What ABC is all about is the allocation of costs to individual products, individual components, subassemblies, parts, and activities that take place in any repetitive or occasional work operation.

Overhead costs are, of course, accounted for in traditional accounting systems, but in a much more aggregate form. For instance, in traditional accounting systems, budgets are prepared and actual costs are measured for the quality control department, the maintenance department, the personnel department, the janitorial department, the engineering department, the transportation department, the legal department, and the accounting department, and for other overhead activities or services such as water, electricity, gas, other fuels, advertising, and office supplies.

In other words, traditional accounting departments account for the costs of the firm in all areas. What traditional accounting has not done very well is allocate the numerous pockets of costs as outlined above to the products that are being produced.

One illustration of misallocating costs occurred in Advanced Micro Devices' (AMD) Penang plant in Malaysia. The Penang plant produces computer chips for world markets. Based on traditional accounting methods, AMD was under the impression that its most expensive chips cost no more than $2 each to assemble and test. The remaining higher-volume chips, constituting 60% of production volume, were estimated to cost $0.25 each. A detailed ABC approach revealed that its most expensive chips cost as much as $3.50 each to produce. The ABC study also showed that 54% of the Penang plant's chips cost as much as $0.75 to assemble and test. Armed with this valuable information, AMD's Penang plant was able to alter its production mix and adjust its prices to conform to the true costs of production [5].

Another illustration is the determination of the optimum number of wiring harnesses to produce for Chrysler's minivans. Wiring harnesses are assemblies of the vehicle's wiring under the instrument panel, in the engine compartment, or in the trunk. The wiring harness is complex; it looks like spaghetti because of the hundreds of wires involved. Different models of minivan use different combinations of wiring. Theoretically, it is possible to use only one wiring harness configuration. However, this approach produces excess wiring for most models, costs more, weighs more, and increases the chances of error when wiring connections are made.

Nine different departments at Chrysler—assembly, design engineering, purchasing, production engineering, accounting, and others—worked individually on the determination of the optimum number of wiring harness configurations. The assembly department preferred just one harness model; the design engineering group wanted nine different harness configurations for the multitude of different variations of the minivan. Activity-based costing came to the rescue to settle the debate. Activities related to the design, manufacture by supplier, shipping, stocking, inspection, and installation were evaluated and individually costed. The results of the ABC study showed that the optimum number of wiring harness configurations was two. Before the application of ABC, any so-called optimum number was not a true optimum number; it was suboptimum because it was based on one department's estimate of its costs and ignored costs incurred by others [5].

A third illustration involved a problem at General Electric Medical Information Systems (GEMIS). The 2500 technicians who maintain GEMIS' medical imaging systems requested laptop computers for easier access to maintenance manuals. Each service technician carried along 200 pounds of paper manuals in his or her vehicle, and during the actual servicing had to make frequent trips to get the appropriate manual. The technicians estimated that they spent 15% of their time shuttling back and forth between the maintenance job location and their vehicles. However, with traditional accounting methods it was difficult to justify the replacement of the manuals with the laptop computer and its database. ABC came to the rescue. Detailed activity cost analysis showed that substantial savings could be achieved by going to laptop computers. Not only were frequent work interruptions avoided; it was also discovered that the paper manuals were not always kept up to date by the technicians. With a centralized database, all laptop computers could be updated whenever necessary. Thus all maintenance information for all 2500 technicians was identical, and errors caused by outdated technical data were avoided. Switching to laptops raised productivity by 9% for GEMIS. This was equivalent to a $25 million increase in sales with no increase in cost [5].

These three examples clearly illustrate the value and importance of activity-based costing. Firms not switching to it run the risk of not identifying opportunities to save substantial costs, opportunities to alter product mix, and opportunities to develop profitable new products.

Allocating Costs in Flexible Manufacturing Systems

We now give a brief description of the problems associated with activity-based costing in flexible manufacturing systems. The most common form of a flexible manufacturing system is a manufacturing cell. The manufacturing cell consists of a number of numerically controlled machines that collectively perform all the operations on a part to prepare the part for use in a subassembly or component. These machines are flexible so that they can be quickly changed over to perform all the necessary operations on a part belonging to the same part family. In other words, a manufacturing cell can perform all or nearly all necessary machining and other operations on parts belonging to a common part family.

Because the costs incurred for operating manufacturing cells is virtually entirely indirect labor and overhead, the traditional method of using direct labor cost for allocation of overhead costs is not just inappropriate; it does not work.

In flexible manufacturing systems, we can consider two main cost categories: direct material cost and transformation cost. The components of transformation costs can be classified as follows:

1. Equipment depreciation expenses
2. Operating expenses (allocated by space utilized)
3. Operating expenses (allocated by machine center costs)
4. Service department expenses
5. Amortization expense of capitalized programming costs
6. Production setup expenses

The first four transformation cost components are allocated to a product on the basis of machine-hours used. The fifth transformation cost item is allocated to a product on the basis of number of units produced during a product's life. The sixth transformation cost item is allocated to a product on the basis of average number of units per lot processed through the work center for the particular product.

The benefit of the above approach is that once the basic calculations for the cost allocation model have been performed, it is relatively straightforward to arrive at the manufacturing unit cost. The derived manufacturing unit cost is based on true cost under normal operating conditions. This derived cost can be used for pricing, for determining product mix, and for general management purposes.

Appendix B illustrates the method of cost allocation for flexible manufacturing systems [6].

Conclusions

In this chapter we have analyzed, described, and illustrated activity-based costing methods. Activity-based costing is a philosophy and technique whose time has come. Firms that ignore the ABC approach, and instead continue to depend on traditional cost accounting methods, do so at their peril. Several illustrations were presented that showed how costly mistakes occur for firms that ignore ABC methods.

The use of computer-based software by itself is a dangerous alternative for solving the activity-based costing problems of a firm. What is needed is a restructuring of the cost and management accounting function, from cost calculation and determination to detailed cost studies of the internal and external activities of the firm, to determine how the overhead costs are produced and how they should be allocated to the products produced by the firm.

Discussion Questions

1. What is the primary objective of activity-based costing?
2. What would profit or loss for each of the three products in Table 21–1 be if overhead costs were allocated on the basis of material and parts utilized by each one of the three products?
3. Suppose indirect labor costs (Table 21–1) were allocated on the basis of direct labor costs. What would total manufacturing cost be for each one of the three products?
4. Based on question 3, what would profits for products A, B, and C be if the overhead cost allocation was based on total manufacturing cost?
5. Based on question 3, what would profits for products A, B, and C be if the overhead cost allocation was based on actual overhead costs?
6. Identify and describe the six components of transformation costs.
7. Explain why proper cost allocation is important to a product.

References

1. Cooper, R., and R. S. Kaplan. "Profit Priorities from Activity-Based Costing." *Harvard Business Review,* May-June 1991, 130–135.
2. Dhavale, Dileep G. "Product Costing in Flexible Manufacturing Systems." *Journal of Management Accounting Research,* Fall 1989, 66–88.
3. Drucker, Peter F. "We Need to Measure, Not Count." *Wall Street Journal,* April 13, 1993, A16.
4. Kelly, Kevin. "A Bean-Counter's Best Friend." *Business Week/Quality,* 1991, 42–43.
5. Paré, Terence P. "A New Tool for Managing Costs." *Fortune,* June 14, 1993, 124–129.
6. Turney, P. B. B. "Using Activity-Based Costing to Achieve Manufacturing Excellence," in B. J. Brinker (ed.), *Emerging Practices in Cost Management,* Warren Gorham Lamont, Boston, MA, 1991.

Part five

New Trends and Developments in Total Quality Management

Innovation in Product Design and Development	22
External Sourcing and Global Movements in Manufacturing	23
The Future of Total Quality Management	24

Introduction

The first chapter in this brief section covers innovation in product design and development. For firms to remain competitive, freshness and newness in designs of products and services is important. Designs not only need to be efficient and effective, but also attractive in terms of aesthetics.

The second chapter focuses on sourcing of components, supplies, and services by firms and organizations. Specialization requires that firms do considerable amounts of outsourcing. And outsourcing is frequently the most effective and efficient way to remain competitive. However, in core competence areas, firms must remain technically competent, and excessive outsourcing in core competence areas could weaken a firm.

The final chapter provides a review of total quality management and also takes a peek into the future of total quality management. Although the term total quality management may change, the improvement activities that make up total quality management will not soon disappear.

Chapter twenty-two

Innovation in Product Design and Development

Outline

Introduction
What Does Creativity Contribute to Innovation?
Innovation in Basic Products
Innovation—New Products
Innovation in Health Care Information Technology
Innovation in Biotechnology
Innovation in Digital Technology
Innovation in Computer Hardware and Software
Conclusions

Introduction

We will begin this chapter with two quotations that are relevant to the importance of innovation in the design and development of new products. Too much attention has been paid to the importance of marketing of existing products and to the marketing of modifications of existing products. The field of innovation and industrial design of new products has received insufficient attention in the popular press and especially in management education.

The first quote is from Seth Banks, manager of market communications and industrial design at General Electric Medical Systems: "Industrial design understands the needs of the customer and knits the customer into the fabric of our product development" [7]. To some extent, one can quibble with this statement. In essence, it asserts that the industrial designer knows more about what the customer wants than the customer. It also implies a belief that the industrial designer's creation will create a want or need in the buyer, a need that the buyer was not aware of.

The second quote is from Charles L. Jones, head of Industrial Design/Human Interface Strategy at Xerox Corporation: "Coupling the needs of users to advanced technologies is the key to our growth and survival" and "industrial design links the two" [7]. Jones essentially supports Banks' statement implicitly. We cannot leave it up to customers to communicate to us what their needs are because before a new product is designed and developed they may not be aware of these needs. Therefore, the industrial design team must come up with newly designed products, and marketing must market them.

The key message from these observations is that firms who solely depend on traditional marketing approaches and ignore innovation and industrial design do so at their peril. Marketing typically depends on consumer surveys, focus groups, and other statistical tools to determine what motivates the customer to buy certain products. Industrial design, on the other hand, takes an anthropological approach, using ethnographic tools such as observing human behavior and the work, play, and home environment of people to determine the potential needs and wants of the consumer [7, 14].

In this chapter we begin by taking a look at creativity. Then we review a number of areas of product innovation, including basic products, biotechnology, health care, digital technology, information technology, and computer hardware and software.

WHAT DOES CREATIVITY CONTRIBUTE TO INNOVATION?

What is creativity? Who possesses it, and who can use it to contribute to the organization? These are questions that are frequently asked. A more proper question is, How can the organization utilize the collective creativity of its employees to enhance the welfare and growth of the organization? Anderson [1] attempts to provide some answers to these questions, and we shall adapt some of his ideas below.

Everyone is born with creative talents. By creative talents we mean that people have ideas to do things differently, to create things, or to experiment. Few organizations have found ways to unlock the treasure trove of ideas in their employees' heads. We have suggestion boxes, quality and productivity improvement teams, and other ways to unlock ideas by individuals. But in nearly all cases the solicited ideas and suggestions are restricted to fairly narrow areas of an individual's job. Hence, only a small percentage of employees' creativity is ever solicited. And even if creative ideas were solicited from employees, how would an organization sift through them and select the worthy ones for feasibility testing? The screening process of most big organizations is highly likely to react negatively to the vast majority of new ideas, even if they have strong potential.

Because of this, many successful ideas are implemented by individuals working with others in fledgling organization. One example is the success of Apple Computer and its personal computer products. Another is Microsoft, which, because of Bill Gates' ideas and organizational talent, has become the dominant software organization in the world. Compaq and its marketing successes are notable. More recent successes in PC marketing are Dell computer and Gateway 2000. In other areas, we find the notable successes of Amway, with direct marketing through large amateur sales forces, and Wal-Mart, the retail giant that changed retailing through its use of information technology, communication technology, and high-volume purchasing-logistics strategies.

These examples show that creativity is not necessarily restricted to new products; it can be applied to methods of transacting business. Successful creative ideas improve competitiveness for firms through delivery of products and services that the customer wants at prices that are highly competitive. Hence, firms cannot ignore the creative potential of their employees. They must find ways to tap into that potential and then screen the generated ideas with care.

INNOVATION IN BASIC PRODUCTS

One of the more successful innovators and developers of basic products is Rubbermaid Inc. of Wooster, Ohio. With 1993 revenues around $2 billion, it is the largest manufacturer and marketer of housewares, toys, and commercial products. Its products are sold through supermarkets and hardware stores but are concentrated at the large-volume retailers such as Kmart and Wal-Mart.

Rubbermaid is a prolific generator of new products. It brings about 365 new products to market each year—a product a day. Its products are designed by about 50 entrepreneurial teams each responsible for a product category. Each team consists of a product manager, research and development engineers, and financial, sales, and marketing executives, usually totalling about five to seven members per team. The teams conceive their own products and then manage the entire design, development, marketing, and manufacturing introduction process until the product hits the marketplace. No test marketing is done, but the team members get heavily involved in the design, utility, shape, appearance, usefulness, and appeal of the product [9, 11].

One of the more successful products Rubbermaid brought to market in 1991 was a litter-free lunch pail for kids, set at a premium price in comparison with other lunch pails. The litter-free box had strong appeal to kids who are brought up not to litter, not to use paper or plastic wrappers, and not throw away cans or other containers. The litter-free lunch pail is attractively designed and has space for three plastic sealable containers that can be used for a drink, a sandwich, and a dessert. Because the containers are sealable there is no need for plastic or paper wrappers, so no waste is generated. When the kids return home, all that needs to be done is a quick wash of the sealable containers before the lunch pail can be used again.

The litter-free lunch pail, available in several attractive colors, was an immediate hit and quickly became a best-seller even though its price was well above the competitors' prices. Larger variations of the litter-free lunch pail were developed for adults [9].

Rubbermaid's ability to bring out a large volume of new products shows how a firm in a household products industry is able not only to remain competitive but also to show a healthy growth rate. It also shows how Rubbermaid uses an entrepreneurial team approach to decentralize its new product and design activities, and how entrepreneurial teams can use a form of concurrent engineering to design and develop new products.

Even in basic industries firms can continue to grow, but they must base their growth on creating and developing new and attractive products at a prolific and rapid rate.

Innovation—New Products

Bringing unique and original products to market is a key to success, and enables a firm to stay ahead of the competition.

The Industrial Designers Society of America holds an annual design contest for its members. The winners receive Industrial Design Excellence Awards (IDEA). In 1992, 753 designs were submitted, and 31 gold awards, 26 silver awards, and 34 bronze awards were given out. Nearly all major corporations make submissions including General Motors, IBM, Apple Computer, Chrysler, Boeing, Hewlett-Packard, NCR, and Nissan, as well as numerous smaller and less well-known corporations [8].

One particularly innovative and successful design was the Hewlett-Packard foldout jet printer. The compact printer fits in a space only half the size of its counter model twin. It is essentially a folded up printer for use by traveling PC notebook users who want to print out reports while on the road. The foldout printer is easy to pack, is attractive, and is easy to use. It uses a simple-to-use paper feeder that takes up little space. It found an unanticipated use in offices where desk space is at a minimum and a printer is only used occasionally. Sales in Japan, where office space for employees is typically more limited, have been surprisingly strong. When the printer is not in use, it can be stored in a drawer [3].

Another award winner is a thermal electric grill designed for people who do not like to use charcoal or gas. It is built by Thermos Company and designed by Fitch Inc. The thermal grill has an attractive appearance, and it requires little electricity because the heat is captured by vacuum-insulation technology developed by Thermos. A domed lid seals in heat, moisture, and flavor. The grill, because of its insulation, is cool to the touch and can be used inside or outside [4].

A third design award winner is the Bioject. The Bioject gives injections without using hypodermic needles. The handheld device uses compressed carbon dioxide to shoot vaccines through the skin, making administration of through-the-skin medications safer, quicker, less painful, and less intimidating. Bioject of Portland, Oregon, developed and (over time) improved the device. To improve its appearance and appeal to customers, Bioject used the industrial design firm Ziba Design of Portland to design the external appearance and other features. Bioject engineers worked with Ziba Design's designers in a concurrent engineering way to bring the product to market [15].

The above are three typical IDEA design award winners. In each case industrial designers worked with design engineers and others in a concurrent engineering fashion to develop new, innovative, and successful products. These products either supplemented older, less effective products or are original applications to areas previously unserved by a product.

Innovation in Health Care Information Technology

One of the most information-laden industries is the health care sector, and one specific area in that industry is the storage and maintenance of medical records. A patient's medical record typically contains a patient's health status and health care record. These records have largely been kept in handwritten, frequently illegible, format. With patients moving from provider to provider and records not being transferred along with them, there is virtually no complete medical record around for any one person.

If the medical information for a person could be recorded and stored in digital format over a patient's lifetime since birth, the accumulated history would be extremely valuable to the health care provider in diagnosing illnesses and prescribing medications and therapies. The accumulated databases would also be extremely valuable for doing research studies on health status, treatments, diseases, and other aspects of health.

One system that is trying to make a beginning at computerizing patient medical records is the Inter Practice system. The system computerizes medical records so that they are instantly available to a health care provider. The Inter Practice system is being used in Health Maintenance Organizations (HMO), organizations that not only insure patients for health care but also provide a complete array of medical services. The Inter Practice system, as used in an HMO or in a medical clinic, automatically sends prescriptions to the pharmacy, relays orders for tests or x-rays to the laboratory or x-ray department, records test results into the patient's electronic record, and triggers the billing system, thus reducing clerical intervention with its associated costs and potential for errors [6].

The Inter Practice system also contains a diagnostic tool. If the health care provider finds symptoms that are difficult to relate to a specific diagnosis, the computer will make diagnostic suggestions. The diagnostic suggestions are presented through a menu on the computer screen. The computer system will suggest treatment guidelines, tests, or medications.

A home version of the Inter Practice system has also been developed. As a patient enters symptoms into a personal computer connected to the Inter Practice system, he or she is asked additional questions by the computer, and informed by the computer whether to use a home remedy or to go and see a health care provider. As the patient arrives at the HMO or at the medical clinic, the health care provider will already know the patient's symptoms and will thus need to spend less time with him or her [6].

The benefit of the Inter Practice system is that it provides an ongoing medical record for the patient. And by involving the patient in the process of recording his or her symptoms, more information will potentially be gathered than by a direct doctor-patient interview.

The Inter Practice system is an initial model of a patient medical record and diagnostic system. Other systems will be developed in the future with a variety of potential extensions. The potential for better medical care is enormous. Substantial benefits will be derived from such systems in the form of more productive medical care systems that will be able to provide a higher quality of care because of more comprehensive medical information availability.

INNOVATION IN BIOTECHNOLOGY

When we discuss topics such as innovation, we cannot exclude the biotechnology sector. Although biotechnology has made waves largely by generating research and development money, the products that have emerged from the biotechnology industry so far are few. Yet some drugs, several superior vaccines, and more accurate diagnostic tests are generating revenues in excess of $6 billion in annual worldwide sales [2].

However, the relatively small current output will soon grow to a substantial industry. Over 100 new medical biotechnology products are in advanced stages of development and will soon come to the marketplace.

The medical biotechnology market is not the only one that will fuel the biotechnology industry. The ability to alter plants to produce fruits, vegetables, and grains of better quality and greater abundance will become a huge revenue-generating industry.

As is now being done with plants, the biotechnology industry will soon be able to alter animals that provide us with meat, milk, eggs, and other products. These changes will improve quality and productivity, thus lowering costs.

Control of insects and diseases that adversely affect human, animal, and plant life in the future will not have to depend on poisons with their devastating side effects. Biotechnology will be able to control many if not all of the adverse effects.

Finally, pollution has devastated many environments in which human, animal, and plant life exist. Biotechnology promises to control pollution, and to reverse the harmful effects of past pollution.

In combination the biotechnology markets promise to generate huge revenues and create employment, and they also promise to significantly improve our environment, health, and standard of living. The latter is especially important for the 76% of the world's population that currently lives in poverty.

INNOVATION IN DIGITAL TECHNOLOGY

The most explosive area in innovation during the next 10 or 20 years will be the area of digital technology as it is extended from computers to sound, video, and communications. By transforming electronic sound or video signals to digital signals, speed, volume, capacity, and quality of transmission can be vastly improved. For instance, the coaxial cable that now carries TV signals has the capacity, or bandwidth, to move one billion bits of data per second. This capacity is enough to transmit the entire *Encyclopaedia Britannica* in about two seconds. Over regular telephone lines, the same volume of material would take 17 minutes to be transmitted [12].

This example illustrates how much potential there is for transmitting virtually any type and any amount of information from a central distribution source to satellite locations such as the home or office.

Another area of potential expansion is the ability to compress data so that they are instantly accessible to the user. Apple Computer is working on a handheld system that will put all maintenance and engineering specifications for a Boeing 747 in the hands of a maintenance worker or engineer. The equivalent paper documents for this information now take up 10 feet of shelf space [12]. A related use would be the entire *Encyclopaedia Britannica* loaded on a similar handheld or book-size computer so it is instantly accessible to the student whether he or she is at home, on the bus, or in class.

The most prominent product, because it received so much publicity, is the personal data assistant (PDA) developed by Apple and named Newton. It is a book-size device measuring 6 × 8 inches. It uses liquid crystal display technology and is built by Sharp Electronics in Japan using Apple's software. It has no keyboard because it is programmed to recognize handwritten printing. It can also transmit written or sketched material, similar to a fax machine. Newton understands certain key words programmed in by the user, such as "fax to John," and is also able to receive data from other computers via a cellular modem [10].

Sharp is planning to bring out its own version of Newton using Apple-licensed software. Other manufacturers are also working on similar systems.

Another digital electronic product that will appear on the market during the next few years is interactive television. It will select which of up to 500 channels you should watch based on your choice of such key words as game show, western movie, entertainment news, talk show, current news, weather, and so on. Eventually, for a price, you will be able to select your own movie from a huge library that far exceeds what is available now in your video rental store. It will be downloaded and stored in the memory of your TV set in less than a second, and you will then be able to watch it at your leisure.

New digital technology will not only improve the sound of your music but will also mimic the music source location, whether it is a concert hall, a large auditorium, or an outdoor theatre. Optional video enhancements will accompany the music.

The most extensive changes will occur in the educational field. Books as we know them will gradually be replaced by handheld, book-size, computer-based teaching materials. The video screens will not only show the text, tables, and graphics of current textbooks but also will contain video versions of the material being studied. For instance, a history book will provide video clips of battles, demonstrations, speeches, parades, and so on. A book on production management will show videos of manufacturing, shipping, warehousing, wholesaling, maintenance, operations, and retailing. At the elementary school level, learning to read, write, and do arithmetic will be brought alive by creative and interactive media.

Another significant development will be improvement in ease of use of digital electronic devices. The user-friendliness of most computer-based digital products, including VCRs, electric appliances, and CD players, is in many cases deplorable or nonexistent. Instructions are too lengthy, too difficult, or too confusing to most users. User-friendliness has taken a backseat in the development phase of most digital and electronics-based products. The reason this has occurred is not because these products cannot be made user-friendly, but because the developers are so familiar with the devices that they tend to ignore the needs and desires of the end user. User-friendliness takes additional work and expense on the part of the developers, but the end user is usually willing to pay for it.

INNOVATION IN COMPUTER HARDWARE AND SOFTWARE

Innovations constantly occur in all industries, but probably no industry produces more innovative products than the computer hardware and software industry. A listing of innovative products recently highlighted by *Fortune* [5, 13] will be discussed below.

The first product is from Apple Computer. It consists of a powerful laptop computer that can be inserted into what Apple calls a Duo Dock, which includes a full-size color monitor, an expanded keyboard, a laser printer, and a slot into which the laptop can be inserted. The laptop then becomes a full-fledged desktop computer. The combined package is called the Macintosh PowerBook Duo. It is an ideal solution for those people who need to carry a laptop and who also need a desktop computer. The Duo's best feature is that the need for transferring files from desktop to laptop or vice versa is done automatically.

Another innovative hardware product is Intel's Pentium computer chip. It is one of the densest, most complex chips ever made. It carries 3.1 million transistors and is able to do more than 100 million instructions per second. It is as fast as a modern mainframe and is compatible with the software written for PCs that use earlier versions of Intel chips.

Sharp's Pen-Based Wizard is another innovative and specialized product. It is a type of personal organizer and telephone book. It can hold 2000 addresses or short memos, and its memory capacity is expandable with memory cards. The Wizard is able to communicate with printers, on-line data services, PCs, and other Wizards. Because of these and other features, it is widely used by salespeople who need access to databases and who need to keep notes during their daily calls and other activities. It essentially provides a limited set of services normally provided by a PC, but at a much lower cost.

A software product that has received a lot of attention is Lotus Notes. It enables large groups of users in a company to collaborate on projects. The users share access to common files, and Lotus Notes keeps the information up to date in the network. Documents can be created, revised, and exchanged without the need for face-to-face meetings. Lotus Notes provides opportunities for many people in the organization to be involved in the same project, or at least to be informed about the status of the project. It is, therefore, a medium for concurrent engineering, at least for small-scale projects not requiring the need of computer-aided design.

The four illustrations above show innovative products. Each has had wide impact on the way computers are used to organize work, transmit information, and assist in doing daily work in the information age.

CONCLUSIONS

In this chapter we have explored the major contributions made to the health and growth of corporations by the design and development of new and often radically different products.

Consumers' wants and needs are seemingly insatiable. As long as the means are available to acquire new products, they will be purchased. New product development, especially new products that improve productivity, raise the standard of living in those societies using them. It is only through increased standards of living of the world's population that demand for new products will continue unabated.

Three areas in which rapid and possibly explosive growth of new products will occur are digital technology, information technology, and biotechnology. These three areas have the potential to substantially enhance the quality of life, reduce environmental pollution, and increase the health and welfare of the population on our planet.

Discussion Questions

1. Describe the two different approaches used by marketing and industrial design in the development of new products.
2. Would you want to combine marketing and industrial design in one department? Why or why not?
3. Discuss how creativity of employees can be utilized and managed in the organization.
4. The information highway promises to provide a whole array of new products and services in the future. Use your creativity to come up with at least three products or services that can become available in the home.
5. Visit the showrooms of two competitive automobile dealers and inspect the interiors of two comparable automobiles—one at each dealer. Identify features that make one stand out in relation to the other. Describe your findings.
6. What kinds of innovative products will be developed in the future to improve the efficiency and effectiveness of medical care and health care?
7. Digital technology holds great promise for the future. Describe how digital technology will affect libraries, elementary education, and high school education.
8. Develop an idea for a potential new innovative product for which a market may exist.

References

1. Anderson, J. V. "Weirder than Fiction: The Reality and Myths of Creativity." *Academy of Management Executive*, 6(4), November 1992, 40–47.
2. Hamilton, Joan. "Mutating into a Second Era." *Business Week/Reinventing America*, 1992, 175.
3. Hof, Robert D. "A Fold-Out Printer." *Business Week*, June 7, 1993, 61.
4. Jones, Sandra. "The Cleaner Patio Sizzler." *Business Week*, June 7, 1993, 61.
5. Luscombe, Belinda. "Products that Make Markets." *Fortune*, June 14, 1993, 82–84.
6. Magnet, Myron. "Who's Winning the Information Revolution?" *Fortune*, November 30, 1992, 110–117.
7. Nussbaum, Bruce. "Hot New Products." *Business Week*, June 7, 1993, 54–57.
8. Nussbaum, Bruce. "Winners—The Best New Designs of the Year." *Business Week*, June 7, 1993, 58–59.
9. Rebello, Kathy. "Apple's Daring Leap into the All-Digital Future." *Business Week*, May 25, 1992, 120–122.
10. Reitman, Valerie. "Rubbermaid Turns Up Plenty of Profit in the Mundane." *Wall Street Journal*, June 11, 1991, B6.
11. Schiller, Zachary. "At Rubbermaid, Little Things Mean a Lot." *Business Week*, November 11, 1991, 126.
12. Schwartz, Evan I. "Your Digital Future." *Business Week*, September 7, 1992, 56–61.
13. Sherman, Startford. "The New Computer Revolution." *Fortune*, June 14, 1993, 56–80.
14. Taylor, W. "The Business of Innovation." *Harvard Business Review*, March-April 1990, 102.
15. Yang, Dori Jones. "A Shot in the Arm for Sales." *Business Week*, June 7, 1993, 64.

Chapter twenty-three

External Sourcing and Global Movements in Manufacturing

Outline

Introduction
The Pros and Cons of Outsourcing
Local Sourcing by Japanese Transplants in the United States
Reducing the Number of Supplier Firms
High Cost of German Production
High Quality Level in Mexican Automobile Plants
Conclusions

Introduction

In this chapter we will explore the pros and cons of outsourcing, including when it is desirable to outsource and when it is not. In evaluating this question, we can no longer look at strictly local outsourcing; we must also consider global sourcing. For instance, for components used in electronic and computer products, the source is usually located in Japan or some other Asian country. Hence, when we evaluate the decision of whether or not to outsource, we also implicitly might be making a decision of whether or not to import the component in question from abroad.

If the question were asked, To which country are a lot of manufacturing plants moving? most people would probably reply correctly: to Mexico. But if the question were asked, Which is potentially the most explosive market for the developed industrial world? not many people would answer Mexico.

According to Mexican economists, the potential of Mexico's per capita income quintupling in the next decade is not farfetched. At present, Mexican manufacturing hourly wages average about $2.50, compared with double that figure in Hong Kong, Singapore, and Taiwan. The U.S. hourly manufacturing wage is about $17, and the German average manufacturing wage is about $25. Needless to say, Mexico appears mighty attractive to serve the huge U.S. and Canadian markets as well as the growing

Mexican market. Not only are wages low in Mexico, but the young labor market is easily trainable and training is not expensive.

This is creating problems for manufacturing plants in Germany, the United States, Canada, Japan, France, and other countries where labor costs are high. Manufacturers in these countries are evaluating their worldwide operations to determine where to manufacture and source their parts, components, and subassemblies.

Below we will look at outsourcing in general, at the manufacturing success in Mexico, at Germany's high-cost manufacturing problems, and at the restructuring of outsourcing practices.

The Pros and Cons of Outsourcing

Whether to outsource or not has been heavily debated in the popular business press for the past few years. There have been concerns about the hollowing of the corporation. By definition, the hollowed corporation only does assembly and depends on supplier firms for all of its components.

The problem with using outsourcing is the type of outsourcing a firm uses. If a firm with a high-technology product outsources all components and has its suppliers do all technological development of the component, the product firm will soon be competing against its suppliers for the same final product or depending on the supplier for the product and the product's development. This will place the suppliers in a strong bargaining position and will lower the product firm's competitive position. In other words, product firms that turn much or most technological product development and responsibility to supplier firms may lose competitive advantage in the marketplace.

An example of the above outsourcing problem is the outsourcing of U.S. computer firms for flat-panel displays from Japanese firms. The Japanese firms design, build, and improve this important component of all laptop computers. The American firms buy from their Japanese suppliers, but have no knowledge or expertise in the flat-panel technology at all. As a result, in the long run, the U.S. firms will probably have to withdraw from the final product market.

A study by Bettis et al. [4] has shown that excessive outsourcing, especially of technological products, is an important cause for the continuing decline of international competitiveness by Western firms.

There are, of course, areas where outsourcing is highly desirable. In cases where specialization and experience provide lower costs for the supplier, it is nearly always desirable for the firm to outsource. For instance, in such areas as information systems, communication, building maintenance, office cleaning, and building security, outside suppliers can usually provide these services at a much lower cost than if the firm decides to staff these areas itself. Outsourcing, by lowering costs, probably provides increased competitiveness [11].

As a rule of thumb, we can say that a firm should not abandon the design, development, and manufacturing capability of critically important high-technology components. Being on the forefront of the technology of these components is usually a requirement to also be on the forefront of the assembled final products in which these high-technology components are used.

Local Sourcing by Japanese Transplants in the United States

Japanese automobile companies have captured well over 20% of the U.S. automobile market plus a much smaller percentage of the U.S. truck and passenger van markets. Yet their total purchases of U.S. parts, components, and subassemblies amounts to only 10% of the $100 billion automotive suppliers market. The balance of their parts, components, and subassemblies come from their own plants and their suppliers in Japan plus selected purchases from suppliers in other countries.

A large component of the U.S. trade deficit with Japan is generated by these enormous automotive parts imports from Japan. Despite strong pressures from the U.S. government, the Japanese automobile companies have resisted making large increases in U.S. automotive supply sources.

There are good reasons why the Japanese resist the wider use of American suppliers. To maintain quality, an automobile firm must have strong control over the supplier's production processes, and the automotive parts suppliers must have strong, effective, high-quality, low-cost operations. Unfortunately, not many of the 4000 major U.S. parts suppliers satisfy these requirements. U.S. automobile manufacturers historically have selected automotive parts suppliers on the basis of low cost and have avoided involvement in the suppliers' internal engineering and management activities.

There are, however, serious changes in the works. Most automobile manufacturers are now switching to the Japanese automobile manufacturers' practice of using no more than two or three suppliers for each part, component, or subassembly. By limiting the number of suppliers, the automobile manufacturers can afford to become more intensively involved in the suppliers' internal operations. Closer control can be exercised over internal quality processes, and assistance can be provided to the suppliers in the areas of efficiency improvement, management training, and other productivity improvement activities.

One example of an American automotive supplier to Toyota is the automobile bumper manufacturer called Bumper Works of Danville, Illinois. With the help of a team of manufacturing experts supplied by Toyota, lean manufacturing techniques were introduced and other manufacturing and engineering approaches were introduced over a period of time.

Productivity at Bumper Works increased 60% and the number of defects was reduced by 80% within one year. This example illustrates how critical it is for the major automobile producers to become more actively involved with their parts, components, and subassembly suppliers [12]. Benefits are accrued by the supplier as well as by the automobile companies because lower costs generated by productivity and quality improvements are always shared between supplier and buyer.

Reducing the Number of Supplier Firms

Parts, component, and subassembly suppliers to manufacturers of finished products, such as automobiles, appliances, machinery, equipment, and other mechanical, electric, or electronic products, have always been an important link in the supply chain leading to the finished product. According to the U.S.

Bureau of the Census, in 1991 the cost of materials in U.S. manufacturers' factory shipments amounted to between 50% and 55% of the value of the products shipped. Many finished product manufacturers make a high percentage of their own parts, components, and subassemblies. Others, however, buy nearly all parts, components, and subassemblies from suppliers and restrict the work they do largely to final assembly, painting, and merchandising [6].

In the U.S. automobile industry, it is estimated that General Motors, including its company-owned supplier plants, produce as much as 70% of G.M. parts, components, and subassemblies. At Chrysler and at many Japanese automobile plants, the parts, components, and subassemblies manufactured in-house may be as low as 30%. The general direction of the industry appears to be toward less in-house manufacturing and a reduction in the number of suppliers.

The model for supplier-buyer relationships in the U.S. automobile industry in the future seems to have been set by Toyota. Toyota has two suppliers for each part, component, or subassembly it does not manufacture itself. The two suppliers compete heavily against each other, and Toyota encourages them to do so. Toyota also works closely with its suppliers to encourage quality and productivity improvements. It sends teams of industrial and manufacturing engineers into its supplier plants and works closely with them to lower cost. This lowered cost is then, of course, shared by Toyota [5, 10].

General Motors has also begun to send teams of engineers into its supplier plants. But because of G.M.'s high costs, it is also insisting that its suppliers cut contract prices across the board [8].

General Motors' restructuring of its supplier relationships is also creating opportunities for those plants that already have high productivity and low costs. In the short run, G.M.'s across-the-board price cutting will hurt the profits of the low-cost part suppliers. In the long run, however, they stand to gain substantial additional business as G.M. moves to the Toyota model of only two or possibly three parts suppliers for each part, component, and subassembly.

The beneficiaries of the restructuring of the automobile industry will eventually, of course, be the buyers of automobiles. The competitiveness among suppliers and manufacturers can only result in eventual lower prices for the final product.

HIGH COST OF GERMAN PRODUCTION

There is little question that German industry is in trouble because of high labor, energy and pollution control costs, and high taxation. These high costs will not affect those industries where Germany's highly technically trained labor force is critical. Germany is still the world's largest and strongest exporter. However, in industries where Germany's highly technically trained labor force is not critical, there will be serious difficulties because of high overall costs.

Specifically, the average German worker cost in wages and benefits is about 50% higher than the average labor costs in the United States, Japan, France, and the United Kingdom. German labor costs are five times higher than in Portugal. Corporate taxes are about 50% higher than those in the United States, Japan, and France. German factories pay 20% to 40% more for energy than competitors in the European community. And German environmental protection costs are 60% higher than the average in the European community [3, 7, 9].

These costs pose a formidable challenge to German industry. They are causing an exodus of German manufacturing and a switch of German parts, component, and subassembly sourcing to other countries. Although the exodus has not yet reached a stampede, it could become one if the powerful German labor unions do not modify their wage demands. They may even be forced to take wage reductions.

Part of the reason for Germany's high wages and benefits is the high technical training level reached by much of Germany's labor force. Germany's apprenticeship system, together with classroom training, has created the world's highest technically trained labor force. For firms that manufacture high-quality, precision-engineered machine tools, the high wages may be justified because they depend on a highly trained labor force.

To the German manufacturing segment that produces automobiles and other high-volume products, the high level of technical training could prove to be a major hindrance. Mass-production techniques require only modest skill levels. The present German manufacturing structure may make it extremely difficult to reduce manufacturing costs to the level required for German firms to compete successfully.

The German manufacturing situation is quite problematic. Unless the powerful labor unions realize the economic situation and can convince their membership to accept lower wage levels, there is bound to be serious trouble on Germany's manufacturing employment horizon.

HIGH QUALITY LEVEL IN MEXICAN AUTOMOBILE PLANTS

The rapid movement of U.S., European, and Japanese manufacturing plants to Mexico has not been widely publicized. The automobile companies nearly all have assembly plants in Mexico, including Ford, General Motors, Nissan, Mercedes-Benz, and Volkswagen. Many of them are there ostensibly to supply the Mexican automobile market, which is growing at double-digit annual rates. But the real markets all automobile assemblers are after are the automobile markets in the United States and Canada.

There are extensive debates going on now about the desirability, the details, and the rate of implementation of the North American Free Trade Agreement (NAFTA). But in reality, NAFTA has already been in effect in a de facto way for a number of years. Even extensive modification of NAFTA will not stop the large manufacturers from staying in or moving into Mexico.

There are three main reasons why the world's automobile manufacturers are in Mexico or flocking to it. The first reason is its willing-to-learn, low-cost, young labor force. The second reason is that Mexico is potentially the fastest-growing automobile market in the world in terms of absolute numbers. The third reason is that the low-cost Mexican worker is easy to train, and costs little to train because of his or her relatively low wages. These three reasons justify the massive investments being made in Mexico by automobile manufacturers (as well as by numerous other manufacturers).

The low cost of training is particularly attractive to many firms. Today's automobiles are precision-crafted machines that are expected to be defect free and to provide reliable service for a long period of time. As manufacturers have discovered over the past decade, the only way to obtain good quality and dependability is to start with a good design and to use a highly trained and motivated workforce to manufacture and assemble the products. The trained Mexican workforce is providing just that.

The rapidly developing markets for many products in Mexico are also not as farfetched as many like to believe. Mexican workers in non-Mexican manufacturing plants are receiving wages that are substantially above the national level in Mexico. Hourly wages of $3 per hour are not uncommon, and weekly wages of $80 per week are the norm. With low cost of living there is the potential for substantial savings, and a resultant demand for low-cost secondhand automobiles. This demand will grow rapidly and be followed by a demand for low-cost new cars. In addition, the savings of the high-wage (by Mexican standards) workers will generate a demand for imported products [1, 2].

Before long, wages in the Mexican labor market will inch up. The current labor cost is so low in comparison with U.S., European, and Japanese standards that even a doubling of current wage levels in Mexico will still make Mexican plants highly attractive. And remember that the more the Mexican worker makes, the sooner he or she will become an automobile owner.

Conclusions

The rapid exodus of many manufacturing plants from Germany, Japan, Canada, and the United States is a temporary phenomenon. To believe that all manufacturing will leave these four countries is foolish. You could even argue that many of the larger manufacturers, such as the automobile manufacturers, have already made their moves. Of course, many smaller firms will be moving there during the next decade, not only because of lower wage costs but also to take advantage of Mexico's rapidly growing industrial, commercial, and consumer markets.

Mexico's average income levels are increasing rapidly, and with these increases the cost gap will narrow and the demand for products will increase. If Mexican wages were to double (and they could do that very quickly), Mexican wages would be at Korean and Hong Kong levels. And we will then not see many manufacturers, with the possible exception of the Japanese, move their manufacturing operations to these markets.

The migration of manufacturing to Mexico is creating temporary displacements in many labor markets in Germany, Canada, and the United States, but in the long run, all countries, including Mexico, will benefit from the increased trade and from the value creation.

Discussion Questions

1. Describe several ways the United States and Canada could benefit from closer trade ties with Mexico.
2. Large manufacturers like to have close ties with their suppliers, including influence over internal operations practices. Why do these large manufacturers

not manufacture more of the needed parts, components, and subassemblies themselves?
3. How could Germany's highly trained technical labor force be a threat to continued growth in the German economy?
4. Will Germany's labor unions be willing to agree to more modest wages in the future? Explain your rationale.
5. Explain why Mexico is popular as a location for parts and assembly plants for the world's large automobile manufacturers.
6. Will NAFTA remain restricted to Canada, Mexico, and the United States? How might it expand?
7. American sports shoe manufacturers extensively use external sourcing (Korea, China, Indonesia). Will this affect their competitive position in their Western markets? Explain your rationale.
8. Several U.S. personal computer manufacturers extensively use external sourcing (Japan, Hong Kong, Korea). Will this affect their competitive position in their Western markets? Explain your rationale.

References

1. Baker, Stephen, David Woodruff, and Elizabeth Weiner. "Detroit South." *Business Week,* March 16, 1992, 98–103.
2. Baker, Stephen, Geri Smith, and Elizabeth Weiner. "The Mexican Worker." *Business Week,* April 19, 1993, 84–92.
3. Benjamin, Daniel. "Germany Is Troubled by How Little Work Its Workers Are Doing." *Wall Street Journal,* May 6, 1993, A1.
4. Bettis, R. A., S. P. Bradley, and G. Hamel. "Outsourcing and Industrial Decline." *Academy of Management Executive,* 6(1), February 1992, 7–22.
5. Freece, James B. "The Lessons G.M. Could Learn for Its Supplier Shakeup." *Business Week,* August 31, 1992, 29.
6. Hill, R. C., and S. M. Freedman. "Managing the Quality Process: Lessons from a Baldrige Award Winner." *Academy of Management Executive,* 6(1), February 1992, 76–88.
7. Kelly, Kevin, Zachary Schiller, and James B. Freece. "Cut Costs or Else." *Business Week,* March 22, 1993, 28–29.
8. Roth, Terence. "German Firms Bemoan Production Costs." *Wall Street Journal,* January 29, 1992, A8.
9. Schiller, Zachary, David Woodruff, Kevin Kelly, and Michael Schroeder. "G.M. Tightens the Screws." *Business Week,* June 22, 1992, 30–31.
10. Templeman, John, Gail E. Schares, Jonathan Levine, and William Glasgall. "Germany Fights Back." *Business Week,* May 31, 1993, 48–51.
11. Welch, J. A., and P. R. Nayak. "Strategic Sourcing: A Progressive Approach to the Make-or-Buy Decision." *Academy of Management Executive,* 6(1), February 1992, 23–31.
12. White, Joseph B. "Japanese Auto Makers Help U.S. Suppliers Become More Efficient." *Wall Street Journal,* September 9, 1991, A1.

Chapter twenty-four

The Future of Total Quality Management

Outline

Introduction
Quality as a Focus for Management Improvement
Mentofacturing—Mento-Manufacturing—Mento-Operations
How Did Wal-Mart Do It?
Virtual Reality—What Is It?
The Workplace in the Twenty-First Century
Quality Experts, Consultants, and Associations
Conclusions

Introduction

Total quality management, by whatever name, has made and will continue to make a major impact on product manufacturing, service industries, retailing, and many other industries.

The focus of the TQM movement is changing somewhat from quality to productivity, but for most successful utilizers of TQM quality and productivity have always gone hand in hand.

The reason the focus is changing is probably caused by quality having become a given requirement. In most strongly competitive industries, firms must be able to reach a certain quality level in order to be competitive. Once that quality level is attained, it is not surprising that firms refocus their efforts on productivity.

Productivity, however, is affected by many factors in the organization; as a result, the means used and the areas attacked to achieve improved productivity are quite broad. Techniques such as benchmarking, concurrent engineering, reengineering, cycle-time reduction, product innovation, and customer focus are being used extensively in order to achieve improved productivity and increased competitiveness.

In this final chapter, we will review the Baldrige award and observe how it serves as a focus to not only improve quality but also productivity. Next we will look at how

Wal-Mart is maintaining its double-digit growth and how it is managing its enormous operations. Then we will take a look at a new technology: virtual reality. Virtual reality is here and will become more prominent in the next few years. What will the twenty-first century workplace look like? We take a peek at it. And finally, we will look at the leading organizations involved in quality and productivity education, training, and consulting.

QUALITY AS A FOCUS FOR MANAGEMENT IMPROVEMENT

If there is one specific milestone in the U.S. product or service quality movement, it is most likely the decision by the U.S. Department of Commerce to institute the Malcolm Baldrige National Quality Award.

Whatever the expectations of the Baldrige award were, they have been exceeded by far. The application process for the award is tedious and time-consuming and consists of some 75 pages of questions that must be answered. A firm has to think twice to determine if applying for the award is worth the time and effort.

Initially, interest centered on the Baldrige award itself. Since then, firms have found that the Baldrige award application process helps the firm in identifying where its weak points are—in all areas, not just product quality.

The result is that firms now use the Baldrige award application process not only in an effort to win the award but to help them identify weaknesses in their various operating divisions. Motorola also requires its suppliers to go through the application process so they can identify their weaknesses and correct them. Although this may seem to be an imposition, it not only helps Motorola but also its suppliers [7].

The important attributes on which the Baldrige award application focuses are listed in Table 24–1. As you can see, just filling out the application form quickly reveals whether an applicant has any chance of winning. If a firm cannot satisfy all the criteria, the chance of winning the award is zero. Yet hundreds of firms request the Baldrige award application packets each year. So it is clear that the benefits of the application process far exceed the work involved in filling out the forms [8].

As with any national attention getter such as the Baldrige award, there are critics. Some people feel that companies spend too much time and energy on the work involved in preparing the application. Some people claim that the time spent on preparing the award application packet could be more effectively used on quality improvements in the firm, or on focusing on customers' wants and needs. What these critics ignore is the fact that the work involved in preparing the application packet is actually a quality and productivity improvement process.

Still other critics feel that the Baldrige award focuses too much on quality and not enough on productivity. This may be partially valid, and changes in the application packet could focus more on productivity. What the critics do not realize, however, is that focus on quality and resultant improvements in quality in most cases result in concomitant increases in productivity as well [2].

THE FUTURE OF TOTAL QUALITY MANAGEMENT

Table 24-1
Typical Baldrige Award Criteria

Attribute	Does Applicant Satisfy Award Criteria?
Quality focus	Actively supports quality focus in all areas by all levels of management
Supplier relations	Actively working with suppliers to improve the quality of products or services and the productivity of their operations
Employee training	Has programs in place for training of employees in quality techniques
Quality control	Has systematic quality control in place to ensure all products are of highest quality
Product or service quality	Its product or service quality is similar to or better than its competitors' quality
Customer satisfaction	Customer satisfaction ratings are similar to or better than its competitors' rating
Market share	Market share is increasing
Product cycle time	Product and process cycle times are decreasing

Source: Malcolm Baldrige National Quality Award. "1994 Award Criteria." U.S. Department of Commerce, Technology Administration, National Institute of Standards and Technology, 1994.

MENTOFACTURING—MENTO-MANUFACTURING—MENTO-OPERATIONS

The term *mentofacturing* was introduced by Forward et al. [3] to indicate the importance, if not critical importance, of utilizing the mind in the manufacturing process at all stages.

Mentofacturing means making or producing things by using the mind, whereas manufacturing means making or producing things by hand.

I believe a better term would be *mento-manufacturing* or *mento-operations*. Both of these terms describe the importance of the mind, the intellectual contribution of humans, to the manufacturing or operations process.

Mentofacturing is defined by Forward et al. [3] as developing organizations that emphasize learning, human development, risk taking, and technology transfer.

Organizations that practice mento-manufacturing or mento-operations will be technology driven, will foster employee involvement, will encourage new ideas, will support employee education and training, will be actively involved with both customers and suppliers, will be innovative, and will satisfy most of the criteria found in the Baldrige guidelines.

Although the term *mento-manufacturing* is just another way to describe how American industry is going through a major metamorphosis, it may also help industrial managers think differently of what is happening in their organizations, and what needs to happen in order for their organizations to remain competitive.

How did Wal-Mart do it?

How does a huge organization that is widely dispersed across the entire United States effectively manage its operations while it is simultaneously expanding at double-digit annual rates? Wal-Mart, exclusive of its Sam's Wholesale Clubs, had 1800 stores in operation in 1992. These stores were located not in large urban areas close to major airports, but in smaller cities where the nearest airport is typically accessible only by small propeller aircraft.

Despite these travel limitations, Wal-Mart believes in frequent personal contact by its regional vice-presidents with the managers and employees that have made Wal-Mart what it is today. It is the largest department store chain in the world, with sales approaching $50 billion in 1992. Each one of its 15 regional vice presidents spends an average of four days per week visiting his or her approximately 120 stores. He or she does this travel using Wal-Mart's own airline, which consists mainly of twin engine propeller aircraft. These aircraft are able to land at the smaller airports not accessible by larger aircraft [9].

Figure 24–1 shows the Wal-Mart organization. There are 15 regions, each headed by a regional vice president. Each region consists of approximately 120 stores managed by 11 to 15 district managers. Each store in turn is managed by a store manager, who is assisted by 2 or 3 assistant managers and 15 department heads.

Centralized control is maintained by the regional vice presidents, who, through their frequent visits to stores, maintain a strong personal connection with the store managers and the store employees. All regional vice presidents reside near the Bentonville, Arkansas, headquarters and return to headquarters every weekend for group meetings with senior management. This type of personal contact is considered critical for Wal-Mart to provide its employees with a feeling of belonging to the Wal-Mart family.

However, the personal contacts are not the only means of managing at Wal-Mart. Store managers receive a large amount of central support through Wal-Mart's computer-based sales reporting, inventory reordering, and other information technology services provided by Wal-Mart's central computers. Through tracking the sales levels of every item in Wal-Mart's stores, reordering of fast-moving items is speeded up, and slow-moving items can be marked down for quick sales.

Also supportive of each store's operations is Wal-Mart's satellite television station, which provides new employee training, retraining of current employees, and new and standard approaches at how to display merchandise for every department. Videos of all programs are available so that store managers have high flexibility in offering video-based training and operations planning sessions for all affected employees.

In other words, Wal-Mart manages its far-flung operations through three main means: personal contact with all employees by central management, information technology to manage sales and merchandise replenishment, and television and video production and technology to train employees and to provide guidance in the day-to-day operations of each Wal-Mart store.

Figure 24-1
Wal-Mart's Organization Chart

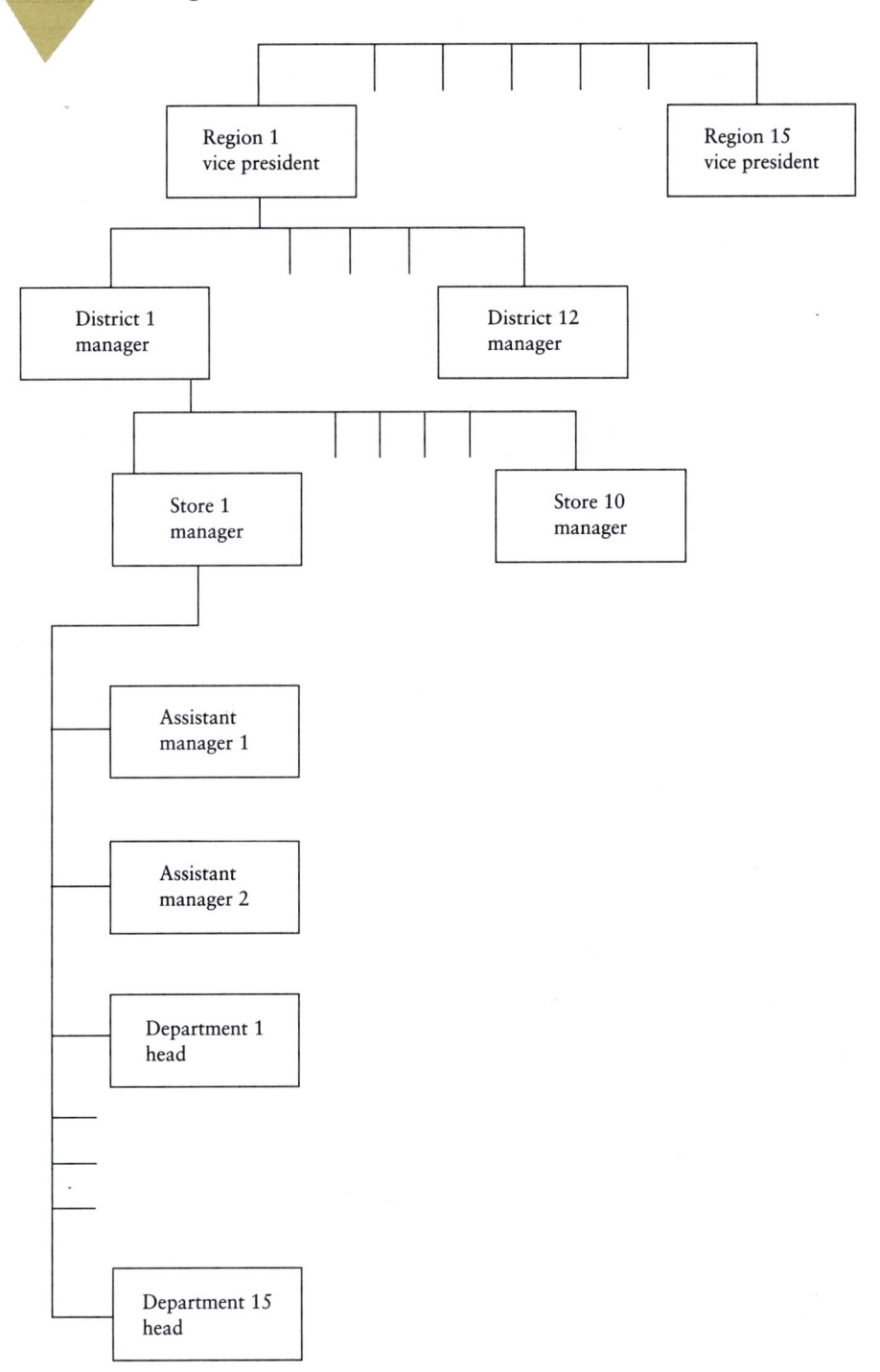

```
                    ┌──────┬──────┬──────┬──────┬──────┐
                    │      │      │      │      │      │
            ┌───────────────┐                   ┌────────────────┐
            │   Region 1    │                   │   Region 15    │
            │ vice president│                   │ vice president │
            └───────────────┘                   └────────────────┘
                    │
          ┌────┬────┼────┬────┐
          │    │    │    │    │
    ┌───────────┐        ┌────────────┐
    │ District 1│        │ District 12│
    │  manager  │        │   manager  │
    └───────────┘        └────────────┘
          │
     ┌────┬─┼──┬──┬──┐
     │    │ │  │  │  │
  ┌─────────┐         ┌──────────┐
  │ Store 1 │         │ Store 10 │
  │ manager │         │ manager  │
  └─────────┘         └──────────┘
       │
       ├──────┌─────────────┐
       │      │ Assistant   │
       │      │ manager 1   │
       │      └─────────────┘
       │
       │      ┌─────────────┐
       ├──────│ Assistant   │
       │      │ manager 2   │
       │      └─────────────┘
       │
       │      ┌─────────────┐
       ├──────│ Department 1│
       │      │    head     │
       │      └─────────────┘
       │
       │      ┌─────────────┐
       └──────│Department 15│
              │    head     │
              └─────────────┘
```

Virtual Reality—What Is It?

Virtual reality is being made available to us through the cooperative efforts of computer software designers and behavioral scientists using computer power that is just now becoming available.

Virtual reality is often compared with artificial intelligence, which, at least as an idea with rather crude applications, has been around for approximately 30 years. So far, artificial intelligence has not lived up to its promise, though it probably eventually will. Virtual reality, on the other hand, is here now. It is still in its infancy, but it will be a growth industry during the balance of the 1990s and into the twenty-first century. Unlike artificial intelligence, which will take decades to fully develop, virtual reality will explode on the scene in a wide variety of applications, including training airline pilots, training military personnel, industrial training, recreation, and, yes, even managerial training.

The reason we can be so confident about the future of virtual reality is because of its enormous success in training airline pilots on flight simulators and its more recent success in training the military in battlefield situations. Much of the success of Desert Storm's drive into Kuwait can be attributed to the extremely well-trained U.S. military, whose officers were trained in virtual simulation systems designed and developed for the military (at a cost of hundreds of millions of dollars).

The U.S. Army is spending well over a hundred million dollars per year on simulations, mostly battlefield simulations. These simulations are multimedia, multiscreen experiences that make the participants see and feel as if they are in the middle of a battlefield. These simulations also include interactive features that allow battlefield commanders and officers, and potentially also the infantry, to make decisions in the midst of simulated but realistic battle conditions [4]. The benefits of this type of training, as a substitute for and enhancement of real-life training, are substantial and enormously cost-effective. In addition, what makes someone proficient at a complicated task with many unpredictable outcomes, such as functioning on a battlefield or piloting an airplane, is repeated training. Virtual reality, achievable in these highly developed simulation situations, provides this training at very low cost.

Other applications of virtual reality have been developed for training power plant engineers, security traders, salespeople, and business negotiators. The success of virtual reality is partly based on the fact that the brain processes information much better when it is presented as sight, sound, touch, and smell instead of text or numbers. Also, hand-eye coordination and the ability to recognize movement are encoded in our genes, not learned abilities. The more successful virtual reality simulators take all of these factors into account [4].

With employee training budgets in some cases approaching 4% of total costs, virtual reality training systems are appearing on the scene none too soon. The potential market for virtual reality systems to assist in employee training is enormous.

The Workplace in the Twenty-First Century

Will everybody be part of a work team at the start of the twenty-first century? Not likely. In fact, the explosive formation and utilization of work teams we see nowadays is probably a transitional phenomena. Yes, there will remain large amounts of cooperative work arrangements. Communication through computer networks will become the standard for most forms of work where interaction is necessary, but the work team as we know it in today's factories eventually will be rendered unnecessary by the automated factory. People will still be needed for maintaining and operating the factory, but much of both functions will be done by individuals or by teams of at most two or three technicians.

Increasingly, we will see the growth of technical experts who will function as the infrastructure to keep our highly technical information, communication, and production sector functioning. These technical experts will work closely together in design and development areas, such as in product and especially in software design. The term software design will have to be expanded to include more than just computer software. Development of nonphysical entertainment, educational, and recreational products will become a much larger industry than it is today. As groups of software development experts, these individuals will work closely together through concurrent engineering approaches but probably will do most of their communication by electronic means. Hence, many of them will physically work apart from their fellow team members.

This does not imply that people will not continue to work together in offices. Most people will continue to do so more because of social and personal interactive socialization needs than work needs. The technical software, information, or maintenance specialist of the future will probably work more effectively from his or her home, hotel room, or vehicle. And many will do so with much more flexibility in their daily and personal schedules. Couples with children will schedule their work around their parenting duties, thus providing at least a partial solution to today's frustrations of two parents who both work the same hours.

Other changes to occur are the reduction in average size of companies, at least as measured in terms of employees. Information technology will reduce vertical integration because service or product suppliers are more specialized and can supply the firm at lower cost. First-line supervisors or lower middle managers will gradually disappear. The disappearance of large concentrated workforces will obviate the need for the lower middle manager. The remaining middle managers will manage people by means of telecommunications or, if they are located in a single location, by means of persuasion, trust, training, and humane treatment. These managers must also be technically proficient in the work their subordinates are doing. Pure managing will be largely the task of senior management. In other words, even MBA training will need to become increasingly technical as well as behavioral. The manager needs behavioral skills to manage people, but he or she also must be proficient in those areas of expertise in which the people he or she supervises are engaged [5].

QUALITY EXPERTS, CONSULTANTS, AND ASSOCIATIONS

Who are the quality experts and how can they be used? The quality training and consulting industry was booming back in 1991, and by all indications has expanded considerably since then.

Most of the quality trainers provide quality training instead of quality consulting. The major player was Philip Crosby Associates. The best known consultants, on the other hand, were Deming and Juran, who traveled to Japan in the 1950s and spread the quality gospel there. Deming died in 1993; Juran is in his eighties. Juran will probably have a more visible legacy because of the Juran Institute, which Juran founded. Deming, on the other hand, is acknowledged as *the* quality movement guru.

The expectations are that all quality training firms will become more heavily involved in consulting during the balance of the decade. Most firms are finding that employee training is useful, but only up to a point. Quality program implementation—the most difficult part—must then begin. It is anticipated that quality program implementation assistance will become a huge consulting industry in the future. Productivity follows quality; the two go hand in hand.

Table 24–2 lists the names of the top 11 consulting firms in 1991 as reported by Byrne [1] in *Business Week*. Also listed are the top six professional quality associations.

Table 24–2
Leading Quality Consulting and Training Organizations

Leading Quality Consultants and Trainers	Professional Quality Associations
1. Philip Crosby Associates, Winter Park, FL	1. American Society for Quality Control, Milwaukee, WI
2. Development Dimensions, Pittsburgh, PA	2. Association for Quality and Participation, Cincinnati, OH
3. United Research, Morristown, NJ	3. Quality and Productivity Management Association, Schaumburg, IL
4. Gunneson Group, Landing, NJ	4. American Productivity and Quality Center, Houston, TX
5. ODI, Burlington, MA	5. American Supplier Institute, Dearborn, MI
6. Ernst and Young, New York, NY	6. Goal/QPC, Methuen, MA
7. Walker Customer Satisfaction, Indianapolis, IN	
8. Qualtec, Palm Beach, FL	
9. General Systems, Pittsfield, MA	
10. Juran Institute, Wilton, CT	
11. Zenger Miller, Joiner and Associates, New York	

Source: Adapted in part from Byrne, John A. "High Priests and Hucksters." *Business Week/Quality 1991, 52–57.*

Conclusions

How will TQM evolve over the next decade? I believe TQM as a term will disappear. What is happening at the present time is just too extensive and too varied to be covered by the term TQM. I believe someone will coin a more comprehensive term to reflect the numerous activities, tools, and techniques that are now covered by TQM.

Total quality management, as a term, was fine when the main focus was on quality improvement. But as we have shown in this book, nearly everything that is going on, and is relatively new or unique, seems to fall under the TQM term. Does it make sense to use the term TQM for such diverse activities as benchmarking, reengineering, concurrent engineering, customer satisfaction, product innovation, cycle-time reduction, restructuring, and organization flattening?

Whatever the future term will be for all these activities is immaterial. It is clear that management in the foreseeable future will remain focused on all of them. Not to do so will be too risky. After all, competitiveness is the key word. And to remain competitive will mean that the firm must continue to change, adapt, reform, and restructure. The status quo is no longer an option.

Discussion Questions

1. Why and how are quality and productivity related? Describe in detail.
2. Does the current focus on productivity mean that quality is no longer important? Explain in detail.
3. Describe and discuss the eight Baldrige award criteria.
4. Describe mentofacturing, or mento-manufacturing. Do you think the terms will become commonly used?
5. Describe and discuss how Wal-Mart uses three management and technological means to manage its 1800 retail locations.
6. Why is virtual reality as reflected in sophisticated simulators so potentially valuable for future employee training?
7. What are the economic benefits to a firm of having employees work from their homes instead of in office locations?
8. Speculate on what terms will be used in the future to focus on quality and productivity improvement activities. Develop five alternatives.

References

1. Byrne, John A. "High Priests and Hucksters." *Business Week/Quality 1991*, 52–57.
2. Carey, John, Robert Neff, and Lois Therrein. "The Prize and the Passion." *Business Week/Quality 1991*, 58–59.
3. Forward, G. E., D. E. Beach, D. A. Gray, and J. C. Quick. "Mentofacturing: A Vision for American Industrial Excellence." *Academy of Management Executive,* 5(3), August 1991, 32–44.
4. Hamilton, Joan, Emily T. Smith, Gary McWilliams, Evan I. Schwarz, and John Carey. "Virtual Reality." *Business Week,* October 5, 1992, 97–105.
5. Kiechel, Walter, III. "How We Will Work in the Year 2000." *Fortune,* May 17, 1993, 38–52.
6. *Malcolm Baldrige National Quality Award.* "1994 Award Criteria." U.S. Department of Commerce, Technology Administration, National Institute of Standards and Technology, 1994.

7. Neff, Robert. "Going for the Glory." *Business Week/Quality 1991*, 60–61.
8. *Profiles of Malcolm Baldrige Award Winners.* Allyn and Bacon, Boston, 1992.
9. Saporito, Bill. "A Week aboard the Wal-Mart Express." *Fortune*, August 24, 1992, 77–84.
10. Smith, Emily. "Doing It for Mother Earth." *Business Week/Quality 1991*, 44–49.

Part six

Appendices

Evaluation of Functioning Productivity Teams   **A**

Using Activity-Based Costing to Achieve Manufacturing Excellence   **B**

Appendix A

Evaluation of Functioning Productivity Improvement Teams

Outline

Introduction
Status of Implementation
Level of Activity
Effects of Staffing
Operational Impact
Changes in Employee Attitudes
Conclusions

Introduction

When management invests resources to train work teams, productivity improvement teams, or any other type of organized group activity, it is of utmost importance that an accounting be made on a regular basis of the group's activities. How this accounting and evaluation process can be done and how it can be institutionalized is addressed in this appendix. The focus will be on the productivity improvement team.

Management must be assured that the initial investment and ongoing expenditures for productivity improvement teams are justified. This requires an evaluation process that can be performed on a continuous basis.

The productivity improvement team evaluation process can be divided into five segments:

1. Status of implementation
2. Level of activity
3. Effects of staffing
4. Operational impact
5. Changes in employee attitudes

For each of these segments, an evaluation form is applicable. In the following sections we present rudimentary examples of these forms for use as models by productivity improvement team programs in organizations.

Status of Implementation

When initiating a productivity improvement team program, a time schedule should be developed to govern the rate of implementation. Organizations normally start with a pilot program of a few productivity improvement teams. During this pilot phase, management can evaluate the process as well as the operation of each pilot productivity improvement team. Errors in grouping members or in the process or organization can be identified and steps can be taken to correct them.

In the monthly accounting of the implementation process, the statistics to be recorded include the number of productivity improvement teams in operation, the total number of productivity improvement team members, the average productivity improvement team size, the range of productivity improvement team membership size, the number of trained leaders, the number of trained facilitators, the number of supporting staff for productivity improvement team operation, and the total expenditures per month. To determine the impact of productivity improvement team implementation, it is also necessary to calculate the number of potential members and the percentage of employees involved.

Table A–1 shows the form on which the implementation evaluation material can be recorded. Scheduled or budgeted data for a hypothetical organization have been entered on the form to show how it can be used.

Table A–1
Productivity Improvement Team Implementation Status Form

Description of Implementation Measures	Scheduled or Budgeted	Actual[a]
Number of teams in operation	15	14
Number of team members	120	112
Average team size	8	8
Range of team membership size	5–11	4–12
Number of trained team leaders	16	16
Number of trained team facilitators	8	8
Number of supporting team staff	1	1
Total team expenditures per month	$8500	$9000
Potential team members	1200	1200
Percentage of team members	10.0%	9.3%

[a] Actual data as of 30 April 1993.

The table shows that the number of productivity improvement teams scheduled and the number actually implemented differ by 1. The implemented average productivity improvement team size is identical to the planned average size, and the range in the number of members per productivity improvement team is somewhat wider (4–12) than planned (5–11). Total productivity improvement team expenditures per month exceed the budgeted figure by $500. Finally, the actual penetration or coverage rate is 9.3% as compared with the planned 10.0%.

Completion of the productivity improvement team implementation status form on a monthly basis not only provides a history of the implementation but also keeps management informed of the status of implementation.

LEVEL OF ACTIVITY

Each productivity improvement team should keep a record of its activities. This record can then be combined with other activity records in reporting collective projects.

The statistics on productivity improvement team activities can be extensive. Table A–2 shows a form that can be used to record activities of a productivity improvement team. The form contains cumulative statistics for a 16-month period, from 1 January 1992 to 30 April 1993. Cumulative statistics are preferred because one problem could take several months to resolve, and problems can overlap. Statistics for relatively short periods thus would have a tendency to distort the actual level of productivity improvement team activities.

Table A–2
Form Showing Level of Productivity Improvement Team Activities

Description of Activity Measures	Quantitative Measure[a]
Number of problems analyzed	12
Number of problems resolved without management involvement	6
Percentage of problems resolved without management involvement	50%
Number of problems resolved with management involvement	4
Number of problems analyzed but not resolved	1
Percentage of problems analyzed but not resolved	8.3%
Number of problems awaiting management action	1
Number of problems presently under analysis	2
Number of management presentations	4
Number of productivity improvement teams on which statistics are based	1

[a] Cumulative figures as of 30 April 1993, covering period since 1 January 1992.

APPENDICES

Table A-3
Form Showing Aggregate Level of Productivity Improvement Team Activities

Aggregate Level of Productivity Improvement Team Activities Description of Activity Measures	Quantitative Measure[a]
Number of problems analyzed	128
Number of problems resolved without management involvement	66
Percentage of problems resolved without management involvement	50.6%
Number of problems resolved with management involvement	38
Number of problems analyzed but not resolved	12
Percentage of problems analyzed but not resolved	9.4%
Number of problems awaiting management action	12
Number of problems presently under analysis	26
Number of management presentations	36
Number of productivity improvement teams on which statistics are based	14

[a] Cumulative figures as of 30 April 1993, covering period since 1 January 1992.

Table A–3 shows the aggregate activities of 14 productivity improvement teams during the 16-month period from 1 January 1992 to 30 April 1993. The form used for the aggregate statistics is the same as that used for individual productivity improvement team activities and provides a summary of all productivity improvement team activities operations in the organization.

EFFECTS OF STAFFING

Productivity improvement teams have considerable impact on employees' morale, motivation, cooperation, and interest in their jobs. In order to determine the extent of such impact, it is necessary to keep statistics for a variety of staffing measures.

There are eight staffing measures that should be maintained on a monthly basis. These can then be compared for different time periods to determine the changes that have taken place. Some of the staffing measures are directly observed or reported figures; others are derived from the reported figures. The eight measures are (1) the number of staff resignations, (2) the number of layoffs, (3) the number of staff members, (4) the annualized turnover rate, (5) days lost through absenteeism, (6) percentage of absenteeism, (7) the number of grievances filed, and (8) the number of reported staff accidents.

Table A–4 shows the eight staffing measures with corresponding data. The first two, number of resignations and layoffs, are recorded figures for the four-month period ending 30 April 1993. The third, the number of staff members, is the average employment level during the four-month period. The fourth, annualized

Table A–4
Form for Reporting Staffing Statistics

Staffing Statistics	
Description of Staffing Measures	Quantitative Measure[a]
1. Number of staff resignations	35
2. Number of staff layoffs	24
3. Number of staff members	1450
4. Annualized staff turnover percentage[b]	12.2%
5. Days lost through absenteeism	6460
6. Percentage of absenteeism[c]	5.1%
7. Number of grievances filed	23
8. Number of reported staff accidents	29

[a] Cumulative figures for period 1 January 1993 to 30 April 1993.

[b] Annualized turnover percentage = 100 × ([line 1 + line 2] × 3)/line 3.

[c] Percentage of absenteeism = 100 × (line 5/[line 3 × 88]).

staff turnover, is derived from the first three measures by the following formula:

$$\text{ATOP} = 100 \times \left[\frac{(SR + SL) \times 3}{SM} \right]$$

where ATOP is the annualized turnover percentage, SR is the number of staff resignations, SL is the number of staff layoffs, and SM is the number of staff members. Multiplying by 3 converts the four-month period to an annualized period, and multiplying by 100 changes the result to a percentage.

The fifth staffing measure lists days lost through absenteeism during the four-month period. In Table A–4 the cause of absenteeism is not identified, but a more detailed analysis could expand this measure to distinguish absenteeism because of sickness from absenteeism due to time taken off without pay.

The sixth staffing measure, percentage of absenteeism, is derived from statistics on days lost through absenteeism and statistics on the staffing level. Percentage of absenteeism is derived from the following formula:

$$\text{PA} = 100 \times \left[\frac{DLA}{SM \times 88} \right]$$

where PA is the percentage of absenteeism, DLA is days lost through absenteeism, and SM is the number of staff members. In this formula, 88 is the number of working days in a four-month period, and multiplying by 100 changes the result to a percentage.

The seventh staffing measure is the number of grievances filed. Our hypothetical organization is unionized, with a formal grievance procedure. If there are no unions or if an organization is only partially unionized, an alternative staffing measure for employee complaints or dissatisfaction should be obtained.

The eighth and final staffing measure is the number of reported staff accidents. Although many minor accidents are not reported, this is still an important statistic because productivity improvement teams can identify unsafe conditions and propose actions to eliminate potential accidents. Risk managers and safety officers are the best sources of such information.

OPERATIONAL IMPACT

Management must make the decision to invest in the training of productivity improvement team facilitators, leaders, and members. Once they are established, the productivity improvement teams require time, which translates into cost of operation. As a result, management expects a return on its investment, and the question of benefits to be derived from the productivity improvement teams arises very early. For this reason, it is important that detailed statistics be kept of activities that relate to productivity improvement teams.

The five operational impact measures proposed here consist mainly of complaints generated by customers, suppliers, and others. Complaints emanating from customers, suppliers, and others are important impact measures because they present more directly external perspectives.

Table A–5 lists the five productivity improvement teams impact measures with hypothetical data. To obtain this data, there must be an organized way of collecting complaints every month from customers, suppliers, and others. The reported statistics apply to a four-month period, but separate monthly reports similar to this cumulative report can also be kept.

The purpose of these reports is to indicate if change occurs in the complaint rates as a direct or indirect result of the operating productivity improvement teams. The cost savings generated are listed on an annualized basis, that is, for the calendar year. The statistics are based on 14 productivity improvement teams in operation.

Table A–5
Form Showing Operational Impact Statistics

Description of Impact Measures[a]	Quantitative Measure[a]
1. Number of customer complaints	658
2. Number of supplier complaints	23
3. Number of other complaints	58
4. Number of staff complaints	141
5. Cost savings generated (annualized)	$147,000

[a] Cumulative figures for four-month period ending 30 April 1993.

Exhibit A-1
Employee Questionnaire—Job- and Self-Related Questions

Employee Questionnaire

For each item, circle the number between the two indicated responses that best expresses your opinion or feeling

My job:

is boring	1 2 3 4 5 6	is stimulating
has a lot of responsibility	1 2 3 4 5 6	has little responsibility
is difficult	1 2 3 4 5 6	is easy to do
is demanding	1 2 3 4 5 6	is not demanding

I view myself as an employee who:

works very hard	1 2 3 4 5 6	takes it easy
never is absent	1 2 3 4 5 6	frequently is absent
is generally satisfied	1 2 3 4 5 6	is generally dissatisfied

CHANGES IN EMPLOYEE ATTITUDES

Important measures of the effects of productivity improvement teams can be obtained through surveys that reveal changes in employee attitudes and opinions over time. An attitude survey administered before and then again six months or a year after productivity improvement team implementation can show how much the attitudes and opinions of productivity improvement team members have changed over the period.

Exhibit A–1 is an example of a job- and self-related attitude and opinion questionnaire that can be used with employees. The upper part of the questionnaire asks questions about the employees' jobs, and the bottom part inquires about the employees' feelings about themselves in relationship to their jobs. Exhibit A–2 is a survey form focused on employees' feelings about management, their fellow employees, and the staff's commitment to serving the customer.

CONCLUSIONS

By monthly application of the evaluation process described in this appendix, information can be derived to determine the effects of productivity improvement teams over an extended period of time. At the same time, monthly data points can be compiled to establish trends for critical measures of the productivity improvement team process.

Evaluation is an integral part of the productivity improvement team implementation process. When management installs productivity improvement teams or any other organized team activities, it makes an investment of resources, and it expects an accounting of that investment.

Exhibit A-2
Employee Questionnaire—Management- and Other-Related Questions

Employee Questionnaire

For each item, circle the number between the two indicated responses that best expresses your opinion or feeling

Management is:

lenient	1 2 3 4 5 6	demanding
accessible	1 2 3 4 5 6	not accessible
considerate	1 2 3 4 5 6	not considerate

My fellow workers are:

demanding	1 2 3 4 5 6	not considerate
helpful	1 2 3 4 5 6	not helpful
friendly	1 2 3 4 5 6	not friendly
cooperative	1 2 3 4 5 6	uncooperative
willing to share expertise	1 2 3 4 5 6	unwilling to share expertise

My fellow workers' commitment to customer service is:

excellent	1 2 3 4 5 6	poor
dedicated	1 2 3 4 5 6	indifferent
professional	1 2 3 4 5 6	unprofessional

Discussion Questions

1. What are the five segments of the productivity improvement team evaluation process?
2. What importance weights would you assign to each of the ten implementation measures on the implementation status form?
3. What importance weights would you assign to the ten activity measures used in Tables A–2 and A–3.
4. What importance weights would you assign to the eight staffing measures used in Table A–4?
5. What importance weights would you assign to the five impact measures used in Table A–5?

Appendix B

Using Activity-Based Costing to Achieve Manufacturing Excellence

Peter B.B. Turney

Outline

Introduction
Traditional Systems
Activity-Based Costing
What Is Manufacturing Excellence?
Objectives of Continuous Improvement
What Do Managers Need?
Product Costs
Conventional Product Costing Systems
Overhead Activities Unrelated to Volume
Overhead Rates Based on Direct Labor
Activity-Based Costing Systems
The Search for More Accurate Product Costs
Eliminating Cross-Subsidies
The Location and Consumption of Activities
Using Activity-Based Costing to Focus Manufacturing Strategy
The Impact of Sourcing Decisions
Impact of New Process Technologies
Using Activity-Based Costing for Product Design
Using Activity-Based Costing for Continuous Improvement
Performance Measurement
Using Activity-Based Costing for Behavioral Change
Reducing Lead Times
Is Activity-Based Costing Consistent with Manufacturing Excellence?
Conclusions

Introduction

Achieving and sustaining a competitive advantage via manufacturing excellence require continuous improvement in all aspects of performance. But to achieve continuous improvement, managers must have information to help them identify appropriate strategies, improve product design, and remove waste from operating activities.

Traditional Systems

Traditional product costing systems provide little information on these sources of competitive advantage. Product costs generated by these systems are often so inaccurate they encourage management to adopt strategies that inhibit the improvement of manufacturing [1]. Product designers may also react to inaccurate cost information by selecting designs that (in the eyes of customers, at least) fail to add value [2]. Finally, managers may be encouraged to manage the allocation and absorption of overhead rather than striving to eliminate waste [3].

Activity-Based Costing

In contrast, activity-based costing is a costing technology that provides information for continuous improvement in manufacturing. Activity-based costing traces costs to products according to the activities performed on them. The results are:

- Accurate cost information for strategic and design purposes
- Information that describes the range, cost, and consumption of operating activities throughout the manufacturing organization

This appendix examines the role of activity-based costing in achieving manufacturing excellence. It describes manufacturing excellence and the product cost information requirements of managers who seek to achieve it. It shows how conventional product costing fails to meet these needs and demonstrates how activity-based costing corrects these deficiencies. It explains how managers in manufacturing companies can use activity-based costing. Finally, this appendix lays to rest fears that activity-based costing may be too costly and complex to be compatible with manufacturing excellence.

The recent emergence of activity-based costing is timely because rapid technological change and global competition have increased the need for accurate cost information. At the same time, declines in the cost of processing and capturing data have reduced the cost of building new systems.

What Is Manufacturing Excellence?

Manufacturing excellence is the deliberate and continuous improvement of all activities within a manufacturing company with the goal of achieving a competitive advantage. Continuous improvement takes place within the framework of a competitive strategy that uses market, environmental, and technical opportunities to achieve a favorable competitive position in an industry.

Manufacturing excellence requires success in three broad types of activity. First, managers must select and implement strategies based on an understanding of the relative profitability of those strategies. Second, products must be designed that profitably meet the needs of customers identified by the chosen strategies. The resulting product designs must facilitate excellent manufacturing. Third, managers must strive for continuous improvement in all operating activities.

Objectives of Continuous Improvement

Continuous improvement has several objectives [4]:

- Eliminate waste
- Reduce lead times for customers, materials, tooling and engineering changes, and new product introduction
- Increase quality
- Reduce cost
- Develop people by increasing skills, morale, and productivity

A manufacturing company that implements a successful program of continuous improvement generally sees a simultaneous change in key operating characteristics. Costs come down, quality goes up, and the gain in flexibility enhances customer service. These improvements increase the odds that the company's strategy will be implemented successfully.

What Do Managers Need?

Managers need product cost information to help them achieve manufacturing excellence. They need accurate costs for strategic and product-design purposes. They require information on operating activities to guide continuous improvement in these activities. They need information that will motivate decisions that are consistent with the firm's manufacturing strategy. These needs must all be provided by a system whose cost does not exceed the benefits provided.

Product Costs

Product costs are used by managers to make strategic and design decisions. More accurate product costs reduce the chances that incorrect decisions will be made. The greater the competition in the firm's markets, the higher the cost of making incorrect decisions and the greater the need for accurate product costs [5].

Managers also need activity-level information from the product costing system to guide continuous improvement. Activity-level information allows managers to identify and eliminate waste from operating activities [6].

Product cost information should be designed to encourage managers to make decisions that are consistent with the objectives of manufacturing excellence. Managers should be encouraged to introduce and design products that support manufacturing improvement. They should also be encouraged to focus on the elimination of waste.

Managers who are working hard to simplify manufacturing and eliminate waste do not wish to introduce a product costing system that is excessively costly to design, implement, and run. This cost should not exceed the perceived benefits of the system. Nor should the system be more complex than is necessary to achieve the required benefits [7].

Conventional Product Costing Systems

Conventional product costing systems assume that *individual products cause cost*. They, therefore, make individual product items the focus of the cost system design. Conventional systems use cost drivers [8] that are attributes of the product item, such as direct labor hours, machine hours, or material dollars [9].

Conventional product costing systems may report accurate product costs where overhead activity is consumed in relation to production volume. Benefits for direct employees may be related to direct labor, for example, and power costs may be related to machine hours.

Overhead Activities Unrelated to Volume

Product costs may be inaccurate, however, where overhead activities are not related to volume. Activities unrelated to volume (e.g., setups and engineering changes) are common in many manufacturing settings [10]. There are a number of documented examples of such settings where conventional systems report inaccurate product costs [11].

When volume-unrelated activities are significant, conventional product costs do little to enlighten managers' understanding of the relationship between the operating activities that generate the overhead cost and the products. In the absence of proper information, managers tend to rely on across-the-board overhead cuts to control spending.

Such well-intentioned efforts are doomed to failure. They do not address the demand for overhead resources—the activities that keep people busy. Deterioration in the quality of service and pressures on an overburdened staff prompt renewed spending and overhead creeps up again.

Overhead Rates Based on Direct Labor

Conventional systems also convey messages that may encourage decisions that conflict with manufacturing excellence. An overhead rate based on direct labor, for example, may cause design engineers to believe that product design should focus on eliminating direct labor cost. This happens because the costing system tells product designers that direct labor is very expensive. Where the direct labor overhead rate is 500%, for example, a design change that will remove $1 of direct labor cost from a product will result in an apparent savings of $5 of overhead [12]. In reality, however, a design change that removes $1 of direct labor is likely to increase overhead due to the increased demand for activities relating to engineering changes.

Activity-Based Costing Systems

The assumption that *activities consume resources and products consume activities* is fundamental to activity-based costing.

Activities are procedures or processes that cause work. Examples of activities include:

- Establishing vendor relations
- Purchasing
- Receiving
- Disbursing
- Setting up a machine
- Running the machine
- Reorganizing the production flow
- Redesigning a product
- Taking a customer order

The performance of these activities triggers the consumption of resources that are recorded as costs in the accounts. The activities are performed in response to the need to design, produce, market, and distribute products [13].

The Search for More Accurate Product Costs

This view of the economics of manufacturing is radically different from the conventional view and may report more accurate product costs. Consider the case of a company that produces products in both small and large batches. Activity-based costing traces the costs of setup-related activities to the production batch that created the demand for those activities. The cost of setting up the batch is then spread over the units contained in the batch. (See Table B–1.) Product A, the low-volume product, incurs a heavy penalty for setup whereas the high-volume product *B* incurs little setup cost.

Traditional costing, on the other hand, considers batch-related costs to be incurred each time a unit of the product is manufactured. The example in Table B–1 accomplishes this by allocating an equal amount of setup cost to each direct labor hour. Each unit of A or B receives an equal amount of setup cost because each product requires two direct labor hours.

A similar situation occurs where two different products require different levels of attention from engineering (see Table B–2). Product C uses a lot of direct labor. Since it has been in production for some time, however, most bugs have been eliminated. By contrast, product D is a new product that is designed to require very little direct labor. D still has production and quality problems that require a number of engineering changes.

Activity-based costing traces the costs of engineering change activities to the product (primarily D) that receives the benefit of this activity. Traditional product costing, however, allocates engineering cost using a volume-related measure such as direct labor. This approach traces an equal amount of engineering each direct labor hour. Since C accounts for most of the labor hours, this product incorrectly picks up most of the engineering cost.

In both of these cases, traditional product costing distorts product cost. This is because volume-related cost drivers fail to trace volume-unrelated activities

Table B-1
Activity-Based Costing and Conventional Costing Contrasted

	Product A	Product B	Total
Production volume	50	1,000	
Cost per setup	$1,000	$1,000	
Number of setups	1	2	
Batch size	50	500	
Total cost of setups	$1,000	$2,000	$3,000
Direct labor hours per unit	2	2	
Total direct labor hours	100	2,000	2,100
Setup cost per direct labor hour ($3,000/(2,100))			$1.43
Activity-Based Costing overhead cost per unit (A = $1,000/50; B = $1,000/500)	$20.00	$2.00	
Conventional overhead cost per unit ($1.43 × 2 direct labor hours)	$2.86	$2.86	

Table B-2
Activity-Based Costing and Conventional Costing Contrasted: Costing Engineering Changes

	Product C	Product D	Total
Production volume	1,000	500	
Cost per engineering change	$1,000	$1,000	
Number of engineering changes	2	10	
Total cost of engineering changes	$2,000	$10,000	$12,000
Direct labor hours per unit	3	2	
Total direct labor hours	3,000	1,000	4,000
Engineering cost per direct labor hour ($12,000/(4,000))			$3.00
Activity-Based Costing overhead cost per unit (C = $2,000/1,000; D = $10,000/500)	$2.00	$20.00	
Conventional overhead cost per unit (C = $3.00 × 3 direct labor hours; D = $3.00 × 2 direct labor hours)	$9.00	$6.00	

correctly. The result is a cross-subsidy: One product picks up cost that rightly belongs to another.

Eliminating Cross-Subsidies

In contrast, activity-based costing eliminates cross-subsidy by using volume-unrelated cost drivers to trace the cost of volume-unrelated activities to the product. For example, activity-based costing may use the number of setups to trace the cost of setup activities to the product. Similarly, engineering change notices may be used to trace the cost of engineering change activities to the product.

Designing and implementing an activity-based costing system yield a wealth of information on operating activities that managers can use to eliminate waste. This information includes an identification of activities performed in the organization, a determination of the cost of each of these activities, an identification of where in the organization the activities are performed, and the consumption of these activities by individual products.

The Location and Consumption of Activities

For example, in Figure B-1, the activity-based costing system shows that two activities are performed in the process engineering department: performing setups and making engineering changes to products. Each of these two activities is performed in two different departments (Departments 1 and 2). In each department, the activities are consumed by products according to the demand for setups and engineering changes of each product [14].

The greater accuracy of product costs in activity-based costing avoids the problem of inappropriate messages that may be conveyed by conventional systems. In addition, the designer of an activity-based costing system has the ability to choose cost drivers that are behaviorally consistent with the firm's manufacturing strategy. For example, the designer may choose the number of vendors as a cost driver in order to emphasize the need to reduce the number of vendors.

Using Activity-Based Costing to Focus Manufacturing Strategy

Activity-based costing can radically change how managers determine the mix of their product line, price their products, identify the location for sourcing components, and assess new technology. This is accomplished by providing a realistic economic picture of the impact of these decisions on activity consumption.

Consider the circuit board division of an electronics company that changed its product mix by introducing low-volume specialty products into its line. Each of these products consumed engineering, procurement, quality, setup, and other activities. Introducing one or even a handful of these products did not require hiring a new engineer, purchaser, inspector, or setup person. But over time, as new products were added, the demand for these activities increased to the point where new staff were required.

Figure B-1
Information on Operating Activities in an Activity-Based Costing System

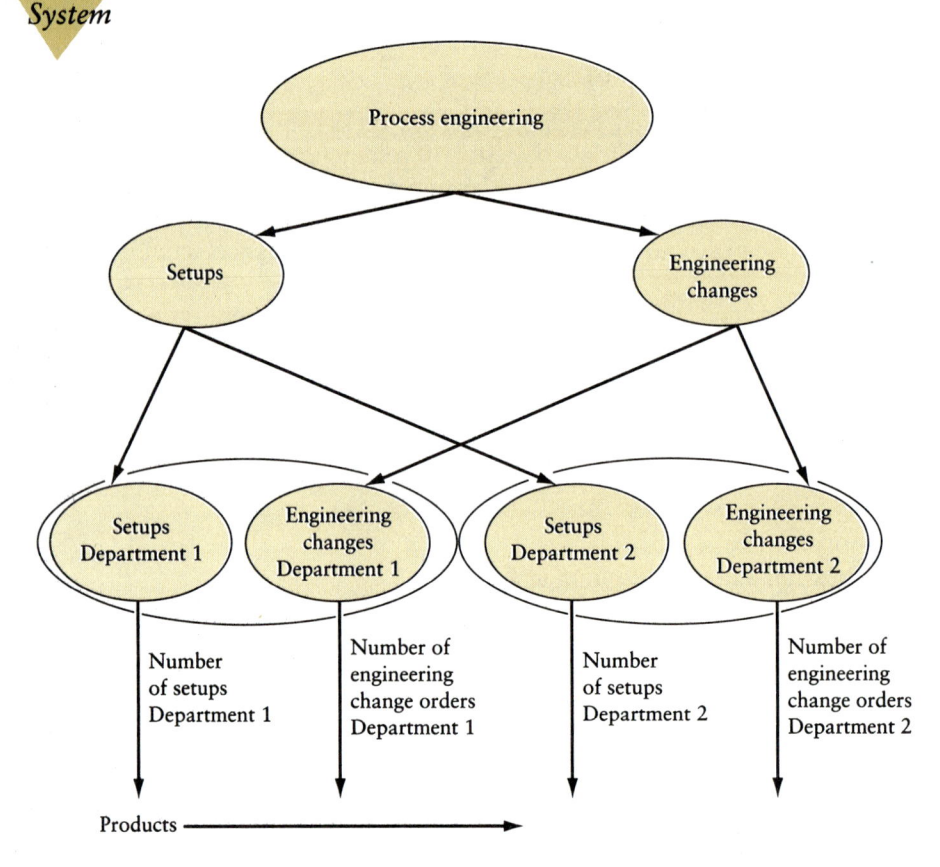

Introducing these low-volume specialty products was, in part, a response to information reported by the division's conventional product costing system, which was based on machine hours. This system showed that the low-volume specialty products cost about the same to produce as the high-volume standard products. The cost system, therefore, reported that the low-volume specialty products were among the most profitable products sold by the division.

Orders received from the customer service division of the company for replacement circuit boards, for example, were typically for volumes of one or two. One replacement board was transferred to this division based on a standard price of less than $3. The board contained hundreds of parts, however, and required a special engineering effort to produce it.

When the company installed a new activity-based costing system, however, it showed that low-volume products such as these were more costly than had been previously thought. Using this information, management was able to consider a range of alternatives—such as dropping certain products, increasing their price, or changing their design—to simplify manufacturing or compensate the company for the additional activities required by the products. The circuit board for the service division, for example, was repriced at more than 100 times the old price.

The Impact of Sourcing Decisions

Activity-based costing also helps management understand the impact of sourcing decisions. Sourcing decisions often focus on the savings that come from eliminating direct labor by using outside sources. What are often ignored, however, are the additional activities required to coordinate with the vendor. These activities may include:

- Qualifying the vendor to make the subassembly
- Shipping components to the vendor's plant
- Receiving and processing the completed subassemblies
- Monitoring quality and delivery
- Processing purchase orders and invoices

Activity-based costing provides the insights needed to weigh the impact of these activities on the sourcing decision.

Impact of New Process Technologies

Activity-based costing also allows managers to understand the impact of new process technologies. Introducing a new technology (e.g., designing surface mount equipment, improving quality to reduce inspection, and reorganizing the plant layout to create a continuous linear flow of product) has a major impact on the type of activities required and the way they are performed. Activity-based costing can model these changes accurately and provide management with the data required for an economic analysis.

Using Activity-Based Costing for Product Design

Using activity-based costing to understand the impact of alternative product designs is the key to using design as a tool for manufacturing excellence because product design determines the activities that are consumed by the products.

Activity-based costing allows design engineers to understand the impact of different designs on product cost and flexibility. Product cost can be reduced by using designs that diminish the demand for high-cost activities. Product cost can be reduced and manufacturing flexibility improved by designing families of products that use many of the same activities.

For example, one company designed a new oscilloscope to fit on a bench or be mounted on a rack. The bench and rack versions were built on the same production line using the same components and subassemblies. The only difference between the products was the placing of a rackmount kit in the box of the rack version during packing. Consequently, the rack option had little impact on activity requirements. In contrast, the bench and rack versions of an older product of the same company were produced on separate production lines, with different components and subassemblies, so they, therefore, shared few activities.

Using Activity-Based Costing for Continuous Improvement

Activity-based costing provides critical information to support continuous improvement in manufacturing. Activity-based costing maps the company's activities and describes the cost structure of products in terms of activity consumption.

Identifying the activities that are performed in each area of the company provides management with insights into eliminating activities or improving the efficiency of activity performance. One company, for example, used activity-based costing to identify recommended changes in procurement activities and to monitor progress when the changes were implemented. Before the changes, the buyer received a weekly printout of the production plan and material requirements. The buyer visited the stockroom to compare the requirements with the quantity on hand. If there was a shortfall, the buyer called the vendor and placed an order.

After studying the cost of this procurement activity as reported by activity-based costing, it was proposed to replace the procedure described above with a trigger based on Kanban quantities in the assembly area. A red flag on a Kanban was the trigger for a call to the vendor to replenish the parts on the Kanban. Manufacturing proposed to track the impact of this change using activity-based costing.

Performance Measurement

The activity-based product cost structure in activity-based costing also provides important performance information for management. This cost structure, which is referred to as the bill of activities, describes each product's pattern of activity consumption.

The bill of activities may summarize activities consumed by a product into economic or functional groupings such as receiving, procurement, engineering changes, and quality. (See Table B–3.) The bill may also provide detailed information on the activities themselves. (See Table B–4.) In both cases, the bill of activities is a source of information for setting manufacturing excellence targets for process and design improvement.

In the case of a screw-machine shop, for example, review of the bill of activities of screw-machine parts showed that the movement of parts was a costly activity. This insight led management to move a heat-treatment facility (which had been a mile away) adjacent to the screw-machine manufacturing area to eliminate the cost of moving the parts [15].

Using Activity-Based Costing for Behavioral Change

Some companies use activity-based costing as a behavioral tool to focus attention on one or two critical aspects of manufacturing excellence. In one case, for example, a division used activity-based costing to drive down the part count and the number of vendors. These reductions were considered critical to accomplishing cost, quality, and flexibility goals of their manufacturing excellence program.

This division used the number of part numbers as a product driver for procurement, storage, receiving, and part database maintenance activities. Since each part number received the same cost regardless of volume, the cost per part was much less for high-volume part numbers than for low-volume part numbers. This made it more expensive for the product designer to use a low-volume, unique component than a high-volume, common component.

As a result, design engineers started using substantially fewer unique components in their product designs. In three years, the part count for the

Table B-3
Sample Summary Bill of Activities

Activity	Cost
Receiving	$1.87
Procurement	2.19
Raw material inventory	2.99
Finished goods inventory	1.34
Engineering changes	4.75
Rework	2.88
Quality	1.34
Setup	5.21
Manufacturing—Department 1	4.12
Manufacturing—Department 2	2.02
Total product overhead	$28.71

division fell from about 6000 to 1500 while the number of vendors fell from over 1500 to less than 200 in the same time period. Procurement overhead fell, quality improved, and several products that had previously been produced on separate lines could now be produced on the same line [16].

Table B-4
Sample Partial Detailed Bill of Activities

Activities	Cost
Raw material inventory	
Number of raw material shipments	$1.02
Number of purchased part shipments	1.33
Number of setups	0.64
	$2.99
Quality	
Number of setups	$0.88
Number of purchase orders received	0.45
	$1.34

Reducing Lead Times

In another case, a manufacturer of power supplies used cost drivers to focus attention on reducing the elapsed time from when orders for components were placed to when the finished product was shipped to the customer.

Order lead time for components was used as a cost driver to trace the cost of procurement activities to the product. Manufacturing cycle time was used to trace manufacturing overhead to the product. This focus on elapsed time was consistent with a manufacturing strategy that emphasized cost, quality, and flexibility—all three of which the company believed were a function of time.

Is Activity-Based Costing Consistent with Manufacturing Excellence?

A company that implements activity-based costing adds a new system that requires design, training, and maintenance resources. An important test of a new system is whether it contributes to the goals of manufacturing excellence: eliminating waste and improving quality and flexibility. Otherwise the system adds unnecessary complexity and becomes a waste itself.

Robert W. Hall made this point well in his discussion of Shigeo Shingo's seven wastes of manufacturing: "Were he more familiar with Western manufacturing, Shingo might have added an eighth waste: unnecessary measuring, recording, and managing in an effort to deal with unnecessary complexity" [17].

The experience of managers who have used activity-based costing in a variety of manufacturing situations indicates that a properly designed activity-based costing system does not add unnecessary complexity. It is a tool for the reduction of waste and the improvement of manufacturing:

1. *Activity-based costing helps managers understand and eliminate complexity.* Activity-based costing provides a road map to the complexity of a manufacturing organization. It describes and costs the activities being performed. It helps management understand an important source of complexity—the demands placed on the organization by a diverse range of products. Once managers understand what is keeping the organization busy and where the demands for activities come from, they focus on eliminating both the demand for the activity and possibly even the activity itself.
2. *Activity-based costing helps prevent product design and marketing from placing unreasonable demands on production.* Activity-based costing is a tool for communicating to product design and marketing the impact their decisions have on production. With the information activity-based costing provides, the engineers can avoid designs, such as those with a high part count, that create complexity (as measured by activity-based costing) without adding features valued by the customer. Marketing can pick strategies that avoid product proliferation that creates complexity unjustified by added customer value.
3. *Activity-based costing system design avoids unnecessary complexity.* The cost of designing, implementing, and maintaining activity-based costing can be reduced by simplifying its design. The activity-based costing designer can avoid using data that are not already available within the company. In some companies, for example, a designer can take advantage of data that already exist in the manufacturing database (e.g., the number of production runs). The activity-based costing

designer can also take advantage of design rules that simplify the system without sacrificing the accuracy of product cost. For example, tasks that are performed at the same time, such as changing the tools on a machine and inspecting the first part, can be combined as one activity with one cost driver, such as the number of setups [18].
4. *The complexity of an activity-based costing system matches the complexity of manufacturing.* A complex manufacturing organization will require a system that is sufficiently detailed to capture the patterns of activity performance and consumption. A simple manufacturing organization—such as one where products of similar design are built on a single line as a family of products or where manufacturing improvement programs have eliminated such activities as incoming inspection and receiving—requires a simple activity-based costing system. For example, in one organization that was well advanced in its manufacturing-improvement program, the activity-based costing system used just two product drivers—cycle time and part numbers—to measure the consumption of activities by the products.

Conclusion

Activity-based costing is used in a number of ways to support manufacturing excellence. It provides information for making long-term, strategic decisions about such things as product mix and sourcing.

Activity-based costing allows product designers to understand the impact of different designs on cost and flexibility and to modify their designs accordingly. Activity-based costing supports the continuous improvement process by allowing management to gain new insights into activity performance by focusing attention on the sources of demand for activities and by permitting management to create a behavioral incentive to improve one or more aspects of manufacturing.

Activity-based costing is a tool for managing complexity in manufacturing. Activity-based costing provides activity-based information to help managers understand and eliminate complexity. It is also a communication tool between the production, marketing, and product design functions that helps minimize product changes that create unnecessary complexity.

The benefits of activity-based costing can be achieved without designing a system that is more complex than necessary. Systems designers can use the rules of activity-based costing design to simplify the system without sacrificing the accuracy of product cost. A well-designed activity-based costing system provides no more detail than that required by the manufacturing environment. An activity-based costing system for a simple manufacturing setting, for example, will be a simple system.

Experience shows that activity-based costing is a strategic weapon in the ongoing quest for competitive advantage in manufacturing. For progressive companies, activity-based costing is an indispensable, flexible, and cost-effective tool for manufacturing excellence that is tailored to the needs of their competitive and manufacturing conditions.

Notes

1. R. Cooper. "Schrader Bellows." Harvard Business School No. 9-186-272 (1986).
2. R. Cooper and P. B. B. Turney. "Tektronix: The Portable Instrument Division (A), (B), and (C)." Harvard Business School No. 9-188-142/3/4 (1988).
3. Turney and Anderson, "Accounting for Continuous Improvement," *Sloan Management Review* (Winter 1989), pp. 37–47.
4. R. W. Hall, *Attaining Manufacturing Excellence* (Homewood, IL: Dow Jones-Irwin, Inc., 1987). p. 22.
5. Cooper, "Cost Management Concepts and Principles: The Rise of Activity-Based Costing—Part Two: When Do I Need an Activity-Based Cost System?" *Journal of Cost Management* (Fall 1988), pp. 41–48.
6. Johnson, "Activity-Based Information: Accounting for Competitive Excellence," *Target* (Spring 1989), pp. 1–9.
7. Cooper (Fall 1988). *op. cit.*
8. In this context, a cost driver is a measure of the consumption of activities by the product.
9. Cooper, "Cost Management Concepts and Principles: The Rise of Activity-Based Costing—Part One: What Is an Activity-Based Cost System?" *Journal of Cost Management* (Summer 1988). p. 45.
10. *Ibid.*, pp. 45–54.
11. See, e.g., R. Cooper (1986), *op. cit.*
12. Direct labor overhead rates in excess of 500% are not unusual in today's manufacturing environment where direct labor has declined and overhead has increased as a percent of manufacturing cost.
13. Much of this section is based on the work of Robin Cooper. See, e.g., Cooper (Summer 1988), *op. cit.*
14. There are technical terms that describe each of the elements of an activity-based costing system. For a listing and explanation of these terms see Cooper, "Cost Management Concepts and Principles: The Rise of Activity-Based Costing—Part Four: What Do Activity-Based Costing Systems Look Like?" *Journal of Cost Management* (Spring 1989), p. 38–49.
15. R. S. Kaplan, "John Deere Component Works," Harvard Business School No. 9-187-107/8 (1986).
16. Turney and Anderson (Winter 1989), *op. cit.*
17. R. W. Hall (1987), *op. cit.*, pp. 24–25.
18. Cooper, "Cost Management Concepts and Principles: The Rise of Activity-Based Costing—Part Three: Determining the Number and Nature of Cost Drivers." *Journal of Cost Management* (Winter 1989), pp. 34–46.

Source

Appendix B is reprinted with permission from *Emerging Practices in Cost Management*, Barry J. Brinker, ed. Warren, Gorham & Lamont, Boston, 1991.

Index

A

Abita, J. L., 203
Activity-based costing (ABC), 217–24, 266–78
Adaptability in strategic alliances, 185–86
Advanced Micro Devices (AMD), activity-based costing, 221–22
Affinity charts, 85–86
Agile Manufacturing Forum (AMEF), 184–85
Agile manufacturing systems, 184–85
Alaska Airlines, customer focus, 32–33
Allegheny Ludlum Steel, cross–functional teams, 72
American National Standards Institute (ANSI), 137
American Productivity and Quality Center, 160
American Society for Quality Control (ASQC), 137
American Telephone and Telegraph (AT&T)
  benchmark activities, 19
  integration of functional areas, 213
  quantified improvements achieved, 27
AMP
  flexibility, 24
  quantified improvements achieved, 27
  work with suppliers, 22
Anderson, J. V., 228
ANSI/ASQC Q90, 137
A.O. Smith, quality circles and work teams, 12
Apple
  innovation in development, 232–33, 233–34
  value pricing, 36
Asia, Brown, Boveri, Inc.
  anticipating customer needs, 22
  teams, 19
  working with suppliers, 22
A.T. Kearney, 160
Autocratic leader, 62
Averages control chart, 108

B

Baldrige award, 25, 45, 245, 246
BancOne Mortgage, reengineering management information systems, 193
Banks, Seth, 227–28
Bar diagrams, 87–89
Barnard, C. I., 59
Benchmarking, 18, 19
  achievements of, 157
  in the administrative sector, 159
  defined, 155–56
  networks, 160
  pitfalls, 159–60
  the process, 158–59
  process of, 158
  the product, 157
Bergdorf–Goodman, customer focus, 36
Berwick, Donald M., 33
Bettis, R. A., 238
Bioject, innovation in development, 230
Biotechnology, 231–32

BMW, value pricing, 36
Boeing
  customer focus, 29
  reengineering, 196–98
Boundarylessness, 9
BP America, customer focus, 33
Brainstorming, 84–85
British Airways, customer focus, 29
British Telecom
  employee training, 23–24
  participative leadership, 19
Bumper Works, outsourcing, 239
Business Week, 252
Byrne, John A., 252

C

CAD/CAM, 203
Camp, Robert, 156
Cartwright, D., 58
Caterpillar, product modularization, 184
Cause and effect diagrams, 97–100
C-chart, 114
Champion leader, 62
Champy, J., 159
Charles Schwab and Company, customer focus, 34
Chrysler
  activity-based costing, 222
  developing manageable units, 23
  flexibility, 24
  outsourcing, 240
  productivity through empowerment, 151
  quantified improvements achieved, 26, 27

Cigna Property and Casualty Insurance, customer service improvement, 20
Clausing, D., 128
Cleveland area hospitals, 33
Coca-Cola, profitability, 24
Computer hardware industry, 182–83
Concurrent engineering, 23, 201–14
Control charting, 108
  averages, 108–11
  error, 114–16
  proportional, 112–14
Corning
  employee training, 24
  just-in-time operations, 174–75
  training as investment, 44
Cost graph approach, 209–10
Crosby, 45
Cross-functional teams, 72
Customer focus
  adaptive and flexible corporations, 186–87
  cycle-time reduction, 163
  defined, 29–30
  in financial services, 34–35
  in health care, 33–34
  in Japan, 31–32
  in package delivery service, 34
  quality function deployment, 128
  in retailing, 35–36
  in travel services, 32–33
  through value pricing, 36
Customer needs, anticipating, 22
Customers, developing loyal, 22
Custumer satisfaction, 37
Customer service improvement, 18, 20
  Cigna Property and Casualty Insurance, 20
Cycle-time-based competition
  in day-to-day operations, 164–65
  in new product designs, 165–66
  and the U.S. armed forces, 166–67
Cycle-time reduction, 164–68

D

Data gathering, 87–89
Decision rules for process variation control, 118–22
Deere and Company
  integration of functional areas, 213
  quantified improvements achieved, 27
Deming, W. Edwards, 5–6, 16, 31, 45, 252
Deming award, to Toto Limited, 31
Deming's 14 points toward quality control, 7
Digital Equipment Corporation (DEC), organizational flexibility, 182
Digital technology, 232–33
Disney, customer focus, 31
DuPont, benchmark activities, 19

E

Eastman Chemical Company, teams, 19
Eastman Kodak, teams, 19
Eaton Corporation
  improvement from employees, 18–19
  participative leadership, 19
  profitability, 24
  quantified improvements achieved, 27
  teams, 19
Educated workforce, 41–42
Electronic data interchange (EDI), 174
Employee development, 53–54
Employee improvement, 18–19
Employee training, 23–24, 41–47
Epperley, W. Robert, 203
Error control chart, 112, 114–16
Evaluation of productivity improvement teams
  changes in employee attitudes, 263
  effects of staffing, 260–61
  level of activity, 259–60
  operational impact, 262–63
  overview, 257, 264
  status of implementation, 258

F

Facilitators, 68–70
Federal Express
  customer focus, 33
  reengineering, 193–94
  training as investment, 43
Feigenbaum, A. V., 16
Fidelity Financial Services
  anticipating customer needs, 22
  customer focus, 22, 33–34
  profitability, 24
  quantified improvements achieved, 27
  utilizing information, 23
Fish-bone diagram, 97–100
Flexibility
  in computer hardware industry, 182–83
  of operations, 17, 24, 179–87
  organizational, 182–83
  through product modularization, 183–84
Flowchart approach (to problem solving), 209–10
Flow-process charting, 89–91
  application of, 92
  proposed-method, 92–93
  recording entries, 91
Follett, M. P., 59
Ford Motor Company
  benchmarking, 19, 157, 159
  concurrent engineering, 202, 203
  cycle-time-based competition, 165
  improvement from employees, 18, 19
  integration of functional areas, 213
  product modularization, 183
  productivity through engineering, 152
  productivity through management, 152
  profitability, 24
  program management, 203
  quantified improvements achieved, 26, 27
  reengineering, 194–95
  strategic alliances, 185–86
Fortune, 11
Forum Corporation, anticipating customer needs, 22
Forward, G. E., 247
Four Seasons Hotels, customer focus, 32
Fujitsu Network Transmission System
  profitability, 24
  work with suppliers, 23
The Functions of the Executive, 59

G

Gaither, Norman, 172
General Electric
  integration of functional areas, 213
  productivity through engineering, 152
  total quality management, 6–7, 9
  Work-Out program, 63
General Electric Medical Information Systems (GEMIS)
  activity-based costing, 222
  innovation in development, 227
The General Managers, 167
General Motors, 19
  benchmark activities, 19
  developing manageable units, 23
  flexibility (of operations), 24
  flexibility in plant utilization, 181–82
  joint program meetings, 203
  NUMMI, 4, 10–11
  outsourcing, 240
  quantified improvements achieved, 26, 27
German model (for apprenticeship training), 45–46
Germany
  apprenticeship training, 45–46, 241
  cycle-time-based competition, 166
  educated workforce, 41–42
  outsourcing, 240–41
  productivity compared to United States, 149–50
Global sourcing, 140–41
Godfrey, A. Blanton, 33
Goodyear Tire and Rubber
  participative leadership, 19
  teams, 19
Gordon, J. R. M., 148
Graicunus, V. A., 59
Group dynamics, 57–64
Group structure, 62–63

INDEX

H

Hallmark Cards, reengineering management information systems, 193
Hammer, M., 159
Hampton Inns, customer focus, 32
Hardware, 182–83, 233–34
Harvard Business Review, 128
Harvard business school, 167
Harvard Community Health Plan, 33
Hauser, J. R., 128
Hawthorne studies, 59
Hayes, Robert H., 203
Head Start, 42
Health care, 230–31
Hewlett–Packard
   customer focus, 33
   innovation in development, 230
   organizational flexibility, 182–83
Histograms, 87
Holiday Inn reservation optimization (HIRO), 23
Holiday Inns Worldwide, utilizing information, 23
Home Depot, customer focus, 35
Honda, cycle-time-based competition, 165
Horizontal team, 64
Human resource management, 41–47

I

IBM
   Baldrige award, 1990, 25
   benchmark activities, 19
   developing manageable units, 23
   flexibility, 24
   ISO 9000 standards, 141
   organizational flexibility, 182
   quantified improvements achieved, 26, 27
   reengineering, 195–96
Implementation of teams, 69
Improvement from employees, 18–19
Industrial Designers Society of America, 230
Industrial Design Excellence Awards (IDEA), 230
Information, utilizing, 23
Innovation
   basic products, 229
   biotechnology, 231–32
   computer hardware and software, 233–34
   creativity, 228–29
   digital technology, 232–33
   health care information, 230–31
   introduction, 227–28
   new products, 230
Instrumental leader, 62
Integration of functional areas
   alternative means of achieving, 203–4

comparison of alternatives, 212
implementation of, 212–14
introduction, 201–3
proposed frameworks for, 206–11
proposed product development routing, 206
traditional approach vs., 204–5
Intel, innovation in development, 234
Intermountain hospital, customer focus, 33
International Benchmarking Clearinghouse, 160
International Management, 202
International Organization for Standardization (ISO), 137
Interorganizational team, 64
Inter Practice system, innovation in development, 231
Interrelationship diagram, 85, 86
Ishikawa, 45
ISO 9000 standards, 18, 20, 81
   components of, 138–40
   described, 137–38
   global sourcing, 140–41
   productivity, 141–42

J

Japan
   educated workforce, 41–42
   employee development, 53–54
   NEC and QFD, 133
   Nissan's European plant, 51–52
   operations flexibility, 180–81
   origins of TQM, 16–17
   participative management, 50–51, 54–55
   productivity compared to United States, 149–50
   quality circle, 49
   quality function deployment, 128
   vs. American management, 52
Japanese Toyota system, 4
JC Penney, customer focus, 36
Johnson Controls
   anticipating customer needs, 22
   developing customer loyalty, 22
   employee training, 23–34
Joint program meetings, 203
Jones, Charles, 227–28
Juran, Joseph M., 16, 31, 45, 100, 252
Juran Institute, 33, 252
Juran on Quality by Design, 16
Just-in-time (JIT)
   at Corning plant, 174–75
   defined, 171
   in Japan, 17
   philosophy, 171–73
   purchasing, 173–74
   in retail chain stores, 175–76

K

Kanbans, 172, 173
Kotter, John P., 167

L

Labor vs. capital, 55
Leadership roles, 76–77
Leadership styles, small work groups, 61–62
Lehigh University's Iacocca Institute, 184
Lehrer McGovern Bovis Inc. (LMB), cross-functional team, 72
Lewin, Kurt, 59
L.L. Bean, benchmarking, 159, 160
Lockheed Missile and Space Company, span of control study, 59
Lotus Notes, innovation in development, 234

M

Malcolm Baldrige National Quality Awards, 25, 45, 245, 246
Marriott Corporation, customer focus, 32
Management
   to improve productivity and quality, 3–13
   styles, 11–12
   of time for the manager, 167–68
Market response system (MRS), 23, 176
MasterCard, customer focus, 33
Matrix organization, 203, 206
Mayo, Elton, 59
Mazda
   strategic alliances, 185–86
   reengineering, 195
MBNA America, customer focus, 33
Mellon Bank of Pittsburgh, bench-marking, 159
Mentofacturing, 247
Mercedes, value pricing, 36
Mexico
   growing market, 237
   outsourcing, 241–42
Milestone chart, 207
Mitchell, Russell, 202, 203
Mitsubishi, cycle-time-based competition, 165
Motorola
   benchmark activities, 19, 157
   customer focus, 29–30
   ISO 9000 standards, 141
   process variation, 117, 118
   six sigma challenge, 123–25
   timeliness, 24
   training as investment, 44–45

INDEX

N

National Cash Register (NCR)
  integration of functional areas, 213
  quantified improvements achieved, 27
National Demonstration Project
    (health care), 33
NEC, quality function deployment, 133
New England Corporation
  process analysis technique (PAT), 20
  process management, 20
New United Motor Manufacturing, Inc.
    (NUMMI), 4, 10–11
New York Life Insurance
  anticipating customer needs, 22
  developing customer loyalty, 22
  participative leadership, 19
  teams, 19
Nissan
  European plant, 51–52
  operations flexibility, 181
North American Free Trade Agreement
    (NAFTA), 241

O

Operations flexibility in Japan, 180–81
Out of the Crisis, 16
Outsourcing
  pros and cons, 238
  Japanese transplants in U.S., 239
  number of supplier firms, 239–40
  in Germany, 240–41
  in Mexico, 241–42

P

Pareto, Vilfredo, 100
Pareto analysis, 100–104
Pareto diagram, 101–103
Parker Hannifin, customer focus, 33
Participative leadership, 18, 19, 62
Participative management, 50–51, 54–55, 70
Phillip Crosby Associates, total quality management, 251
Polite stage of team development, 77
Pontiac, productivity through engineering, 152
Pratt and Whitney
  concurrent engineering, 23
  participative leadership, 19
  quantified improvements achieved, 27
Primary improvement strategies, 15, 18–21
Problem analysis, 97–104
Problem identifying, 84–85
Problem solving, 87–93
Process Analysis Technique (PAT), 20
Process control chart, 118
Process management, 18, 20

Process variation, 117
Procter & Gamble
  developing customer loyalty, 22
  profitability, 24
Production, 203
Productivity and quality improvement team, 67–73
Productivity improvement teams
  evaluation of, 257, 258–63
  Japanese model, 54
  maximize human resources, 55
  objectives, 68–71
  from quality circle, 49
  success factors, 71–72
  western view of workers, 52, 53
Product innovation, 227–34
Productive stage of team development, 77
Productivity
  of American economy, 149–50
  defined, 148–149
  ISO 9000 standards, 141–42
  through empowerment, 150–51
  through engineering, 151–52
  through management, 152
Profitability, 24
Program management, 203
Proportion control chart, 112–14
Putnam, Arnold O., 202–203

Q

Quality, as focus for managment improvement, 246
Quality circle, 16, 39, 49
Quality experts, consultants, and associations, 251
Quality function deployment (QFD), 127
  application of, 133–34
  description of, 128
  illustration of, 128–33
  Taguchi method, 134
Quality loss function (QLF), 134
Quantified improvements achieved, 26, 27

R

Reengineering
  at Boeing, 196–98
  at Ford Motor Company, 194–95
  at IBM Credit Corporation, 195–96
  in packaged goods transportation, 193–94
  management information systems, 192–93
  pitfalls, 192
Registrar Certification Board, 138
Reliance Electric, customer focus, 33
Reverse engineering, 157
Review-oriented approach, 206–7

Richardson, P. R., 148
Romm, Joseph J., 165
Ross, A. M., 157
Rubbermaid Inc., innovation in development, 227

S

Saturn Corporation
  cycle-time-based competition, 165
  productivity through empowerment, 151
  quality vs. productivity level, 17–18
Schonberger, Richard, 5–6
Schonberger's 19 principles of TQM, 8–9
Scollard, W. E., 126
Sears
  organizational flexibility, 182
  value pricing, 36
Secondary improvement strategies, 15, 20, 22–25
Seidman, L. W., 148
Selectron, training as investment, 43–44
Self-managed work team, 40
Sequential engineering, 204–5
7-Eleven chain, customer focus, 31–32
Shapiro, Benson P., 201
Sharp Electronics, innovation in development, 232, 233, 234
Sign-off stages, 203
Singapore Airlines, customer focus, 32
Six sigma challenge, 123–25
Skancke, S. L., 148
Small work groups
  leadership style, 61
  size, 61
Smith, John F., 19
Software, 233–34
Southwest Airlines, customer focus, 32
Span of control, 60–61
Special causes (of error), 117–18
Standardized appliance measurement satisfaction (SAMS), 30
Statistical control charting, 107–25
Steiglitz, J., 59
Stevenson, William J., 209
Steward, Thomas A., 180
Strategic alliances, 185–86
Strategic Planning Institute Council on Benchmarking, 160
Struggle-for-power stage of team development, 77
Supportive leader, 62

T

Tabulation, 87–89
Tactical business team (TBT), 72
Taguchi method of QFD, 134
Taylor, Frederick, 10, 59

INDEX

Team development, 57–64, 68–71
   stages of, 77–78
Team spirit, 78–79
Teams
   establishment of, 69
   pitfalls of, 63
   types of, 64, 72
Teamwork, 18, 19, 39–40
Tectronix, activity-based costing, 218
Thermos Company, innovation in development, 230
Three-managerial-level approach, 208–9
Timeliness, 24
Toshiba, operations flexibility, 180–81
Total Quality Control, 16
Total Quality Management (TQM)
   defined, 4–6
   future of, 245–52
   in terms of reported practice, 15, 18–26
   introduction, 1, 3–4
   origins, 16–17
Toto Limited, customer focus, 31
Towers Perrin, 160
Toyota
   just-in-time operations, 175
   NUMMI, 4, 10–11
   operations flexibility, 181
   outsourcing, 240
   production system in U.S., 10–11
   product modularization, 183
Training as investment, 43–45
Training of team members, 68–69
Turney, Peter B. B., 265
Tuttle, Howard C., 202

U

United Airlines, customer focus, 29
United Kingdom
   educated workforce, 41–42
   ISO 9000 standards, 142
   Nissan plant, 51–52
United Parcel Service (UPS)
   customer focus, 33
   reengineering, 194
United States
   educated workforce, 41–42
   need for worker training, 46
   view of worker vs. Japanese view, 52–53
Units, developing manageable, 23
U.S. Army
   cycle-time-based competition, 165
   training as investment, 44
   virtual reality, 250
USAA, customer focus, 33

V

Value decade, 6–7
Vertical team, 64
VF Corporation
   flexibility, 24
   just-in-time operations, 175–76
   market response system (MRS), 176
   quantified improvements achieved, 27
   utilizing information, 23
Virtual reality, 250
VISA, customer focus, 33

W

Wal-Mart
   customer focus, 35
   marketing response system (MRS), 23, 176
   reengineering, 194
   total quality management, 248
Wausau Paper Mills Company, time-based competition, 187
Welch, Jack, 6–7, 9, 63
Western view of workers, 52
Westinghouse Corporation, benchmarking, 159
Wheelwright, Steven C., 203
Whirlpool
   concurrent engineering, 202
   customer focus, 30
Why-are-we-here stage of team development, 77
Winston, Stephanie, 168
Woodruff, David, 183
Work grops, small, 61
Work-Out program, 63
Workplace in the twenty–first century, 250–51
Work with suppliers, 22–23

X

Xerox
   anticipating customer needs, 22
   benchmarking, 19–20, 157, 158–59, 160
   customer focus, 33
   innovation in development, 227
   ISO 9000 standards, 141

Y

Yamaha, cycle-time-based competition, 165

Z

Zander, A., 58
Ziba Design, innovation in development, 230